# THE SHORTCUT

# THE SHORTCUT

**HOW TO START YOUR BRAND WITH ZERO EXPERIENCE**

**DYLAN TRUSSELL**

## CULPRIT 🎩 PRESS

COPYRIGHT © 2026 DYLAN TRUSSELL
*All rights reserved.*

THE SHORTCUT
*How to Start Your Brand with Zero Experience*

FIRST EDITION

ISBN   978-1-5445-5105-0   *Hardcover*
           978-1-5445-5104-3   *Paperback*
           978-1-5445-5106-7   *Ebook*

*This book is dedicated to:*

*You. You're investing the time to read this. If you give me your word you will finish it, I give you my word it will change your life.*

# CONTENTS

How to Start Your Brand......................................................................... 13

Introduction ............................................................................................. 15

**PART ONE: GETTING THE PARTY STARTED**

1. Let Your Anger Fuel You................................................................... 21
2. Start with Why ................................................................................... 29
3. Think Bigger ....................................................................................... 33
4. How to Think ...................................................................................... 37
5. Think from First Principles .............................................................. 43
6. Life Is Tragically Short ...................................................................... 47
7. Overestimate Yourself ...................................................................... 51
8. Be Your Own Best Friend ................................................................. 53
9. Deal with Your Shit ........................................................................... 57
10. Determination > Intelligence ........................................................... 61
11. Fight Your Greatest Adversary: You ............................................... 65
12. Fuck How You Feel ............................................................................ 69
13. It's Too Late for You .......................................................................... 71
14. Experts vs. Pioneers .......................................................................... 73
15. The Advantage of a Disadvantage ................................................... 77

| | | |
|---|---|---|
| 16. | Ability vs. Opportunity | 81 |
| 17. | Your Most Precious Resource | 83 |
| 18. | The Best ROI in the World | 87 |
| 19. | Good Input Leads to Good Output | 91 |
| 20. | To Get Out of the Hole, See Your Career as a Whole | 93 |
| 21. | Passion Overpowers Pain | 97 |
| 22. | Have a Mentor | 103 |
| 23. | The Company You Keep | 107 |
| 24. | Hire A-Players | 109 |
| 25. | Have Charisma | 113 |
| 26. | No Excuse for Excuses | 119 |
| 27. | Find Someone Who Believes in You | 121 |
| 28. | Find the Right Co-Founder | 123 |
| 29. | Build Real Relationships | 127 |
| 30. | Invite Trusted Criticism | 131 |
| 31. | Hardest Is Easiest | 135 |
| 32. | Dare to Be Different | 137 |
| 33. | Don't Go Chasin' Waterfalls | 141 |
| 34. | Be Unfair | 143 |
| 35. | Lifetime Value | 151 |
| 36. | The Indirect Path | 153 |
| 37. | Cut the Gordian Knot | 155 |
| 38. | Specialization Is for Birds (and Those Bugs That Look Like Sticks) | 159 |
| 39. | What Doesn't Change | 165 |
| 40. | Let the Critics Think You're Crazy | 167 |
| 41. | Bet on Yourself | 171 |

**PART TWO: THE PARTY**

| | | |
|---|---|---|
| 42. | The Secret to Beating the Odds | 177 |
| 43. | The Audacity! | 179 |
| 44. | Comfort Is a False God | 185 |
| 45. | Be Decisive | 191 |
| 46. | Have a Bias for Action | 195 |
| 47. | There Is No Speed Limit | 199 |

| | |
|---|---|
| 48. Burn the Boats | 205 |
| 49. Ready, Set, Fail | 207 |
| 50. You Can Launch More Than Once | 209 |
| 51. Test the Market | 213 |
| 52. Experiment | 215 |
| 53. Trace Your Success | 217 |
| 54. Your Moral Obligation | 219 |
| 55. Brand Storytelling | 223 |
| 56. The Peak-End Result | 227 |
| 57. Direct Response Video Ads | 231 |
| 58. Start a Cult | 237 |
| 59. Tap into FOMO | 241 |
| 60. Above the Influence | 243 |
| 61. Full Court Press | 249 |
| 62. Demonstrate Greatness | 253 |
| 63. Be Memorable | 255 |
| 64. Have Main-Character Energy | 263 |
| 65. Your Goals Are Dumb | 267 |
| 66. Raising Money and the Art of Closing Deals | 269 |
| 67. Pitching Your Product | 275 |
| 68. Retain Control | 281 |
| 69. Don't Use Your Own Money | 285 |

**PART THREE: THE HOUSE IS ON FIRE**

| | |
|---|---|
| 70. It's Supposed to be Hard | 289 |
| 71. Give Up! | 295 |
| 72. Sit Shotgun, Let Your Ego Drive | 299 |
| 73. Don't Sniff Your Own Farts | 305 |
| 74. Be Unrealistically Optimistic | 307 |
| 75. Playing by the Rules | 311 |
| 76. The Boring Road to Success | 315 |
| 77. If You Don't Ask, You Don't Receive | 317 |
| 78. Your Most Sacred Bond | 319 |
| 79. Sunlight Is the Best Disinfectant | 321 |

| | | |
|---|---|---|
| 80. | Never Lose a Single Customer | 325 |
| 81. | Live and Die by Word-of-Mouth | 329 |
| 82. | The Tall Grass Gets Mowed | 333 |
| 83. | The Root Cause | 335 |
| 84. | The No-Assholes Rule | 337 |
| 85. | Stay in Your Lane | 343 |
| 86. | Don't Make Swimwear | 345 |
| 87. | How to Handle Your Competitors | 351 |
| 88. | Avoid Problems Duh | 357 |
| 89. | Never Have a Single Point of Failure | 361 |
| 90. | The Hidden Opportunity | 367 |
| 91. | Conception vs. Execution | 371 |
| 92. | Cause No Harm, but Take No Shit | 373 |
| 93. | Slow Is Fast | 375 |
| 94. | Always Have a Parallel | 377 |
| 95. | Organize Your Organization | 379 |
| 96. | Give Just the Tiniest 💩 About the 🌍 | 383 |
| 97. | How to Negotiate | 385 |
| 98. | Never Jump into a Contract | 389 |
| 99. | Cap Your Downside, Not Your Upside | 391 |
| 100. | Watch Your Costs at All Costs | 393 |
| 101. | Pedal to the Metal | 395 |
| 102. | Always Have a Buffer | 399 |
| 103. | What to Do in a Drought | 403 |
| 104. | The Value Equation | 411 |
| 105. | Incentivize | 415 |
| 106. | Make Group Decisions | 421 |
| 107. | The Most Dangerous Foe | 423 |
| 108. | Hit the Ground Running Every Day | 425 |
| 109. | Leadership | 427 |
| 110. | Break the Chain of Command | 431 |
| 111. | Be a Dictator | 435 |
| 112. | Take Care of Your Team | 437 |
| 113. | Risky Business and the Business of Risk | 439 |

**PART FOUR: THE AFTERPARTY**

114. Don't Let the Grind Affect Your Mind ..............................................447
115. Say Yes to No ..............................................................................451
116. Don't White Label ........................................................................455
117. The Other Sure Thing ...................................................................457
118. Keep the Champagne on Ice .........................................................459
119. Exit Strategy ...............................................................................467
120. Take the Stock ............................................................................471
121. The Unusual Happens, Usually .....................................................473
122. Get Lucky ...................................................................................475
123. The Art of the Pivot .....................................................................477
124. You Don't Deserve It ...................................................................479
125. Remember the Hard Times ..........................................................481
126. Send the Elevator Back Down .....................................................483
127. Novice vs. Master .......................................................................485

Almost the End, My Friends ................................................................489
Acknowledgments ...............................................................................491
About the Author .................................................................................493

# HOW TO START YOUR BRAND...

**Step one:** Don't.

If I had known how hard it was going to be, I wouldn't have started. Actually, if you had told me how hard it was going to be, my stubborn ass wouldn't have believed you.

Not only am I stubborn as a mule, I'm disorganized. I drink too much. My memory works better for useless facts than the details of my own life. My ADHD will transport me to another dimension when you're telling me something important. I'm gullible, too trusting, and I take unnecessary risks. If I can be successful, so can you.

Every lesson I've learned the hard way is in this book. Luckily, you're not just learning from my dumb mistakes; you're learning from the smartest founders who've ever lived. Think of me as the DJ playing the greatest hits from history's wisest entrepreneurs, adding remixes of my own—and not the shitty dubstep kind. If I had this book when I was starting out, it would've saved me ten years of pain. It'll do even more for you. Ready to build your empire? To become the generational inflection point of your bloodline? Strap in and get ready to be catapulted a decade ahead of your competitors who haven't read it. There are no shortcuts in life. Except this book.

# INTRODUCTION

Why am I worth listening to? I'm a college dropout. But I've spoken at Harvard Business School. I'm a successful Hollywood director. But I've never been paid for the movie I made, or the TV show I sold. So, I went back into marketing with my tail between my legs to save my house from foreclosure. I've directed commercials for Starbucks, launched the Stories feature for Instagram, had my work featured on the largest billboard in America for Beats by Dre, shot for Virgin Atlantic, Spotify, Coca-Cola, and a Super Bowl ad for Mercedes. Then I got tired of making other people rich. Exhausted from the endless treadmill of hustling and not building anything, I decided—on that spiteful whim—to launch my own brand with zero knowledge of fashion, manufacturing, e-commerce, internet marketing, finance, raising money, or business in general. Our first year, my brilliance made us two million dollars. Two years later, that same *brilliance* got us into five million dollars of debt. Or should I say *hubris*? It's hard to say where confidence ends and arrogance begins. But it's easy to pinpoint exactly when humility enters the ring and smashes you over the head with a metal folding chair.

You're about to learn every landmine I stepped on and how to avoid them. And you'll be learning from people way smarter than me. I've learned a lot in my fifteen-year career. But I've learned even more in the past two years than in the prior thirteen. One day, I stumbled across the *Founder's* podcast with David Senra, and it changed the trajectory of my life. Within a year, I had listened to all 360 episodes. It boiled down the best lessons from the most successful people who've ever lived. Which I've boiled down even further for you. Is most of this book just stuff I've heard, read, and regurgitated to you? In short, yes. I'm not ashamed either. I'm writing this to remind myself of these ideas, not just help you out. It's so I don't have to reread hundreds of books, podcasts, or relive my own hellish experiences via nightmares when I take too much melatonin. Instead, I get to skim my own book, get inspired to solve impossible problems, get off my ass, and take action. So, criticize me all you want for having very few original thoughts, but keep in mind, there's no such thing as an original thought. Even that idea I stole from Mark Twain.

Why did I write this? It wasn't to vent. I wrote it to prevent other founders from going through hell. The Campbell's Condensed Soup that is this book is stocked with great advice, including wishful thinking like: never get into debt—good advice like: okay, now you're in debt, here's what to do—bad advice such as: okay, here's how to keep the debt collecting wolves at bay till next week. And worse advice: well, we'll get to that. Some advice contained herein is contradictory because there are multiple ways of doing things. This book is here to guide you, not decide for you.

The following lessons contain everything you'll need to start a brand, except how to handle the pressure, stress, and physical pain you'll have to go through to get to the finish line that is beyond what you think you're currently capable of. Although I will give advice on how to handle the pain as well (hint: alcohol).

I've divided the book into four sections, which correlate—somewhat—to the four stages of running a business:

**Getting the Party Started:** If you've yet to launch your business or taste your first spoonful of success, this section will build your foundation. Everything from how to choose the right business, what to focus on, how to stoke the fires of your passion, how to instill belief in yourself, how to design a product that will sell, and how to mentally prepare for all that lies ahead. Including the lies you've already told yourself. Already mastered this part? Read it anyway for a quick refresh.

**The Party:** Getting off the ground is the hardest part. Now it's time for the fun part, where anticipation blossoms into reality. In this section, you'll learn how to be audacious, how to market your product, market yourself, and raise money—the most important skills in the early stages of your company.

**The House Is on Fire:** An inevitable shitstorm is coming. Make sure you're wearing a poncho. Your sales will suffer, your cash will burn, the ceiling will be on fire. Everything that can go wrong will. Even things that could only go right will go so unbelievably wrong. Smooth seas never made a skilled sailor. After this section, you'll be ready to brave a hurricane in a tinfoil canoe.

**The After-Party:** It might take twice as long as you'd hoped, but one day, you'll need this advice. The after-party covers what to do when you're ready to take all that you've learned and all that you've built and turn it into cold, hard, unemotional cash. Should you sell to the highest bidder? Go public? Hang on to it for life? All the answers are here. If you're not there yet, read this section to help you visualize getting there.

Alright, now that you've been slightly titillated and sufficiently warned, let's get this party started.

# PART ONE

# GETTING THE PARTY STARTED

# #1

# LET YOUR ANGER FUEL YOU

*"Chips on Shoulders put chips in pockets."*
—JOSH WOLFE, INVESTOR, CO-FOUNDER OF LUX CAPITAL

Where to begin?

How about what inspired me to write this book?

I just received a call from a lender threatening to put a UCC hold against my company, which would freeze my only source of revenue: Shopify. This would ruin me. My employees' paychecks would bounce, their healthcare would be canceled, I'd lose my house, and my underwear company, currently valued at over $30 million, would be worthless.

Am I stressed? No. Just angry. I consider starting a rival, more founder-friendly financing company purely out of spite...which coincidentally is how I started my current company: Culprit Underwear (seeing a pattern here?). But instead, I take three deep breaths, pop some ashwagandha—which does nothing—and drive to the gym. I'm too pissed off to drive. I pull over. I'm currently on the side of the road, fuming in my 1962 Lincoln Continental. Like most things in my life, it's impractical. It's missing seatbelts. Instead of cupholders for every passenger, it has five ashtrays. I'm starting to wish the overturned protein shake dripping into my car's carpet was a bottle of scotch. But the answers at the bottom of either bottle are the same: a temporary escape from a problem that will still be there whether I wake up with sore muscles or a sore head.

How did I fuck my company up so badly? In due time. What matters is how I convert this anger into something positive. This is a living nightmare. I ask myself out loud, "How do I make sure other founders never go through this?" It starts pouring out of me. I write "The top ten things to know before you start your business." Is this an article? The sun sets as my list of ten swells to thirty. It clicks. I'm writing a book! I look up. It's dark outside. I never made it to the gym.

I went home to continue writing in the hopes that you, dear reader, could copy my successes and avoid my seemingly endless swath of mistakes. I still might start a rival inventory financing company because of the daily torture the lender put me through. I probably can't mention their name legally, but it's Ampla. And in my humble opinion, they're predatory pieces of shit. So much inspiration has come from frustration and angst that I could write a book on it. So I did.

It's almost as if, In The Beginning...God said, "Let there be spite"!

In 1928, Walt Disney took a week-long ride on a locomotive to New York to meet with his distribution partner's new husband, Charles Mintz, who had become his new boss. Disney had created the famed Oswald the Lucky Rabbit character for them and came all the way from Los Angeles to discuss new, more favorable terms, including a small raise for his blood, sweat, and creativity.

Taking control of his wife's studio, Mintz let Disney know that instead of more money per painstaking animation, he'd be getting a pay *reduction*. Mintz said that if Disney didn't accept the new deal, Mintz would take control of the company, including all the animators Disney had personally trained on his own time. Mintz's exact words were, "Either you come with me at my price, or I take your organization away from you. I have all of your key men signed up." Disney would also have no rights to the valuable character he had created.

Imagine traveling for a week on a rickety, coal-burning shit-box to show up freezing your ass off on a cold February morning three thousand miles from home just to have your brief flicker of hope for a better life crushed by the iron grip of a mutinous prick. File that under meetings that should've been an email.

Walt had been betrayed by his partner and his animation staff, and left penniless. He had nothing to his name but a train ticket back and this lesson: make sure you retain control of *everything*. He said to himself, "Never again will I work for somebody else."

On the grueling train ride home, instead of traveling in coach, he traveled in the luxury of sweet, sweet vengeance. Fueled with enough spite to power the train's boiler back to Cali, he drew a little character you might know. Here's that infamous sketch—meet Mickey:

When Elon Musk went to NASA's website on a whim to check their plans for Mars and found nothing, he decided he would do it himself. He wouldn't build a rocket from scratch. That would be far too costly.

Instead, he would start by buying old Soviet ballistic missiles that were once aimed at Washington. He flew to Moscow with rocket experts and found what he was looking for. They wanted $20 million a pop. He offered $20 million for three. They mocked him and drunkenly spat vodka in his face. That was all the motivation he needed.

On the spite-fueled flight home, he made a spreadsheet detailing the raw materials and fuel that went into making a rocket. He realized the amount of metal, components, and fuel you need to make one costs only 2 percent of the price to buy one fully built. Well, he reasoned, with the fresh sting of Stolichnaya on his skin, *Maybe I can't do it for 2 percent of the cost, but I can do it for less than half the price.* The seed that may one day conquer the galaxy and make humans an interstellar species was sown with spite.

There's a proverb that goes, "Anger is like swallowing poison and expecting the other person to die." If you can turn anger into motivation, however, the other person will get sick with envy when they see your success. Necessity is the mother of invention, and the stress of your business imploding will make you the most creative cockroach to ever weather an apocalypse. That's why humans will never fail as a species. It's called The Self-Preventing Prophecy. In the same way millions reading George Orwell's *1984* prevented his premonition from happening, the escalating scariness of climate change will eventually allow us to prevent it. But it's going to take someone really, really fucking pissed off to save the world. So, kids, let the neighborhood bully keep giving you motivational wedgies because things are heating up.

In 2014, I had just started my production company, Culprit Creative. We eventually went on to do cool stuff like global ads for Beats by Dre, Starbucks, and a Mercedes Super Bowl spot, but back then we were fishing for minnows. We wanted to go to the Sundance Film Festival, see what the hype was about, and get a brand to pay for the trip. We had an in at a startup underwear brand, and they loved our idea of people skiing in their underwear. *The Wolf of Wall Street* had just come out, so we made a rambunctious ad called The Wolf of Sundance, which involved my business partner, David Dinetz, and me switching off wearing this wolf mask while skiing the slopes and terrorizing the town. We caused mayhem. I took all my clothes off on the celebrity red carpet and got dragged out by security while yelling at the camera, "I've been kicked out of nicer places than this!" The ad went viral, getting on several fashion and culture blogs.

*"I've been kicked out of nicer places than this!"*

We had killed ourselves for days shooting this and months editing it for just enough money to cover our trip. We fantasized about this being our first retained client as an agency. Not only had we nailed the video, we gave them something they didn't have: a unique brand voice. We had achieved a big success for them and could easily do it again.

Inspiration hit. The next idea was honed, and we spent weeks on a professional presentation deck. We set the meeting, dressed to the nines, and drove an hour in traffic, excited to pitch the next big viral internet hit. As soon as we finished our elaborate song and dance, we waited for the applause that never came. We just stood there awkwardly. The pitch had taken a month to craft, the disappointment only moments.

Finally, their chief marketing officer spoke. "Hmmm, I don't know if it's on brand."

My fuse ignited. "On brand? What do you mean on brand? We just created your brand voice. This is the next installment."

To which Mr. Expert CMO said, "Can't you just film a guy pushing a girl on a skateboard on Venice Boardwalk?"

Most directors would've happily taken their money for a simple shoot and another chance to work with the brand. It made me livid.

I've been that angry only a handful of times in my life. I'm laid back and have an exceptionally long fuse. But when that fuse gets lit, there's no coming back.

**Cut To:** The Parking Lot

**Dylan:** "Fuck them! We're starting our own underwear brand."

**David:** Mmm, I don't know about that. We're directors.

**Dylan:** Culprit Underwear.

**David:** I like the name.

**Dylan:** Get caught with your pants down.

**David:** Oh my God, I see it.

That was it. The genesis that would lead me to stop making other people's dreams come true and start manufacturing my own.

Is there a moment of utter disrespect, an unforgivable insult, or a Pandora's box of unrelenting anger someone in your past opened? What's made you feel slighted could make you a lot of money, help you save the world, or both. Take a ten-second break right now and relive this painful memory.

Now inhale the pain, exhale the passion. Congrats, you have a new weapon in your arsenal.

# #2

# START WITH WHY

"The man who starts out simply with the idea of getting rich won't succeed; you must have a larger ambition."

—JOHN D. ROCKEFELLER

As Rockefeller points out, money is a fantastic outcome, but an awful intention. Make your intention to do what you love, and you will become a money magnet. Hopefully by now, you've had an idea spark. What inspired you? How did it inspire you? What did it make you feel? Why did it make you feel that way? If you're embarking on the most important mission of your life, you'd better know why.

Don't worry about your public-facing mission. Figure out why you *must* found this company, invent this product, and build this business specifically. Why are you the person who must do it? Simon Sinek's famous TED Talk states that people don't buy what you do, they buy why you do it. But before we get to people buying anything, you'll need to figure this out in a way that's authentic to yourself. Or you'll never care enough to be successful. Remember, this will be the hardest thing you've ever done. You better know why you're fighting if you want to survive the war.

Tobias Lütke says he created Shopify as a way of "arming the rebels," giving fresh-faced entrepreneurs a way to compete with the established players. Apple wants to make insanely great products, and SpaceX wants to make humans an interplanetary species. Some brands, like Tom's Shoes and Warby Parker's 1-for-1 model, have more noble missions than others, but remember, these are what the founders are putting out publicly. It's not always the underlying reason why they HAD to found the company. Figure out your personal reasons first: why do you feel you HAVE TO do this? Look inside, find your reason. You don't need to pretend you're curing cancer if you're making rainboots for dogs. It just needs to feel like the most important thing in the world because to you, it is.

When Culprit first got me fired up—as more than a spite store—was when I realized it was the ultimate vehicle for self-expression. I'm an artist who can't draw. I had countless hilarious scenes and characters in my head with no way to get them out until I found the perfect canvas: underwear. My fever-dream designs could come to life in your pants. Once I realized this, I went on a designing spree, hiring a coterie of up-and-coming artists from every corner of the internet. Together, we created 1980s drug-dealing dinosaurs, gun-toting turtles, and sexualized junk food, to name a few. Not only could I now express my creativity unbridled, I was making wearable art. Each print design was like its own mini-movie, had its own storyline, and people noticed! Friends and acquaintances who saw me at parties would excitedly show me which ones they were wearing. And best of all, David and I now had a no-holds-barred approach to our creative process for making videos. Every idea we came up with previously, we always had to run by our clients. Now, whenever we come up with a scene that people on set say is too crazy, I look at David and say, "What do you think? Does client approve?" He gives me a knowing smile and replies, "Client Approves."

I'm not asking what it's going to say on the about page of your website or your press release. I'm asking, why are you going to spend the next decade focused on nothing but bringing this idea to life? And while you think, remember the words of Polaroid founder, Edwin Land, "Don't do anything that someone else can do. Don't undertake a project unless it is manifestly important and nearly impossible." The nearly impossible bit can be ignored unless you're inventing something completely new or disrupting an entire industry. I can't sit here and lie to you that making underwear is nearly impossible. The key part is what makes you, your approach, your *raison d'être*, different from everyone else. It's okay if you never tell another living soul what your real "why" is. As long as you use this moment to be honest with yourself.

# #3

# THINK BIGGER

*"So many of our wildest dreams have turned out to be laughably conservative that it's hard to write anything off as impossible."*
—SID MEIER, CREATOR OF THE CIVILIZATION COMPUTER GAME SERIES

Ready for an insult? You think too small. So did I. If you shoot for the stars, the worst thing that will happen is you'll die in space. If it can't lead to a spectacular, interstellar death, think bigger.

You know the phrase, "Can't see the forest for the trees?" Well, until a few months ago, that was me. I was thinking small and celebrating when I got a $200k loan, paying back $270k just so I could make payroll. After noticing me being happy about just scraping by and getting us into more debt, David said, "Stop thinking so fucking small. That is not a victory!" He said, "Let's think big for fifteen minutes. Who's a brand we love?"

"Liquid Death."

"Let's find out their investor."

We looked it up and found their lead investor was called Science Inc. After some sleuthing, we found the CEO's email address. I wrote the reach-out message in less than ten minutes. It was the best cold email I'd ever written. He wrote back within an hour, and we set up a call. This was that email:

Ladies & Gentlemen of Science,

[that sounds like something Darwin would say, addressing a crowd]

I have your next $700 million company. The good news is it's currently valued at less than 10 percent of that. Perfect time to get in. The water is warm.

It's called Culprit Underwear. It's the most comfortable cloth your loin has ever felt, the cut is so flattering you'll have trouble walking away from your mirror, and the designs are unlike anything you've seen since Lichtenstein kicked the bucket. Each print tells a story, and as each limited edition sells out, it leaves our die-hard audience clamoring for more.

Did I mention we're not an underwear brand? That's right. We're an entertainment company and our videos have been viewed over 300 million times, which, from an April 2020 public launch date, means 3 viewers every second since. For an example: https://www.youtube.com/watch?v=XchWpkXCAAo&t=1s

Let's discuss this mutually golden opportunity, and if you decide it's not for you, hey, at least you'll get some free undies out of it. Whaddyagot to lose?

Looking forward to hearing from you.

Best,

Dylan

This exercise in thinking big took just twenty minutes and yielded us unbelievable results. In fact, because of this one cold reach-out, we raised $2 million and forever changed the trajectory of our fledgling company. I was spending hours every day thinking of how to keep us afloat, do flash sales to pump a few thousand bucks in, chase debt financing, and keep an army of modern-day loan sharks at bay. All I was doing was reacting. I was too busy worrying about how to keep the lights on, I couldn't see how easy it was to build my own power plant. STOP REACTING, START THINKING AND ACTING BIG.

## THINK EVEN BIGGER

*"At the age of six, I wanted to be a cook. At seven, I wanted to be Napoleon. And my ambition has been growing steadily ever since."*

—SALVADOR DALI

When Arnold Schwarzenegger was in the bodybuilding scene in his home country of Austria, everyone was working out just as hard as he was. So why did Arnold become Mr. Universe, and they didn't? Because he thought bigger than them. When they said they wanted to compete in the Mr. Austria bodybuilding competition, Arnold had his eyes on the junior Mr. Europe competition. He entered and placed second! This got him a job at a gym in Germany, where he was able to jump on the next lily pad of success and work out twice as often. This quickly propelled him to his first Mr. Universe and his goal of coming to America. Everyone else was putting in the same amount of work; Arnold's mind was just on another level.

In the 1980s, Oprah Winfrey was a talk show host, but she didn't own the show. She was a hired gun. They paid her a fee for each show, and that was that. It wasn't until she left her agent, who was holding her back, and met her lawyer and mentor—when she was able to think bigger. Instead of simply hosting a show, what if she owned the show? Her lawyer expanded her horizons. They teamed up, made a new show, and took ownership. Together they sold her show in syndication to scores of local and national networks. Without this ability to think and act bigger, Oprah would still be a successful TV host and maybe even a household name. But she wouldn't be one of the most successful women to ever live.

It doesn't take any extra time or effort to think bigger than everyone else. You just need to remove the imaginary ceiling your mind has installed based on your experience and beliefs.

To think bigger, you need to ask yourself bigger questions. Here are some examples: What am I currently working on or dreaming about doing? What does my goal look like ten times bigger? One hundred times bigger? What needs to happen for my business to 10x from where I am? What is the highest level of success in my field? What's even bigger than that? What's the next step to get there?

# #4

# HOW TO THINK

*"There are limitless opportunities open to the man who appreciates the fact that his own mind is the sole key that unlocks them."*
—ROBERT GODDARD, INVENTOR OF THE LIQUID-FUELED ROCKET

Is the author of this book...who never graduated college, photoshopped his degree, and calls himself an entrepreneur, but never had an exit, really tryin' to tell me how to think? Not only am I telling you—I'm also reminding myself.

## BE ON YOUR BUSINESS, NOT IN IT

*"I learned to turn a lot of busy work over to other people. That's an important skill. If you don't develop it, you'll be so busy that you can't get a free hour, a free week, a free month to sit back and think creatively about where you want to be heading and how you're going to get there."*
—PAUL ORFALEA, FOUNDER OF KINKOS

The idea of being on your business, not in it, stems from the founder of Kinkos, who sold copies for a nickel and sold his company for $2.4 billion. That's a lot of nickels!

So, how do you set aside this time when there's so much to be done internally? Put competent people in charge. Delegation is one of the best tools you can learn. If someone else in your organization or an outside agency can do something as good or better than you can, that task should be done by them so you can be freed up to think big picture. Get out of as much busywork as possible and delegate it to your team—you hired them for a reason! As Paul says, "The best way to show people you trust them is to leave them alone." If you can't make time for critical thinking, you're not running your business—your business is running you. Tons of people work hard but don't think hard. The thinking is more important than the work. See where your business is going if you change nothing.

Next, think of where it ought to be instead and how to get there. Time invested in thinking yields far more than time doing busywork. What if your team needs something from you? Paul has an answer for this too: "Staying relatively inaccessible was the only way to stay on my business." I basically just copied everything Paul Orfalea says for this lesson, which is fitting for a man whose business was making copies.

Once you have enough A-players on your team, you won't have to solve smaller day-to-day problems yourself. Making yourself relatively inaccessible, like being on "Do not disturb" or even airplane mode on your phone for several hours per day will set the tone quickly to new hires that they need to figure out how to solve problems themselves. Nothing kills being on your business like an endless barrage of texts, slacks, and calls. You cannot forever be the end-all-be-all problem solver of your company. I usually respond after a few hours or give a call back. Usually by then, they've come up with a solution. It's usually good, so I commend them, building confidence in their abilities next time. If it's not good and not a big issue, I say, here's how to handle it next time. If it's an issue, I teach them how to fix it. They come to me with consistently fewer problems because they've learned how to solve them.

## TURN OFF THE FIREHOSE

Audiobooks and podcasts that actually teach you useful info are fantastic. If it wasn't for the *Founder's* podcast, I wouldn't have written this book. I listen at the gym, driving, hiking, doing the mundane, even while brushing my teeth, but while these are great teaching tools, there is such a thing as too much. If your mind is a chaotic symphony of distractions like mine is, sometimes you'll do anything to prevent your unconscious from bubbling over into conscious thought. But this is not the answer.

Balance the never-ending flow of content with time to let your thoughts form. You must separate yourself from the world and take long, uninterrupted stretches of time to think for yourself. Take a walk or a run with no headphones, drive with no podcast or music, take a shower in silence. Turn off that information firehose for a moment and listen to your subconsciousness. And stay the fuck away from the news.

Humans have not evolved to keep tabs on a twenty-four-hour news cycle. We evolved to be able to keep track of the 150 people in our tribe—that's it. We are not equipped with the goings on of nearly 200 sovereign nations with nine billion inhabitants, thousands of religions, languages, and cultures. Some of these countries have random borders drawn in crayon by the British while they were drunk on power and rum at the end of WWI. The probability of something going seriously wrong somewhere in the world every day for the rest of time is 100 percent. Almost daily, there's a natural disaster, man-made disaster, war, terror attack, mass shooting, missile test, famine, new disease, disease we already cured coming back, threats of a zombie virus thawing in the arctic, a riot over human rights, a worse riot when a sports team wins, a scary AI update, or a newly canceled celebrity. This makes the world seem like a worse place than ever. It's not.

The reality is that things are likely better than they've ever been. We just have too much information now. Too many camera angles. Every tragedy is in 4K. Too many opinions. The dumbest 2 percent make 98 percent of the noise. Your genius ALL-CAPS comment only ignites more anger. We were not designed to handle this level of daily stress. I'm not saying be an ostrich with your head in the sand, or don't be compassionate to your fellow humans who are suffering. I'm saying if you want to accomplish a challenging goal, global news in any kind of media will only distract and depress you. It will break you out of your flow state. So yes, be an ostrich for a year. Mute opinionated accounts, even if you agree with them. It's okay. Focus on your work. On yourself. The next world crisis will still be there when you pop your head back up. And your friends will say, "Have you been living under a rock? Do you really not know about the Dave Grohl cheating scandal or Diddy's 1000 bottles of lube?" And then they'll explain it and show me the memes. And in just one short minute, I get to learn current news in a hilarious, non-stressful way instead of having to follow it in real time.

Some people feel they need a constant flow of distractions because God forbid a thought forms—especially those pesky existential ones—but if you want to build something great, you need to let those thought waves crash on your unsure shores. Some believe you're channeling the divine when you're letting the discovery of gravity or electricity just come to you in a Eureka moment. To get this divine inspiration, you need to turn off the noise. I'm 90 percent sure that when Isaac Newt and Benny Franks made their discoveries, they were not listening to Joe Rogan. However, on shows like Rogan, ideas are shared much faster and openly than before, and a random conversation between two inspiring people you listen to could help you spark the next great discovery. Find the balance between absorbing knowledge and tuning out to process it, and the gold you seek will fall out of the sky and land on your face like fresh bird shit.

> **HACK: DOPAMINE DETOX**
>
> Leave your phone and laptop in a different room. Get a pen and pad. Sit on your bed or a chair and stare at a blank wall. Embrace the boredom. When ideas come, write them down. Set a timer for one hour your first time. Go up to two hours. You will be amazed by the thoughts, unfinished tasks, and ideas that bubble up to the surface. You'll also be insanely focused when you get back to work because your dopamine will be so low that doing work will raise it and reenergize you.

## TAKE A BREAK

*"I have developed techniques for keeping open the telephone line to my unconscious, in case that disorderly repository has anything to tell me. I hear a great deal of music...I take long, hot baths. I garden. I go into retreat among the Amish. I watch birds. I go for long walks in the country. And I take frequent vacations, so that my brain can lie fallow—no golf, no cocktail parties, no tennis, no bridge, no concentration; only a bicycle. While thus employed in doing nothing, I receive a constant stream of telegrams from my unconscious, and these become the raw material for my advertisements."*

—DAVID OGILVY, FAMED ADVERTISER

Austrian designer Stefan Sagmeister famously shuts down his entire company for a year every seven years of work, taking a mini-retirement. He says everything he's made that's any good during that seven-year stretch of work came as an idea during his year off. David Ogilvy didn't take breaks as long; he took them more frequently instead. Sometimes, he would even live among the Amish, where telephones and televisions simply don't exist.

Shutting everything off can be the inspiration you need. Bill Gates takes one week off twice a year with no cell phone, no contact whatsoever—probably in a real baller cabin somewhere—and just thinks. Silence in nature is great. Showering with nothing but the white noise from the water can lead to great ideas. You don't have to live with the Amish. Simple things like driving in a semi-hypnotic state or going for a walk with no distractions can yield fantastic results. You can take the dopamine further and sit in a sensory deprivation float tank for two hours. You might even hallucinate a bit.

## MAINLINE YOUR MEDITATION 💉 🧘

*"Everyone should meditate fifteen minutes per day, and if you're too busy to meditate, do it thirty minutes a day."*

—UNKNOWN

My head is a jungle of current problems, great retorts for ancient arguments, images of a woman I wish I had spoken to ten years ago, movie-style scenarios involving me disarming someone and saving the day, 90s rap lyrics, and depressing thoughts like how many Sunday dinners I have left with my dad. Shutting off the unchaperoned lunatic that lives in my head usually requires tequila and house music, intense physical activity, or being in Yosemite at sunset and seeing two bears getting it on. Meditation helps though.

However, I find unguided meditation difficult. Shutting my eyes and trying to dissolve my ego and sense of self and become one with nothing is frustrating and often impossible. I prefer guided meditation. Tell me what to do, guru daddy. The best way I've ever found to get out of your head is to mainline meditation straight into your soul like a shot of cosmic adrenaline. Listen to Joe Dispenza's already intense "Guided Supernatural Breathing." Except, do it in the sauna. Your first couple of times, do this supervised, or it could be dangerous. It's only twelve minutes, but it's intense. You might pass out and have the sauna turn you into a butt-naked raisin. But damn it works to cool your brain out like nothing I've ever tried. And sister, I've tried almost everything.

# #5

# THINK FROM FIRST PRINCIPLES

*"I don't care what anything was designed to do, I care about what it can do."*
—GENE KRANZ, FLIGHT DIRECTOR ON *APOLLO 13*

Three hundred and fifty years before Jesus was born, Aristotle taught us that a first principle was the basis from which a thing is known. First-principles thinking is a problem-solving technique that breaks down complex problems into their most basic, fundamental elements. Start from the most basic truths and reason up from there instead of relying on assumptions or conventional wisdom. By stripping away all inherited assumptions, such as that electric cars are slow, a smartphone needs a keyboard, space-faring rockets are prohibitively expensive, photographs take time to get developed, and the sun revolves around the Earth, we can consider problems in their most elemental form. In other words, solve problems and invent from scratch. Only use this approach on big problems because it's time consuming.

Experts in any single field are so good at knowing the conventional wisdom, they often miss the fundamental truths. When automobile racing first became a massive sport, the prevailing narrative was that heavier cars held the road better and could handle better at high speeds. They obviously had better traction and stability. Ettore Bugatti challenged this belief with his principle that "weight was the enemy." In 1924, he unveiled the Bugatti Type 35, the lightest car of its day, with an unheard-of power-to-weight ratio. The result was one of the most successful racing cars of all time. He proved that a more agile, lighter car could outperform anything else on the road and single-handedly changed car design forever.

The smartest living physicist, Richard Feynman, told young upstart Ed Thorpe it was impossible to predict the casino game of Roulette. Ed disagreed. He figured predictable forces—such as gravity, inertia, and friction—were at play, so it must be achievable. Think of how insane that is; a cocky kid was questioning the wisdom of the most famous living physicist about *physics*. Then Ed teamed up with Claude Shannon—the inventor of the information age—and, in 1962, made the world's first wearable computer. The device was programmed to calculate where the ball would land based on its speed and the speed of the wheel. A toe switch pressed by the wearer emitted a tone in the wearer's ear letting them know where to place the bet. It gave them a 44 percent edge over the casino. Ed made a lot of money from casinos but had to quit when the mob attempted to kill him. Twice. More on that later.

In the 1940s, when you took a photo on your camera, you'd mail it to Kodak and get it back in two weeks. Imagine not being able to post a selfie for two weeks! Then one day, Edwin Land's three-year-old daughter asked why she couldn't just see the photos now. Edwin thought, *Yeah, what the hell, Kodak? Why are you making my daughter wait weeks? What you got against my three-year-old daughter?* So, he thought from first principles and did what everyone said was impossible. His invention, the Polaroid Camera, made instant photos ubiquitous.

I could write one hundred pages about what was once impossible and is now part of everyday life. But that book would be boring, because you would already know none of that stuff is impossible. It's like, okay, M. Night Shyamalan, I see the twist coming from a mile away. Instead, this book is dedicated to things you don't know yet.

When NASA needed astronauts to write in zero gravity, they took years and millions of dollars to develop the space pen. When tasked with the same problem, the Soviets used a pencil. Okay, that story is actually horseshit. The space pen was invented prior, and graphite pencil dust in zero gravity near electronics is a bad idea. When the Soviets found out how great the space pen was, they showed zero loyalty to their pencils. But the mythology had you going for a second. You can just imagine some underfunded Soviet rocket scientist with vodka permeating from every pore, saying, "Nyet! Stupid rich Americans. We use pencil!"

What's impossible today is only what hasn't been proven yesterday. If you feel there's a stone unturned, there probably is. Is there a problem at your company that's causing a major headache or seems like a gigantic expense? Come at the problem from a new angle, like the Soviets in the fake story. Think from first principles. Invert the problem. Work backward from the answer. What stone are you leaving unturned?

# #6

# LIFE IS TRAGICALLY SHORT

*"Be happy while you're living, for you're a long time dead."*
—OLD SCOTTISH SAYING

At dinner one night, future restaurateur and founder of Shake Shack, Danny Meyer, was relaying to his uncle that he was taking the BAR exam tomorrow but wasn't thrilled about becoming a lawyer. His uncle knew he'd always had a passion for cooking and reminded him, asking why he didn't start a restaurant instead. Danny demurred, talking about how hard he'd worked already in law school and how successful lawyers are, when his uncle retorted, saying, "You're gonna be dead a lot longer than you're gonna be alive."

It clicked instantly. Danny knew no matter how hard he'd worked to get to this point, being a lawyer would never make him happy. Wasting four years on law school was nothing compared to wasting four decades as a lawyer. A lifetime is long, but death is a lot longer. Be happy while you're alive. Meyer took the BAR exam and passed, then immediately quit law and opened his first restaurant, Union Square Café.

When you wake up tomorrow, ask yourself, "If this were my last day on earth, would I spend it doing what I'm about to do?" If the answer is no several days in a row, it's time, my friend, for you to change something. This is what Steve Jobs would routinely do, and while he didn't have a particularly long life, one could argue he didn't exactly spend his time dicking around.

## THE REGRET TEST

*"Ultimately, I had to give it a shot. I didn't think I'd regret trying and failing. And I suspected I would always be haunted by a decision to not try at all."*

—JEFF BEZOS, *INVENT & WANDER*

It's 1994, and Jeff Bezos has the idea to found Amazon. He's at a high-paying, cushy job on Wall Street, months away from a six-figure bonus. He tells his boss he's going to leave. His boss tells him to wait until his bonus. Leaving just before a big bonus is stupid, after all, isn't it? Jeff sees that the internet is growing at 2,500 percent per year. Nothing grows like that. He sees it as the opportunity of a lifetime, so he puts waiting a few months for his big bonus through the regret test.

He asks himself, when I'm eighty, will I regret not jumping on this opportunity right now? When I'm eighty, will I care about this paltry-in-hindsight bonus? He left his safety net and bounced on his bonus to follow his dream of selling books online. Not only did he make his future self proud, he made his future self. He's super jacked and looks like Lex Luthor. Now, instead of selling just books, he sells whatever the fuck he wants. Kudos, Jeff.

Motivational coach Naftali Moses says, "Don't underestimate the monster you will become by settling for less." Filter your decisions through the future you. What would they think? It's not about getting to the end of your life with the most money or accomplishments, but the least number of regrets. If you've done that, you've won the game. Is there a decision you're currently mulling over in your head? Choosing between two paths? Put it through the regret test—will you regret it when you're eighty?

Remember, you only get one shot at this, NO RAGRETS!

As I'm writing this chapter, I've just received news that a good friend died. Of brain cancer. At thirty-seven! He battled it and he beat it. That's what he told me at our last lunch. What a kind soul, talented man, and radiant human being. Being around him was like everyone at laser tag all getting shot at the same time, but with positive energy—that's what he did to a room. He made you stop and acknowledge that you just got tagged with positivity, and you have to pause and smile before you can get back to your life. His name was Marc Becker, and his soul left the planet yesterday. He had a son three months ago. I imagine he must've known since then at least, but tried his hardest to fight it.

Your fate might be just as unexpected. While it's unlikely you'll die three months from now, imagine for a moment you will. What shots that you haven't yet taken would you take? Would you reach out to your crush and ask them on a date? Would you tell the person you're with you love them? Would you spend more time with your family? Would you go to your dream destination you've been putting off? Would you break up with your significant other because the relationship has run its course and you're just going through the motions? Would you race to start your company and launch it as soon as you possibly could so you can taste success for your last meal? Would you write a book and pass on something important to future generations? Figure out what you would do with that time. Write down what it is you would change right now...that shot in the dark you would take or that long overdue course correction.

Once it's written down, ask yourself, "Can I do this right now?" If the answer is yes, put this book down now and go do it. Death is inevitable, so is you living an extraordinary life if you enact this change today.

Go to myshortcut.co and publicly or anonymously comment what change you'll be making. Act immediately because in three months I'll email you and ask how it went. Not all change will be immediately positive. You might make your life worse by listening to my advice. But it will be better in the long run, and at least you'll know what could've been.

# #7

# OVERESTIMATE YOURSELF

> "I'll tell ya my biggest talent. When I believe in something, it's gonna get done. When people say no, I don't hear it. When people say that's a bad idea, I don't believe them. When people say it won't happen, I pretend they're joking."
>
> —JERRY WEINTRAUB, HOLLYWOOD LEGEND, PRODUCER OF *OCEAN'S ELEVEN*

I didn't call this chapter "Fake It Till You Make It," because that conjures up images of wannabe influencers posing with rented Lamborghinis and private jets with the engine covers still on. I'm talking about telling yourself and others you can do something you've never done before and have zero knowledge about. When I started my brand, I knew that dumber people with worse taste had become fashion icons. When I started writing this book, I knew people who couldn't write an Instagram caption that were suddenly *New York Times* Bestsellers.

Stupid people have irrational confidence. So why can't smart people? You must know you can do something well before you figure out how. This is not confidence based on others' validation of your ability to achieve. This is belief in yourself, and belief must come before ability.

If you want to be a high-agency person who doesn't just let the world happen to them, but makes themselves happen to the world, here are the weapons you'll need: Unyielding curiosity, an unshakeable spirit, unbridled positivity, unrealistic confidence in your ability to solve problems, an unparalleled appetite for risk, a disregard for failure, and a supreme dissatisfaction with the inadequacies of the present. Most importantly, you'll need unwavering self-belief. As Charlie Munger says, "Never underestimate the man who overestimates himself." That should be you. It's better to overestimate your ability than to underestimate what you're capable of.

Unwavering self-belief is the greatest tool you possess. And it must come solely from within. It is not that you think you can do something you've never tried before. It is the knowledge that you can do anything you set your mind to. That you can solve any problem that comes up. Rise to any challenge the universe throws at you, no matter the circumstance. It's simply the mindset that when all hell breaks loose, you won't take a step back. You'll take a step forward and crack your knuckles.

Can you guess what record label Jay-Z's first album was on? After being told no by every record company in the business, Jay-Z launched his own, *Roc-A-Fella Records*. He was so sure of his ability, he went around all the gatekeepers and founded his own company. He knew nothing about running a record label. Yet, he was so determined in his quest for greatness, he made his own label to launch his now classic album, *Reasonable Doubt*.

# #8

# BE YOUR OWN BEST FRIEND

*"Don't speak negatively about yourself even as a joke. Your body doesn't know the difference. Words are energy and cast spells, that's why it's called spelling. Change the way you speak about yourself and you can change your life. What you're not changing, you're also choosing."*

—BRUCE LEE

Be the person you would want to be best friends with. Not just charming, brilliant, and hilarious, because those are just bonus traits. Be the person who listens to understand and asks questions when they don't. Who sends money to split a bill without being asked, who takes an interest in others' interests, a stake in their family's well-being, their mental health, their happiness, their success, and *calls them on their bullshit*.

Some of you already are this person, some of you were this and forgot, and some of you never were. This is your reminder. Be the best friend you can be, even when it's inconvenient.

But do this for yourself too. Be your own best friend. Call yourself *on your own bullshit*. Treat yourself with the most respect you've ever treated anyone. Never talk down to yourself. Never tell yourself you're stupid, lazy, irresponsible, or unlovable. Kill it with the negative self-talk.

> HACK: I keep a compliment journal on my phone. When someone gives me a genuine compliment about my character, I write it down. If self-doubt creeps in, I'll open it and remind myself of my redeeming qualities.

## For only $10.99 you can let every visitor to your house know you are struggling

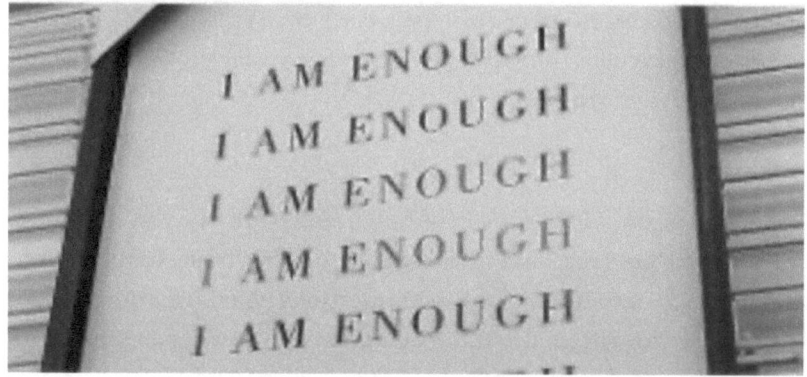

I hate it when people have to tell themselves, "I am enough." Ugh. Enough for who? For someone else? For you?

Screw being enough. Be too much. Be overkill. Take space. Your opinion of yourself is paramount. You don't have to be charming, charismatic, productive, motivated, determined, brilliant, prolific, have all the answers, or be hell-bent on success…*yet*. As long as you know, one day you will be all that and more. You can work backward from the end result you want and fill in the details as you go.

Everything becomes a self-fulfilling prophecy. If you talk shit to yourself, you'll get shit. If you talk yourself up, you'll bring yourself up. It's that simple. You know what else is a self-fulfilling prophecy? This book. I'm not just writing this book for your benefit. I'm writing it for mine. As I type and endlessly proofread these pages, I don't just practice what I preach, I become it. This book is my bible to live by. And I give myself lots of love and tons of props for doing my best every day as I write it. For setting a deadline and sticking to it. I pump myself up, not just thinking I can do it, but knowing I can. The craziest thing is that before I did it, I didn't think I ever could, but as soon as I started, I knew I would. Sounds like some Dr. Seuss bullshit, but he was on to something. Everything in your life can work this way. If you know you can do it, you will do it. Be your own BFF. The most important relationship you'll ever have is with yourself.

With that being said, don't kid yourself either. Don't pussyfoot around the truth. Sometimes the job of a BFF is to tell hard truths. I've had to sit myself down and tell myself things in the mirror I didn't want to hear. I use the Socratic method on myself. I'll ask questions like, "You're almost forty. Is this the level of success you want to be at? Are you going to be the CEO of a fledgling underwear brand when you're forty-five? Is that the grand level of success you envisioned? No? Then what change are you going to make today?"

# #9

# DEAL WITH YOUR SHIT

*"If I got rid of my demons, I'd lose my angels."*

—TENNESSEE WILLIAMS

You already know what drove me to write the first seething sentences of this book, but if you care to know what drives me to chase success in general, read on. In fifth grade, some kid called me a loser. My witty response was, "No, you're the loser." He then went around with his arm around me, asking all sixty kids in our grade who was a bigger loser, me or him. Without fail, everyone said *me*. To my face. This continued until I started sobbing. It was the first time someone had gone out of their way to hurt my feelings. He was my best friend.

I had forgotten that moment—buried it more likely—until I wrote this chapter. I suppose that moment to disprove him has been the rocket fuel to propel me. Maybe one day I'll thank him, but it won't be today, because I still need the motivation. Now he reaches out to me on Instagram for business advice. Maybe I'll send him thirty dollars to buy this book.

# use your demons to your advantage

While harnessing your demons to propel you forward instead of holding you back is vital for success, it's easier said than done. I have had a hard time learning to take criticism and have lashed out at people who love me and are trying to help.

If you have really strong leg muscles from carrying around emotional baggage, and you suddenly let it go, imagine how high you could jump. Paul Orfalea, founder of Kinkos, once said, "When your mind can break free of all the worry and clutter, you'll find yourself coming up with the most improbable and inspired ideas."

Everyone has unresolved trauma in their past. Some trauma holds you back from believing in yourself in the first place. Some results in limiting beliefs that hold you back from higher success, and some prevents you from enjoying your success or believing you don't deserve it. I've been stuck in a pattern recently. Always magically coming up with just enough money to pay just what I need to make it through the week, but never a surplus. I went to dinner with my mom, and we talked about her going broke in front of me over a period of years, from high school to college.

She said, "Wow, that must've been traumatic for you watching me go broke and lose the house."

Until she said those words last month, I had not thought about that in fifteen years. Then, reflecting on it, I wrote the next paragraph.

> Break the cycle. Break the cycle. I tell myself as I take on just one more loan. We'll get out of it this time. Our sales will grow, and we'll be fine in three months when this predatory loan is due. Yeah, just like we were fine when my mom lost our house. I remember her on the phone settling with American Express. And seeing threatening letters from law firms. Amex Vs. Gwen. In my mind, I still see the last moment at the house vividly. I had just left the office of the nightclub where I was being paid sweatshop wages to work at. It was 3:00 a.m. My mom asked me to salvage whatever valuables I could, since we were unable to afford professional movers. Several rooms were still not packed. I stuffed my banged-up 1997 Lincoln to the gills. I drove off into an uncertain future. The only thing I was certain of was that this would not be my life. I would not get in debt, owe credit card companies more than the equity on my house, yet here we are—fifteen years later. What a hole I've dug. Every month it's a puzzle paying the mortgage, and there's always one missing piece. When my parents could no longer pay for my college, I got my first taste of loans and credit cards. And I've been paying them off ever since. Eventually, I got a handle on it though. One day my student loan debt was gone, my credit cards were all paid off, my mortgage was on time, and I was making money as a director. My credit was never better than the day before I launched my own brand. How the fuck will I break the cycle now?

I called up my therapist. She worked with me to face myself as a kid, experiencing that. She put me in a hypnotic state, and I told my younger self it was all going to be okay. And I released that pattern. Some trauma just needs to be dealt with. Some is worse than others. But it's not a trauma-pissing contest, okay? Stop trying to one-up each other at the pity party.

If your trauma—or as some call it, a *spicy memory*—still affects you decades later, maybe it's time you have some personal accountability and deal with your own shit. It's unfair to bring that into your relationships, and especially unfair to pass it on to your progeny. Start the process of healing now. Go find a recommended therapist and do one session. See if it helps. If traditional therapy doesn't work, find a spiritual healer. It's unfair to the people around you if you don't locate and fix the root causes of your destructive patterns. You can't control what happened to you, but you can control your reaction to it, and how you either wither or grow from it. Instead of letting your past define you, let it shape you into the best possible version of yourself. If you take the steps to process it and don't half ass it, your life will forever be changed.

When you're alone, and you get in your own head, control your narrative. Don't reflect solely on what you've done wrong or your defects. Reflect on the things you're doing right, compliments you've received, and milestones you've achieved. Remember, a perfect person has never lived. You will succeed in spite of your flaws. Maybe even because of them. Don't pressure yourself to be perfect. That doesn't mean don't put pressure on yourself at all though. Pressure makes diamonds, baby, and the most expensive diamonds have the most unique flaws.

# #10

# DETERMINATION > INTELLIGENCE

*"Give me human will and the intense desire to win and it will trump talent every day of the week."*

—LARRY ELLISON, FOUNDER OF ORACLE

This equation will serve you well. And if you don't understand simple equations like this, you're not the brightest crayon in the box, but it's alright...that is, as long as you're determined.

Growing up, Sam Bronfman's father owned a small hotel in Canada. Sam noticed their family made more money off cocktails than the rooms they rented. When prohibition was passed in Canada, Sam saw a loophole: existing "wet" hotels could still sell alcohol. He decided to purchase the only available wet hotel.

The problem was that the town's mayor wanted to buy it too. While the mayor did the sensible thing and waited around the hotel for the owner to return from his hunting trip, Sam traveled six days in the snow *by dogsled* to find his campsite. Guess who got the hotel? Was Sam smarter than the mayor? No, just more determined. He simply wanted it more. Then he founded Seagram's Whiskey and became the generational inflection point for his family's wealth. So, how bad do you want it?

To paraphrase Paul Graham's words, if you're super smart, but not that determined, there's no guarantee of success, but if your determination is at a 10/10, you can still be successful even if you're dumb as a bag of hammers. You might not be sending humans to Mars, but you might end up owning a bunch of taxis or garbage trucks. The point is, your grit matters more than your test scores, your grades, or what school you went to. If you have intelligence too, that's just a bonus.

If you're smart but don't have the determination required to be successful, it's time to do something really dumb. Go travel and spend all of your money. *All of it.* To the point where you don't have money for a return ticket. Then figure out how to get home. It's the most fun way to go broke. And being desperately broke is a great tool for building determination. I've gotten to try it many times. Though never on purpose.

> **Determination Hack:** Not ready to strand yourself in a foreign country? Start by learning something hard but beneficial, such as cold-water therapy. Start with a one-minute cold shower, then work your way up to two minutes. Next, it's time to do a one-minute cold plunge. If you don't have access to one, fill a bathtub full of ice water. Work your way up to six minutes. Staying in freezing cold water for that long is purely mental dedication. You are now a determined individual. Bonus points if you can teach yourself this in winter. Ready to go further? Try the mental toughness challenge, *Hard 75*. You can start with thirty days if you must, but if you miss one day, you must start again at day one. This taught me everything.

Instead of waking up every day with the feeling of, "Alright, gotta go grind," change your mindset. You don't *gotta* do this. You don't *have to* work this hard. You don't have to suffer unbelievable amounts of stress, pain, and anguish. You GET TO. You are forging your dream with the steel of your resolve. You're getting out of the rat race. Jumping off the corporate ladder and sneaking up the fire escape. You might be going through hell right now, but it's your hell. No one else put you there. And however bad it is, it's temporary. You're not Sisyphus eternally pushing a boulder up a hill and going nowhere. You've got a chisel and dynamite, and you're sculpting that boulder. You're on your way somewhere, and your achievements, no matter how small, are COMPOUNDING into a sum much greater than its parts. You don't gotta do this, you get to do this. This idea comes from Arnold Schwarzenegger. Early on in his bodybuilding career, he wasn't thinking about how terrible it was that he had to do more reps and push his muscles to the point of failure; he thought about the opportunity he had in front of him. He doesn't have to do innumerable five-hundred-pound squats. He gets to. Because the work you put in is not for someone else; it's for you.

You're moving ever forward toward your goal. While it might seem the road ahead is long and uncertain, you're the one who gets to drive.

My old boss said you could take away all his money and place him on a desert island. As long as he had access to a telephone, he'd make all his money back. That's determination.

Like any skill, determination can be learned. How does one learn determination? Go back to your *why*. The stronger the reason *why* you want to be successful at what you're doing, the more determination you'll have.

# #11

# FIGHT YOUR GREATEST ADVERSARY: YOU

*"There's a guy inside of me who wants to lay in bed and smoke weed all day, and watch cartoons and old movies; my whole life is a series of stratagems to evade and outwit that guy."*

—ANTHONY BOURDAIN

**Disclaimer:** The following paragraph is a rambling, half-drunk internal monologue from the night I battled myself to finish the first draft.

> As I write this, I'm currently battling this demon. One day before the deadline, I gave in to myself and stupidly shared on social media and now have to hit my goal even if it ends up being utterly contrived shit. Now, I have to get this chingadera done even though every cell in my body is telling me to take a shower, get ready for bed, and watch whatever new epically mediocre Star Wars show is on Disney+. I'm tired, had a helluva week, and the last thing I want to do is battle myself. I want to love myself, but I can't.

I need to finish this. Writing something for the first time is fun. Rewriting is torture. Ninety-five percent of writing is rewriting. If when I die, I end up downstairs, and hell is a nonstop living nightmare of your own worst fears, I will spend eternity rewriting something I thought was good, but an executive told me needs work. While rewriting is like a root canal for your mind, having written something you're proud of is one of the greatest feelings in the world. It's almost worth the pain it takes to get there. I've kicked the habit of being healthy and waking up at 6:00 a.m. to write. I went out last night and slept in. I shot guns today and took a small ricochet to the chest and have a bloody ant-sized hole in my shirt. Now I'm drinking wine and listening to Vivaldi to focus. This whole paragraph is garbage. If I was using a typewriter, I'd've rolled this entire section into a ball and thrown it into my trash can like Steven King did with *Carrie*, except I would've missed. If you want to know what else happened today, skip to lesson #88, "Never Have a Single Point of Failure." Guatemala is in political turmoil, and I don't know where my business will be come Monday. Time to get creative and finish. No wonder it took me six years to complete a screenplay that didn't sell. Remember what I said about negative self-talk? Enough of that, I'm God's gift to writing. And as Ben Franklin said, "God helps those who help themselves." Am I making sense? Am I even fucking speaking English?

This chapter is about finding the determination to focus. It seems everyone has some kind of ailment. My ADHD is on full blast. But this isn't about me. This is about you. If you can't focus on the task at hand, focus on the consequences. What happens if you don't do what you set out to do? Regret. This isn't about harnessing your demons either; you've already done that.

This is about quelling that inner voice that says, "I've sweat, bled, and cried enough already, I don't need to work harder, I need a massage, a sandwich, and a nap." That voice will only help you accomplish one thing: failing the regret test.

If you're afraid to sit down and do the work, that's fear telling you it's time to lean in. Author Stephen Kotler says, instead of saying this sucks, say, "I was born for this challenge." Reframe it. Instead of standing in your way, let fear push you. A breath-work guru told me that when you least want to cold plunge, that's when you need it most. Jump in the fucking ice water. It's going to suck, but to be successful, you must embrace the suck. You don't need motivation to start something. You just need to act without thinking. It's your lazy alter ego guarding the gate. The lazy you is *lazy*. And therefore, *easy to beat*. You're not overcoming lazy you for yourself; you're doing it for the world. So, sack up and get on with it.

Book Recommendation: *The War of Art* by Steven Pressfield

# #12

# FUCK HOW YOU FEEL

*"Suffer now and live the rest of your life as a champion."*

—MUHAMMAD ALI

If you tell yourself you need to be in the zone to achieve great things, you won't be prolific. When Eminem goes into the studio to make new music, he does it on a schedule, not when he's inspired. He shows up at the studio at 9:00 a.m. and works till 5:00 p.m. Then he leaves. He doesn't care how he feels. He doesn't care if the artist he's working with shows up on time or not. He does his verse, and he leaves on the dot.

Akon was working with Em once and showed up to the studio casually at 2:00 p.m. Eminem had already been working for five hours. They worked together for a few hours, then right after a take, Eminem said bye and left. Akon was bewildered. He tried to get Eminem to stay because they were in the zone. Em left because he works on a schedule. No matter how he feels, when he's working, he's doing it at the same time every day. Whether he's inspired or hitting a brick wall. If he's on fire and it's time for him to leave, he respects his schedule and knows he'll be back at the same time tomorrow.

You don't need to be great every time, you just need to be consistent. Eminem is consistent and doesn't wait for inspiration to strike. I promise you, if you show up, inspiration will strike more often than if you wait for inspiration and then show up. If you work only when you feel like it, you'll get destroyed by people who put results over feelings. The best thing you can do is stick to the program.

The commitment to the work is more important than how you feel in the moment. Halfway through writing this book, I took a writing course from bestselling author and flow-state researcher, Steven Kotler. He taught me to write at the same time and place every day. I did four hours of writing every weekday from 6:00 a.m. to 10:00 a.m. with my phone off, in the other room. No matter if I was tired, hungover, sad, uninspired, or sick, I'd just pop a couple caffeine pills and get it done. Not being able to accomplish on a regular schedule because you're not feeling up to it will result in you being more likely to quit. Darwin's biggest supporter, Thomas Henry Huxley, said, "Perhaps the most valuable result of all education is the ability to make yourself do the thing you have to do, when it ought to be done, whether you like it or not."

The key to resilience is to work no matter what. The job must get done. The show must go on. Getting your work done when you don't feel like it is more impressive, not less.

# #13

# IT'S TOO LATE FOR YOU

*"I was thirty-eight years old, I had just been fired, my second wife had just left me. I had somehow fucked up. I developed this maniacal passion for wanting to achieve something."*

—JIM CLARK

And achieving something is exactly what Jim Clark did, to put it lightly. At thirty-eight, he founded Silicon Graphics, whose computers were later used to do the VFX in *Terminator 2* and *Jurassic Park*. He made good money when the company went public, but lost control. They stopped listening to him, so he left and formed Netscape at the age of fifty.

Just like it was too late for him, it's too late for you too. Unless you're Henry Ford or Estée Lauder, who started their companies at forty. At the age of thirty-six, Dee Hock considered himself an utter failure after being fired and having to go on unemployment. Then he started a little company called Visa. Christian Dior didn't start his fashion house till he was forty-one. Sam Walton founded Walmart at forty-four. Bob Parsons founded GoDaddy at forty-seven, Adolf Dassler created Adidas at forty-eight, and Bernie Marcus co-founded Home Depot at forty-nine. They were all spring chickens compared to:

- The Dodge brothers made their first car after Horace turned fifty
- Geico Insurance was founded by fifty-year-old Leo Goodwin
- Ray Kroc founded the McDonald's Franchise at fifty-two
- Chaleo Yoovidhya co-founded Red Bull at fifty-three
- Arianna Huffington made the Huff Post go live at fifty-five
- Charles Flint created what would become IBM at sixty-one
- Harland 'Colonel' Sanders gave us KFC at sixty-two
- Bill Porter launched E-Trade at sixty-three
- Henry Leland founded Cadillac at fifty-nine, then Lincoln Motors at seventy-four!

Did you know you're twice as likely to be successful launching a company at fifty than at thirty? While youthful exuberance is great, it's trumped by the wisdom that only comes with age. If you think you're too old for this shit, that's just your old way of thinking. The only old thing—whose time has come to die—is your habit of making excuses as to why you can't, haven't, or shouldn't. You can. You have no excuse. You shall. The only thing that matters is your next move. Get on with it.

# #14

# EXPERTS VS. PIONEERS

*"The experts, to generalize a bit, come along and pick up where the pioneers leave off. Confronted with the unusual, something beyond their rules and special knowledge, their reaction is 'It's never been done' or even 'It can't be done.'*

*"The pioneer says, 'Let's try it.'"*
—CHARLES E. SORENSON, HENRY FORD'S RIGHT-HAND MAN

*"What is an expert anyway? Just some guy from out of town."*
—MARK TWAIN

In 1908, Ford was pioneering new techniques for manufacturing with the goal of getting the price of the Model T so low that everyone could afford one. People were rooting for Ford because everyone wanted a car. It got to the point that whenever the price would drop lower, the newspaper would run a story on it, resulting in more sales, allowing the price to drop even lower.

Since each assembly-line technique Henry Ford created was new, "experts" who had previously run factories became a detriment. Ford's operations were therefore done by people who had no prior knowledge of the subject and didn't have a chance to get on "familiar terms with the impossible," as Henry Ford's right-hand man, Charles Sorenson, puts it. He added, "If one came along who had done well in any other business, we had more of a problem to get him to drop his ideas than fall in line with our progressive manufacturing and assembly." Speaking again on the subject, he said, "When one man began to fancy himself an expert, we had to get rid of him. The minute a man thinks himself an expert, he gets an expert's state of mind, and too many things become impossible."

Experts only know their way of doing things or what's worked before. Pioneers think there must be a better way. Experts propose rigid systems in which rules tend to be paramount. Pioneers put the objective first and the method to accomplish it is always flexible. Be firm in what you want to accomplish, and be flexible in *how* to get there.

When Preston Tucker was making his Tucker car, it was a radical departure from what came before, which was what made it exciting. It used a lightweight helicopter engine, which made it fast, had shatterproof windshields, early standard seatbelts, and a center-mounted headlight that followed the steering wheel around turns. Then, they brought in an auto-industry expert who knew better because they didn't trust someone like Tucker, who had never before manufactured on that scale. The expert changed Tucker's designs to make it more similar to the status quo. He tried to get rid of seatbelts to save money, wasted all of Tucker's money and time, took over his company, and ruined his reputation. Tucker had to go behind his back and make the cars his way. The cars were beautiful, incredibly ahead of their time, and had a hundred thousand pre-orders. Sadly, only fifty were ever made because they brought in an expert who fucked up expertly.

※ ※ ※

Experts told Dyson to hide the cyclone (you know, the only thing that makes his vacuum different!) and that "people didn't want to see dirt."

He said, "Well, how do you know it's working then?"

A board member said to him, "But James, your idea can't be any good. If there were a better kind of vacuum cleaner, Hoover or Electrolux would have invented it." (Dyson, *Against The Odds*)

Typically, for him, this only strengthened his belief in his vision and determination to prove them wrong. He stuck to his guns and now he owns 100 percent of his company. One hundred percent of $10 billion.

Not sure how good your math skills are, but mine are fucking great because my dad taught me math on napkins at McDonald's when I was five, and 100 percent of $10 billion is $10 billion. You can buy a lot of Mickey D's with that. Like the actual restaurants, not just the Big Macs. Fun fact: McDonald's is one of the biggest real estate holders in the world. And they collect rent checks from every single one of their franchisees. Talk about thinking outside the Big Mac box.

When we were getting ready to launch Culprit, every expert we spoke to told me to stop focusing so much on designing the prints. They insisted we'd sell 80 percent basic colors, and our wild prints would only be 20 percent of our sales. We listened and made black the first pair we launched instead of focusing on what made our brand unique. We did $11,000 in sales. In an entire year. The following year, we focused on our prints and made over $2 million. It was exactly the opposite of what they had predicted. These days, we sell over 80 percent prints.

# #15

# THE ADVANTAGE OF A DISADVANTAGE

*"I was a kid born with all the disadvantages to succeed."*

—LARRY ELLISON, FOUNDER OF ORACLE

By adulthood, Thomas Edison was nearly deaf. He didn't view it as a hindrance though. His hearing loss allowed him to concentrate on his work without the distractions from background noise. This intense concentration allowed his productivity and creativity to soar. It also helped in business. He said his condition let him avoid hearing nonsense and let him focus on his thoughts even during meetings. In overcoming this challenge, he reframed his disadvantage as an asset, leading to more resilience and increased determination throughout his life. If Edison could hear perfectly, he might not have over 1,000 patents to his name.

Due to a rare disease, Charles Kettering became too blind to read intermittently throughout his life. In school, his classmates would read aloud to him. With his eyes closed, he harnessed the power of his imagination as they read. He learned to picture things vividly in his mind, saying later, "Without imagination you can't get anywhere." Harnessing this power allowed him to picture his various inventions in detail, such as the electric car starter and automatic transmission.

In high school, I was the class clown, interrupting teachers with epic one-liners that they definitely appreciated. 😉 It made me popular with the kids, but not with the teaching staff. You can imagine I wasn't the best student. In tenth grade, my grades were slipping to the point where my mom intervened because I wasn't going to get into college. She made me take Adderall each morning in front of her. My grades shot up.

The only issue was that my jokes became awful. At the time, I thought they were just too smart, and my friends had somehow gotten dumber. But in reality, the Adderall just killed my sense of humor and personality. I was no longer funny. I was just a smug, methed-out know-it-all. My friends started to avoid me. They would ditch me when I approached a table we'd all hang out at.

I didn't care how good my grades were getting; it wasn't worth it. I started pretending to take the pills in the morning, then spat them out when my mom wasn't looking. I became funny and cool again. I told my friends I stopped taking Adderal, and they started hanging out with me again. I chose my social life over my grades and never looked back. Subconsciously, I must have been thinking, *It's not what you know, it's who you know.* Like an anxious butterfly regressing into a cool caterpillar, my A's turned back into C's. But hey, C's get degrees.

After sifting through twelve rejection letters, one of the envelopes seemed a little thicker. My first and only acceptance. It was CU Boulder. A safety school I didn't even bother to visit. I had no idea what to expect or even what the campus looked like. It was the greatest thing that ever happened to me. On the first day of college, I met my future business partner. Within the first year, I knew what I wanted to do with my life: direct movies.

My disadvantage wasn't all that bad. Millions of people have ADHD. But it led me to realize what's important. My social life was more important than my grades in the same way relationships are more important than money. Since seeing a therapist recently, I've realized, not only is the ADHD that has plagued my working life not a disadvantage. If harnessed correctly, it's a superpower. It helps in pattern recognition and creativity. When a problem arises that my team has no idea how to solve, I come up with an—often unorthodox—solution in seconds.

No matter what cards you've been dealt in life, there's a way to turn your disadvantage into an advantage; your disability into your superpower. Everyone struggles. Some more than others, and some not enough. Those who were born with less-than-average hardship are often less resilient later on. If it's true that whatever doesn't kill you, makes you stronger, then own it. If you've had an especially hard go of it, resist the temptation to see yourself as a victim. Seeing yourself that way can result in a feeling of powerlessness. By focusing on what's gone wrong or who to blame, you won't build the necessary character and grit. So, if you feel you've had it hard in life, be thankful you did, for there are others who were unfortunately, too fortunate. A lack of good opportunities can drive you to create your own better ones; as long as you believe in yourself, you'll have the ability to overcome anything.

# #16

# ABILITY VS. OPPORTUNITY

*"A poor, smart, determined person is not gonna stay poor very long."*
—DAVID SENRA

Ability is evenly distributed across cultures, countries, and classes... opportunity is not. If you have both ability and opportunity, and you are not utilizing both to accomplish something great, you are wasting your one shot at life. If you have the ability but no opportunity, go create the opportunity for yourself.

Coco Chanel and Luxottica founder, Leonardo Del Vecchio, were orphans born with nothing. Both turned their early hardships into a relentless drive that founded multi-billion-dollar empires.

Booker T. Washington, founder of the Tuskegee Institute, was born a slave and died not only free and successful but having bettered conditions for his entire race through supporting Black education and entrepreneurship. Booker T's protégé, A.G. Gaston, was raised in poverty by his grandparents, who were former slaves. He worked in the mines, making paltry wages in dangerous conditions, and faced constant racism. While fighting in World War I, he saw how respectfully he was treated in France. He thought of moving there to live his life comfortably, but felt a moral obligation to come back to America and make things better for his people. Having few opportunities available to him, it was in the lack of opportunity, he saw one. At the time, funeral insurance was unavailable to African Americans, so Gaston put faith in his ability and started a burial insurance company. It served his community and set the stage for his future insurance fortune. His grandparents were slaves, and he died with a hundred million dollars.

You likely have more opportunity than any of them were born with. Now the question is, do you have the ability?

# #17

# YOUR MOST PRECIOUS RESOURCE

*"Time is evenly distributed capital, use it wisely."*
—CHONG JU YON, FOUNDER OF HYUNDAI

Your most valuable currency is the only one you cannot obtain more of, no matter how hard you work.

Spend it wisely, not just on steps to grow your business. Spend it with maximum thrift. Do not make it rain minutes at the strip club of life's distractions. Spend it with family. You won't have as much time as you wish with older family members, and you will miss key times in younger family members' lives as they grow up.

No need to feel guilty about either, though, if you do miss moments. What's done is done. Just do better moving forward. Guilt is an unnecessary emotion built into our brains as a deterrent to being a piece of shit. Use it only as a motivator. Something you've felt in the past that makes you a better person so you can avoid feeling it; once you've done something to feel guilty about, the only thing to do is make it up to the person your mistake has affected. Make amends instead of apologies. Spending time actually feeling this emotion is a waste of time that you should feel guilty about. If you need packing tips like rolling your clothing and then vacuum sealing it so you can fit more in your suitcase, let me know, I'll help you plan your guilt trip.

I cannot stress how important time is. The older you get, the more you realize its value. When you're young, you don't bat an eye about spending time to get money, but the only value you actually receive is experience. Once you have enough experience to feel confident embarking on your own, stop wasting time on building other people's dreams.

Here's how to get more time in each day and manage every second more wisely.

## SOCIAL CALENDAR

*"No such thing as spare time, no such thing as free time, no such thing as down time. All you got is lifetime. Go."*

—HENRY ROLLINS

Throw a monthly or even weekly dinner party. Invite old friends, new friends, romantic interests, and business contacts all at once. A good eclectic mix of people from different industries and walks of life will make the conversation riveting. You'll close deals in business, open up a new romance, all while catching up with friends and getting to know new acquaintances better.

To have even more time, order in or get someone else to cook. You don't need to show off your skills in the kitchen. Or if your budget is limited—or just to change it up—get everyone to contribute. They can bring dishes potluck style, or you can all cook together. If someone else cooks, you can all clean up the kitchen together. It's a bonding experience. Even billionaires or well-known celebrities will enjoy the rare opportunity to roleplay as the 99 percent. But you alone should not do the cooking and cleaning. You'll have no time to connect with your guests, and everyone else will feel guilty that you worked so hard while they enjoyed the evening.

Good friend and behavioral scientist, Jon Levy, throws an epic dinner party with industry leaders being invited to a ten-to-twelve-person dinner where everyone cooks and then cleans together, hosted in one of their houses in an intimate setting. After dinner another fifty influential people come over for drinks, enlivening talks, magic tricks, musical performances, and live entertainment. It's a great way to connect. He often promotes his books or whatever he's working on and lets others promote their creative endeavors. He makes sure everyone brings a bottle of alcohol, so the events cost next to nothing. It's brilliant and everyone's lives are enriched. And best of all, it saves lots of time.

Another friend of mine does things differently. He drops serious coin every month on lavish dinners at restaurants. He invites each one of his close friends who are in town, his family, and important business contacts. Everyone has a blast, and if he gets one lucrative business opportunity out of it per year, the massive tab pays for itself.

## WORK CALENDAR

*"You have to be absolutely brutal in the management of your time."*
—FRED SMITH, FEDEX FOUNDER

When the press wanted to interview Edison, they'd invite him to Manhattan, and he would say, "If I go into the city, I'll lose the whole day. You can come here, and we'll talk while I work."

If a meeting can be a call, a call can be an email, or better yet, a Slack thread or group text, make it so. If you must have a meeting, invite only the most important people. If someone wastes time in a meeting, don't invite them to the next one. If someone is in a different time zone and has a family, let them speak and get off the call first. Not only should you manage your time, respect your team's as if it were your own. They will appreciate this.

## MONEY MANAGEMENT

When Andrew Carnegie realized he was looking at the stock ticker first thing in the morning and checking his investments before his company's, he sold all his stock in other companies so he could focus on his business. He famously said, "The way to become rich is to put all your eggs in one basket and then watch that basket." Saving time applies to outside investments as well.

If you feel you absolutely must have other investments to feel secure, have someone else manage them. Or just pick safe horses and forget about it. Fidelity did a survey and found that the people who had the best record of trading through their platform weren't the most experienced traders or the people who invested the most time into research. The traders with the best-performing portfolios were the ones who had *died*. They weren't able to panic-sell or make decisions based on emotion. If Bill Gates had never diversified and kept all his Microsoft stock, he wouldn't be a billionaire. He'd be the world's first trillionaire. And then you'd really hate him.

# #18

# THE BEST ROI IN THE WORLD

*"There are answers worth billions of dollars in a $30 history book."*

—CHARLIE MUNGER

If you're smart, you won't start out on this journey alone. You'll find a mentor. Hopefully, you'll find someone living, but if not, get help from beyond the grave. As Charlie Munger says, "Make friends with the eminent dead." Books, *especially biographies*, are life's cheat codes. Think about it. In several hours, you can download the accumulated learnings of someone's entire life, their career, their mistakes, their regrets, everything they did right, and the consequences of every major decision they made.

Did you know the entire basis of our digital age came from one creative mofo reading one dusty-ass book?

In 1937, Claude Shannon witnessed a successful circuit board being used to help route phone calls at Bell Labs. Shannon was a voracious reader and had come across the 1854 work from George Boole entitled *An Investigation of the Laws of Thought*. This pre-Civil War book denoted that symbols and equations could be used to translate logic. For example, a system of 1's and 0's denoting "yes" and "no" could further be used to denote "if...then," "And," "Or," and every combination you can think of.

Shannon took this analogue system and, with the inspiration from Bell's phone system circuits, applied it to the precursor of modern-day microchips. The simple 0 or 1 binary code to express logic from Boole's thesis could be translated to digital circuit boards. Instead of using symbols or handwritten equations to represent each yes or no to get to the conclusion, Shannon theorized that this work could be done by switching "on" (1) or "off" (0) any transistor on the circuit. He took a century-old, abstract mathematical concept and evolved it into the spark that lit the fire for the information age. This systematic way to design and analyze digital circuits is the building block of all computers.

Eleven years later, Shannon wrote the paper, "A Mathematical Theory of Communication," which *Scientific American* called the "Magna Carta of the Digital Age." This paper showed that bits—a binary choice such as yes/no or true/false—like a light switch on a circuit board, could break down any piece of information into a series of binary choices. These two states, represented by a single bit: 0 for "off" and 1 for "on," could be combined, representing much more complex information, such as text, images, sound, and even video. This is the basis for all digital storage today, from your laptop to your phone, to the cloud, to the 👻 pics on your Snapchat. To put that into perspective, William Poundstone said detailing Claude Shannon's influence on the information age is "like saying how much influence the inventor of the alphabet has had on literature."

The next book you open at your local garage sale probably won't be as significant to humanity, but it could net you a cool billion. So, enjoy your yacht, you insignificant bastard. You're welcome. And thank you for picking up my book! Speaking of which, learning from history's wisest is a great opportunity to practice gratitude, one of the most important and overlooked traits you can have. In your mind, thank those who came before you for the advancements they've made that help you. Thank them publicly when you get the chance. Gratitude is the precursor to abundance. Here's an email Steve Jobs wrote to himself in 2010:

**From:** Steve Jobs
**To:** Steve Jobs
**Date:** Thursday, September 2, 2010 at 11:08PM

I grow little of the food I eat, and of the little I do grow
I did not breed or perfect the seeds.

I do not make any of my own clothing.

I speak a language I did not invent or refine.

I did not discover the mathematics I use.

I am protected by freedoms and laws I did not conceive
of or legislate, and do not enforce or adjudicate.

I am moved by music I did not create myself.

When I needed medical attention, I was helpless
to help myself survive.

I did not invent the transistor, the microprocessor,
object oriented programming, or most of the technology
I work with.

I love and admire my species, living and dead, and am
totally dependent on them for my life and well being.


Sent from my iPad

In short: learn from the best who've ever done it, the best who've ever lived, and the best you've never even heard of. Isaac Newton expressed gratitude in his famous quote, "If I have seen further [than others], it is by standing on the shoulders of giants." Back then, he was drawing mostly on limited knowledge from those in his field. Today, you get to start in a far superior position, learning not just from those in your field, but from the greatest achievers who've ever walked the Earth. And not just business. Biographies contain something much more valuable than tactics, ideas, successes, and failures. You get to know what's coming *in life*. Many write their stories when they're close to the end. Not only will you know what to expect, you'll learn their regrets so you can avoid them. You'll learn what's truly important because the writer has had decades to reflect. Be grateful you're here now and have this wealth of knowledge on tap instead of having to hack through the jungle of life with a blunt machete.

# #19

# GOOD INPUT LEADS TO GOOD OUTPUT

*"Even a brilliant mind is only as good as the material, the input, fed into it."*
—ROBERT A. CARO IN *THE POWER BROKER*

*"Why steal from anyone but the best?"*
—DAVID OGILVY

Great ideas are not born in a vacuum. If you live in a white-walled room with no art, no internet, and no outside contact, you're not going to come up with the theory of relativity. You need to be exposed to creativity, stories of perseverance and cleverness, ideas, books, music, and business gurus touting the latest e-commerce tools, podcasts, and classic movies.

It's everything you ingest. It's the accounts you follow on social media, the shows and documentaries you watch, the people you hang out with, the coffee table books you flip through, the art exhibits you go to, the events you attend, the seminars, everything. It must be the best to inspire the best in you. There's so much crap out there, so many clickbait articles and videos, mindless celebrity gossip, and reality TV—besides Gordon Ramsay—we love him, don't we? It all sucks your most precious resource: time. So, if it provides zero inspiration, it's not serving you. If it's not serving you, stop doing it. You will not get the next great idea from doomscrolling. You must increase the quality of what you let into your subconscious. If you want to become great, the first step is to expose yourself to greatness.

The same way good input equals good output, take a wild guess what bad input leads to. When Walt Disney was dreaming up Disneyland, he visited every amusement park he could. He would go, get inspired, take notes on what to do and what not to. Early in his research, he visited Coney Island. It was such a tawdry godless shithole that Walt had the urge to quit. It was so bad, it almost altered the timeline and made Disneyland nothing but a broken dream. If Walt had gone to one more place like that, you might not get woken up hungover on a Saturday by your kids. Jumping on your bed. Throwing a tantrum, begging to be taken to the happiest place on Earth. Luckily, one of his next stops was Tivoli Gardens in Copenhagen—an incredible park which served as more great input—causing him to fall back in love with his original vision.

Be careful, even when doing research, of pumping garbage into your brain. You are more susceptible than you think. Only watch TV that makes you smarter. Beyond your friends, only follow social media accounts that provide value. Unfollow the thirst traps. In fact, you can even mute your friends who post dumb or annoying stuff. They might see the unfollow, but they'll never know you muted them. The same way you become the company you keep, over time, you become the media you consume. To be the best, you must only allow in the best.

# #20

# TO GET OUT OF THE HOLE, SEE YOUR CAREER AS A WHOLE

*"Identifying with them and seeing parallels with every stage of my own life enabled me to see my career as a whole and to know that it would turn out the way it has."*

—JAMES DYSON

Dyson said this after looking at the career trajectories of his engineering idols, Buckminster Fuller and Isambard Kingdom Brunel. Whenever he lost faith, he saw that they went through the same hardships. Their careers turned out great, and James knew his would too if he would just press on.

You need to see what you're going through as just a temporary hole you will climb out of soon enough. Your entire journey won't be this tough. Looking at the hardships others you revere have endured will strengthen your resolve. Nowadays, Dyson's company does $10 billion in revenue, and he owns 100 percent. Imagine if he knew that at the time when everything was falling apart, when his ideas were shamelessly stolen, and he was in the middle of multi-year lawsuits with no end in sight. Or the times he used his family's house as collateral for a loan he couldn't repay. Thankfully, he had read about the rock-bottom moments in the careers of his idols and could draw a parallel to his career, avoiding despair.

In 1953, after visiting the US to work on a licensing agreement, Sony founder Akio Morita was overwhelmed. His first thought upon seeing the vastness and industrial might of the US was it would be impossible for his little Japanese company to compete. He then visited Germany and was shocked by how fast they were recovering from the war compared to Japan. They were turning into a mechanized powerhouse, already producing thousands of cars per day. He became even more disheartened.

It wasn't until he visited a small town in Holland where the internationally renowned Philips Corporation was based that he was instilled with a newfound confidence. He realized that if the Philips founder came from a small farming town where they still used windmills and everyone rode bicycles, and founded such a technologically advanced, world-famous company, so could he. He saw that his career could follow a similar path. He immediately wrote his partner, "If Philips can do it, maybe we can too." If it weren't for Akio seeing that someone else could build a great technology company from an obscure part of the world, he may never have built Sony into the powerhouse it is today. And you probably wouldn't be going on a crime spree in GTA 6 on your PlayStation right now while you pretend to read this book.

Looking at the hardships and failures your heroes had to endure to get where they are is an invaluable tool. Whenever you face an insurmountable obstacle, find someone you admire and see how they got through it. All your previous life experiences are preparing you for an opportunity you can't even see yet.

Don't just compare yourself to Mark Zuckerberg and say, "He launched Facebook out of his dorm room and became a billionaire at twenty-three, why aren't I achieving the same rapid level of success?" He is a robot. The rest of us have to struggle. Make a list of your personal heroes and read their stories.

James Dyson looked to his heroes, and after reading his book, *Against the Odds*, he's become one of mine. My struggle pales in comparison to his. It's likely your struggle will pale in comparison to your heroes. It's not a pity party pissing contest—just some much-needed big-picture perspective to patch over the pain.

The next piece of the pain-appeasing puzzle also starts with a P.

# #21

# PASSION OVERPOWERS PAIN

*"Unless you have a lot of passion about this, you're not going to survive. You're going to give up."*

—STEVE JOBS

Buddha said, "Desire is the root cause of all evil." It's also the starting point of all achievement. If you want to live your life like Buddha, I commend you, but you should probably put this book down. You're reading this book because you desire a lot. You want to get more out of life. And you will.

Desire will make you unhappy—Buddha was right about that, but some desires are worth it. Desiring unnecessary things like diamond necklaces or Rolexes will keep you unhappy till you get them, and you'll get only a sugar rush when you do. I know a woman who felt even deader inside when she got the diamond necklace of her dreams. She was like, "Wait, this is all I feel when I get what I wanted?" Ferraris are different though. As the 500-horsepower V12 mounted inches behind your eardrums hits 8,000 RPM, its whining will always overpower your own.

But what will fulfill you beyond anything you can buy? A worthwhile goal. Deep down, ask yourself, "What do I actually desire most?" For me, it's freedom. What do I mean by that? Freedom to express myself to the fullest, to do what I want when I want, to help others, to spend time with my family, and to travel wherever, whenever. However, I also desire never to lose my discipline. And along the way, I want to leave each place I visit and every person I meet, better off than if I had not been part of the cosmic equation.

Accomplishment is another popular one, though less fulfilling than you might think. Winning an Oscar, Grammy, or Nobel Peace Prize is great, but are you really going to be that much happier all-around once you have that gold trophy in your hand? Not long term, though it feels a helluva lot better than a participation award.

Going after your desire and getting it can also make you a great example for your kid or family member, but it's not what motivates me.

Having a challenge is another key to this whole desire thang. You set a goal. The odds are against you. You go and do that thing everyone said you couldn't, and you prove them all wrong. Amazing. Again, it's a short-term sugar rush when you actually get there. It sounds cliché, but the journey really is the best part.

Everyone has a void that needs to be filled. You'll go through a lot of hellish moments in life. What you're suffering through should be worth it. If you were some desireless eunuch, you'd be suffering without cause. At least have a good reason to suffer. As a Buddhist, you could view desire as "a contract to be unhappy," or you can use it as fuel to get out there and bring your dreams to reality. Because living a desireless life sounds miserable. And let's be honest, even Buddha had a desire. He wanted to reach Nirvana. *Nevermind* about that though. Just buy the ticket, enjoy the ride, and let your desire fuel you. If you're not burning with passion about the company you're building or the product you're inventing, you won't have the perseverance to push through to success. You will give up. So if that's you, you might as well give up now and settle for a measly paycheck.

Passion gives you strength, thick skin, and mental fortitude. People in power respect it, and people below you are inspired by it. If you're not currently radiating passion to everyone you meet about what you're doing, it's time to find a new pursuit. You simply cannot attain real, lasting success without passion.

## TURN WORK INTO PLAY

*"What appeared to be hard work to others was simply playing for me. We were playing a game, why not play as hard as you can?"*

—MICHAEL JORDAN

While passion can turn work into play, there's also a positive flywheel; you like doing what you do, so you do it more and get better at it, making the work even easier. Conversely, if you don't like what you do, you'll spend your days hating your life, and you'll want to work less, resulting in less success.

However.

You know the saying "Do what you love, and you'll never work a day in your life." Well, when you're two months behind on payroll, thirty days away from being evicted, and your employee healthcare just got canceled because the state of Florida froze your bank account, the meaning of that cliché goes right out the fucking window. The overwhelming, lower-back pain from stress feels just as shitty...with one key difference: when you're passionate, your suffering has a reason. A marathon runner said, "Pain is inevitable, suffering is optional." There will definitely be days that suck. A thousand of them. You'll just be more equipped to *embrace the suck*.

## LIKE FINDING YOUR FAVORITE FOOD

*"There are many reasons curious people are more likely to do great work, but one of the most subtle is that, by casting a wide net, they're more likely to find the right thing to work on in the first place."*

—PAUL GRAHAM, CO-FOUNDER OF Y-COMBINATOR

Unless your favorite food of all time is breast milk, then you know it takes trying many different things to zero in on what you like. If your favorite food is something exotic and rich like caviar, foie gras, or truffle-butter lobster tail, then you have to try hundreds of other foods first to figure that out. And if your favorite food is a simple cheeseburger and fries, you still have to try foie gras just to make sure. Otherwise, you'll never know if you're hitting the upper limit of your taste buds and will have to live in permanent paranoia of not living up to your snobbiest potential.

The point is, like food, you have to be wildly curious to find your passion in life. If you're not trying everything that interests you, you might be dancing around your destiny without anything ever truly *clicking*. Once it "clicks," you'll know. Finding the one thing that fuels you, that one activity that feeds you and causes your soul to glow, will deliver you away from mundanity toward spiritual contentment. If what you're doing today doesn't feel this way, you're not doing the right thing. Change it up.

Not feeling insanely passionate? Follow your natural drift until you find something that you love doing, that you're good at, which the world needs. If you love doing it and you're great at it, but it serves no purpose to the world, you won't make money. If you're great at it and it makes money, but you don't love doing it, you won't last long. And if it makes money and you love doing it, but you suck at it, either get good fast or keep looking. The intersection of all three is where you'll find purpose... and money.

## WHAT YOU DON'T WANT

*"In life anything can happen, even if you don't have all the things you want, be grateful for the things that you don't have that you don't want."*

—BOB DYLAN'S DAD

If you're still having trouble coming up with what you want out of life, why not try focusing on what you don't want? Instead of hurting your brain thinking about your dream, write down your nightmare. What you don't want to do for a living. How you don't want to spend your days. The legacy you refuse to leave behind. Once you know what you absolutely are not going to do with the time you have left, you can narrow it down. You'll think clearly about what you want to build. Who you want to create it with. What you do want to do with every precious day and ultimately how you want to be remembered. You can even write the epitaph on your gravestone and work backward from there.

# #22

# HAVE A MENTOR

*"Attach yourself to somebody older and wiser than you, learn everything they have to teach, and then move on to your own accomplishments."*

—GEORGE LUCAS

If you don't already have a mentor, get one immediately. Ideally, one who can give you hands-on experience in person.

Before we launched Culprit Underwear, we knew nothing about fashion and even less about manufacturing, e-commerce, inventory management, hiring, management, financials, raising money, or business in general. I'm a film school dropout. When I titled this book, the zero-experience bit means zero experience. The only thing we knew how to do was make videos. Even the videos…they were funny and eye-catching, but we had no clue how to create content that would sell and didn't know what a sales funnel or landing page was.

So, what did we do? We collected mentors. Anyone we knew in fashion got a phone call, every e-commerce whiz got a cold email. We set up weekly mentor calls with a new guest mentor every Tuesday. We did about ten of these calls and wrote down everything they said. This is how we built our knowledge base. Should've done one hundred calls instead of ten though. Would've spilled a lot less blood.

Everyone who's anyone has had a mentor. Without Thomas Edison, famously pushing Henry Ford into overdrive, he may never have changed the face of American transport and heralded in the modern age. One night at a dinner after hearing about Ford's internal combustion engine, Edison blurted, "Young man, that's the thing!" **pounds table for emphasis** "Electric cars must be kept near to power stations, the storage battery's too heavy. Steam cars won't do either, for they have a boiler and a fire. Your car is self-contained, carries its own power plant, has no fire, no boiler, no smoke, and no steam. You have the thing, keep at it!"

Ford's first two car companies failed. Had this encounter with Edison and their ensuing friendship not given him the conviction to persevere, the Ford Motor Company probably wouldn't exist.

To be great, you need the modern equivalent of an apprenticeship first. Do not skimp on this. Whether you believe in nature or nurture, all the best players have had an incredible coach. Michael Jordan was the NBA's leading scorer, but didn't win a championship until Phil Jackson came along. Ditto with Kobe. Who's gonna be the Phil to fill your void?

Greatness is not created in a vacuum; the teachings are passed down to those hungry and curious enough to receive them. Your mentor will not find you; you must seek them. Start by asking for help. It's one of our best survival skills and has been thoroughly discounted in recent times in lieu of appearing strong and independent. People love to help when asked.

Steve Jobs says it better than I can, so this portion is in his words from the book *Becoming Steve Jobs: The Evolution of a Reckless Upstart into a Visionary Leader*.

> I have never found anybody who didn't want to help me when I asked them for help.
>
> I called up Bill Hewlett when I was 12 years old. "Hi, I'm Steve Jobs. I'm 12

years old. I'm a student in high school. I want to build a frequency counter, and I was wondering if you have any spare parts I could have." He laughed, and he gave me the spare parts, and he gave me a job that summer at Hewlett-Packard...and I was in heaven.

I've never found anyone who said no or hung up the phone when I called. I just asked. And when people ask me, I try to be responsive, to pay back that debt of gratitude.

Most people never pick up the phone and call. Most people never ask, and that's what separates, sometimes, the people who do things from the people who just dream about them.

As Jeff Haden of *Inc.* magazine puts it, "Asking for help is not a sign of weakness, but a predictor of success."

Beyond simply asking for help, you can try less traditional approaches like Steven Spielberg. After being rejected from USC's film school multiple times, Spielberg took matters into his own hands.

Legend has it that while on a public tour of Universal Studios Hollywood, he snuck off the tour, and while looking official wearing a suit and tie and carrying a briefcase, he ran into TV executive, Chuck Silvers. Impressed with his passion, Silvers let Spielberg sit in on movie and TV productions on the lot. This experience of seeing major studio feature films being created firsthand allowed Spielberg to gain the knowledge to level up. Inspired, he made a short film, *Amblin*, and through his access with Silvers, got it in front of executive Sidney Sheinberg, who was so impressed, he gave Spielberg a seven-year contract. Without Chuck Silvers' mentoring of Steven Spielberg, you don't have *Jaws*, the first three *Indiana Jones* films, *Saving Private Ryan*, or *E.T.*

Mentors are not only helpful for their access, building up your confidence, and teaching you a thing or two, they can also change your entire outlook. James Dyson, inventor of the Cyclone vacuum, had this to say about his mentor, Jeremy Fry: "Here was a man who was not interested in experts. He meets me, he thinks to himself, 'Here is a bright kid, let's employ him.' And he does. He risks little with the possibility of gaining much."

When Fry had an idea, he wouldn't say, "Let's sit down and work through the calculations and see if it's feasible," he would just go out and create it. He passed this spirit onto his apprentice. When Dyson would imply they needed professional help, saying something like, "We'll need to weld this," Fry would say, "Well then, get a welder and weld it."

Sometimes all you need in a mentor is someone to help you ignore everything you've learned prior. Enthusiasm and an indefatigable spirit can go a lot farther than an indoctrinated education or thinking of yourself as an "expert." Without a mentor, you'll likely fall into the patterns of those around you. Sometimes you don't need someone telling you what to do. What you need is someone telling you what *not* to do. The world wasn't changed by those who think the same. Just make sure you find the right mentor. Not just any old advice off the shelf will do.

What does your mentor get out of the relationship? When a mama eagle dropkicks her toddler eaglet out of the nest, forcing it to figure out how to fly before it hits the ground, and she looks up and sees her baby soar, the pride she feels is the pride your mentor will feel when you spread your wings. Plus, who knows, maybe one day you'll hire your old mentor like Walter Chrysler did.

Still convinced you don't need a mentor? If not for a man named Captain Horace Bixby, Mark Twain would not have become, arguably, the greatest writer in American history. Instead, he would've just been Samuel Clemens, America's first cocaine dealer. Google that. 😉 Albeit, he might've made more money as America's first drug lord.

Don't let the lack of a rich or famous mentor deter you from becoming a legend. Remember, some of the greatest mentors are available to you in a book for thirty dollars or less.

# #23

# THE COMPANY YOU KEEP

*"Associate yourself with people of good quality, for it is better to be alone than in bad company."*

—BOOKER T. WASHINGTON

They say your success will be the average of the five people you hang out with the most, but it goes deeper. If your friend becomes obese, you're nearly 50 percent more likely to gain weight in the next couple of years, but if your friend's friend who you've never even met becomes obese, you're 20 percent more likely to gain weight. This ripple effect of friends of friends of friends goes two more levels deep and can influence everything from your likelihood of smoking to when you have kids. And who you hang out with definitely affects your happiness. Some people have black clouds raining over them and always bring you down just a little. As they say, some people are investments while others are bills.

If you want to be more successful, you need to hang out with successful people. Their ideas and ambition will rub off on you. Their network will expand yours. Cash doesn't rule the world, relationships do! Build relationships with other entrepreneurs and people you look up to. You'll also be happier. Only 15 percent of happiness comes from achievement; the other 85 percent comes from your relationships. If work is half of your waking life, then make those relationships great.

Not everyone you hang out with needs to be rich and successful. I'm not saying ditch your close friends with regular jobs. Just spend more time with inspiring people and become friends. You become the company you keep. So does your company.

This lesson is something I've personally failed at for a decade and am only now realizing what a detriment it's been to my career. I haven't gone out of my way to foster new friendships with other founders. I've sought mentors only when I needed them. For how long I've been at the helm of a successful company, my network is unimpressive. Going out of your way to make new friends who are successful in your field or in wildly different fields will pay dividends you can't even fathom. Just go in with no agenda. Make friends who inspire you. Don't worry about missing out on the party for a while. The party crowd isn't going anywhere. *Literally*.

# #24

# HIRE A-PLAYERS

*"If each of us hires people who are smaller than us, we shall become a company of dwarfs, if each of us hires people who are bigger than we are, we shall become a company of giants."*

—DAVID OGILVY

It's impossible to be perfect; however, there is one field more than any other where you should strive for perfection: hiring. There are few mistakes costlier than hiring the wrong person. Steve Jobs said, "A-players hire A-players, but B-players hire C-players, and C-players hire D-players." He maintained that this loss of focus on hiring leads to a "bozo explosion." Remember, the company you keep will one day dictate if you get to keep your company. If you're letting bozos in the door, even to sweep the floor, you're going to wind up poor.

As much as you hate to realize what your actual job as a founder is, I'll tell you the hard truth. It's not to build or create something great. The creative process loses importance after a successful launch. Your job as a founder is to hire and inspire the best possible team. You must seek the best talent from all corners of the globe. You are now a glorified talent scout. Sorry, I had to tell you this way. It is your people who will make all the difference, and it must be you who chooses the right people. Don't hire people you don't trust, don't like, or don't admire. Before you hire, ask yourself: Will this person raise the average effectiveness of the group they're entering?

Elon Musk interviewed the first 1,000 hires at SpaceX himself. Every single person, from the rocket scientists to the janitors. If you lose focus on hiring only the best, you will experience a gradual deterioration in the quality of your company. Hire well and you'll keep up your spirit of innovation and productivity. High standards of people lead to high standards of work.

Why was Apple in such bad shape before Steve Jobs returned? Because they focused on hiring salespeople instead of top-notch engineers. They focused on revenue over talent. The engineers lost passion due to this approach and the "bozo explosion" that resulted. Many of them left. The salespeople were left with worse products to sell. When Jobs returned, he once again put the focus on talent to design insanely great products, leading to Apple's unprecedented revival.

It's a slippery slope; the first B-player you hire brings the whole company down. What if you're growing too fast and it's too time-consuming to hire A-players? Either hire the world's best headhunter, slow down your growth, or pay people overtime. Sam Walton said, "You should only hire once it hurts." It is better to be slightly understaffed than overstaffed. Teams that are a tiny bit understaffed are more focused and spend less time doing redundant busy work. If you bring on too many people to keep up with growth, you're going to have a rough go of it in the next downturn. You're going to have layoffs. It's going to suck way worse than being temporarily overworked.

Should you do what every other company does and require unrealistic experience to even apply for the job? Absolutely not. Hire for intelligence and enthusiasm over experience ten times out of ten. Inexperienced people are way more capable than they get credit for. Their lack of experience allows them to think from first principles.

Back in the day, David Ogilvy met with the head of Sears. An employee had just made a mistake that cost Sears $10 million. This was the exchange that happened:

**Ogilvy:** "Are you gonna fire him?"

**Head of Sears:** "Hell no, I fire people who don't make mistakes."

This illustrates that it's far riskier to have people unafraid to take risks in the long run. People will learn from their mistakes. If they don't, that's when you fire them. The person who never makes mistakes isn't pushing the boundaries. Some people are too afraid of being fired to take bold action and be decisive. For an innovative business, these are the wrong people to hire. There may be some colossal fuck-ups due to inexperience, and you should especially check people's work leading up to big decisions. Encouraging fresh, bold thinking by hiring the right people will yield incredible results. Let the intelligence and enthusiasm run wild.

# #25

# HAVE CHARISMA

*"It is absurd to divide people into good and bad. People are either charming or tedious."*

—OSCAR WILDE

Most people think charisma is something you're born with. I believe it's something learned early on, leading to charismatic children and non-charismatic or shy kids. Traumatic and embarrassing experiences early on lead to less outgoing, less charismatic adults. But if that describes you, it only describes you in your current state. Shyness and introversion can be unlearned. Charisma can be learned.

Even if you're neurodivergent, I promise you, you can learn charisma. I have a friend with severe Asperger's. To say he was uncharismatic would be an understatement. He made it a point to fix this. After selling his software company for a modest return, he decided he would live in a different country every month for six months. He ended up living three years in a row like this, all over the world, completely by himself. He had to force himself to be outgoing and talkative, learning charisma along the way. The first few countries were complete failures, but there were great moments in each. This inspired him to keep going until it became so much fun for him to challenge himself in new cultures that he is unrecognizable from the person he used to be.

You might not have the money to travel around the world yet, but that was just an extreme example of going from Asperger's to affable to show you what's possible. If you can learn coding, mathematics, or study literature, you can apply the same thirst for knowledge to social skills and make others feel warm and welcome. Although it feels like an art, it's a science like any other. Shyness, coyness, and introversion are not in your DNA. They are learned behaviors, and you can learn other behaviors.

You can still be successful being reclusive or introverted and only letting a select few into your life, but you will increase your surface area for luck if you're out there meeting the best people in your field. You'll find mentors, business contacts, clients, friends, romantic partners, and everyone in between if you master a few basics.

I've always been somewhat social, but as soon as I came across *The Charisma Myth* by Olivia Cabane, I felt the need to master it. While I recommend this book no matter what stage you're at, here are some of my key takeaways to get you started.

## BE PRESENT AF

*"Your entire life consists of the present moment."*

—ECKHART TOLLE

We've all heard we need to be more present, but what that means is being fully engaged in the moment, attentive, and connected with whom you're speaking.

My attention turns into *Flubber* when others are talking. Sometimes I will zone out so intensely, they'll ask me a question, and I'll just nod like I've been paying attention. But I'm usually thinking about utter nonsense like how beavers used to be as big as bears or how sloths were the size of elephants. A useful tip for this is to anchor yourself to the moment. You can do this by focusing on the sensations of your body, such as your breath. My favorite one is to focus on your toes. If you find your mind wandering while someone else is talking, try moving your toes and focusing on that.

## ACTIVE LISTENING

*"Contrary to popular opinion, listening is not a passive activity. It is the most active thing you can do."*

—CHRIS VOSS, FBI NEGOTIATOR, AUTHOR OF
*NEVER SPLIT THE DIFFERENCE*

Show genuine interest in others by nodding while they speak, maintaining eye contact, and asking follow-up questions.

When someone is talking, don't nod like an Adderall-addled weirdo and don't make your eye contact so intense that you're analyzing their soul. Give them real attention and don't focus on what you're going to say next, like 90 percent of people. Actually listen to what they're saying. When they're done speaking, you can take a pause and respond thoughtfully. There's no rush to get your point across or bring up a story they just reminded you of, switching the subject to you.

Want to keep the conversation going? Let them talk about themselves. It's everyone's favorite subject, and the best way to do that is to ask open-ended questions. Not a simple yes or no, or where are you from, but things like: What was it like growing up there or during that time? What was it like having so many siblings or being a middle child? What made you realize that about yourself? Why did you go into that career? What were some of the struggles you experienced founding your company?

Author David Augsburger says, "Being heard is so close to being loved that, for the average person, they are almost indistinguishable." To actively listen is such an important skill. Focus on every word, and only when they are done speaking or have asked you a question should you speak. If it's critical to interrupt, say, "Let me put a benchmark in what you're saying" before adding your thoughts. It's okay to take a pause and think when it's your turn to talk. You do not need to have your next sentence lined up for rapid-fire conversation. Remove that urge from your mind. This is not a movie. You do not need to worry about what eavesdroppers will think of your Tarantino-esque dialogue skills. Not only will this make people like and respect you more, you will also learn and retain more details about the other person. It won't just go in one ear and out the other. You will also appear more charming. Who doesn't want to be charming?

Prime Minister Benjamin Disraeli once went on a date with a woman. His political rival, William Gladstone, took the same woman out on a date that same week. When asked by the press about the difference between the two suitors, she replied, "During our time together, Gladstone convinced me that he was the cleverest person in England. But Disraeli made me feel like I was the cleverest person in England." The difference was that Gladstone spoke, and Disraeli listened. Disraeli asked open-ended questions about his date and let her do the talking. His style of active listening ensured he would recall specific details during their conversation. Disraeli's skills to actively listen and make others feel important did not just help his dating life. There's a reason he became one of the most famous prime ministers in England.

## ELIMINATE DISTRACTIONS

Put your phone away, not on the table, even if it's upside down, because it subtly suggests to the other person you're with that you're not 100 percent there. Put it on airplane mode and keep it in your pocket or bag. Try to sit with your back to the window or to the other people in the venue so you can give your full attention to who you're with.

This one is easy, but a lot of people still get it wrong. If you pick your phone up while I'm telling you my life story, I'm going to get pissed. If you absolutely must check your phone while someone is talking, let them know the reason. "I need to see if my friend is okay." Whatever it is, people will appreciate you giving them the reason you need to check your phone. If you don't absolutely need to check it, don't. If talking to this person is like watching paint dry, either practice your acting skills and pretend you're captivated, or ask better, open-ended questions to get a more entertaining conversation. I bet whoever you're talking to has had an interesting story happen at least once in their life. Dig for it. Every interaction you have moving forward will be better when you do.

> **HACK:** gamify conversations. When bored, dig for one interesting fact or story about the person you're talking to. Also, find one thing you have in common.

## DISPLAY CONFIDENCE

*"I taught him that if you act like you can do something, then it will work. I told him pretend to be completely in control and people will assume that you are."*

—FOUNDER OF ATARI, NOLAN BUSHNELL, ON HOW HE COACHED STEVE JOBS ON RUNNING APPLE

Whether you're naturally confident or not, or having a rare unconfident moment, you can fake your body language to the point that it gives you and the person you're speaking with a real benefit.

By simply standing or sitting tall with your shoulders back and making sure your posture is on point, you can positively affect both your mood and theirs. When your body displays confidence, you become more confident. And they will become more relaxed and comfortable. Energy introduces you before you speak. And when you speak, make sure your voice displays a matching level of confidence. Here are some tips:

- **Voice Control:** Speak with a calm and steady tone to convey authority.
- **Dress the Part:** Wear clothing that makes you feel confident and aligns with the image you want to project.

- **Show Competence:** Share your knowledge and expertise without bragging.
- **A Shot of Tequila:** When all else fails, Dutch courage prevails. Just don't go off the rails.

# #26

# NO EXCUSE FOR EXCUSES

*"You can have results or excuses. Not both."*

—ARNOLD SCHWARZENEGGER

This one I still need to work on, but I'm getting better every day. The reason I haven't fully mastered this yet is because…holy shit, I almost made another excuse.

Quitting excuses is harder than quitting vaping, but necessary. Be diligent about this. Excuses are annoying at best, and no one cares. Especially people who operate at a high level.

If you're going to be late, be transparent about it. Just say, "I'm running fifteen behind." Don't give me a reason why you're late. I prefer to say, "Thank you for waiting" rather than "Sorry, I'm late." And don't tell me why you missed our call or took forever to reply. Admit your mistake, make zero excuses, and make amends. That last part is the most important. No one cares that you're sorry. *Canadians* are sorry. *You* need to make amends. No one cares if you're late because of traffic. They care that you're late. You should know by age twenty-five that traffic is a thing that exists and plan for it. There's a saying, *If You're Going to be Late, Bring Donuts*. The point is, make it up to the person or group you've wronged. That goes with any screwup in life. Making amends is paramount to apologizing.

When you make a mistake, simply say: "Apologies, allow me to make it up to you." They'll say something like, "That's not necessary." Ignore this and go out of your way for this person. Move the fucking Earth, in fact. Go beyond the level of your screwup with the level of your amends. Get them tickets to a show, take them out to dinner, invite them to a cool event—experiences are typically better than things—a personalized gift, or if you have no money…write them a nice note. In short: go way out of your way. They didn't deserve what happened, and you're a good person who makes things right. If you do this properly, your relationship will be better off than if you hadn't fucked up in the first place. In fact, if you did such a good job making amends, you'll have carte blanche to ruin things in the future. That's the sweet spot I've thrived in my whole life. See you at the next colossal screwup. You're welcome.

There's an exception to the no-excuses rule: if you're presenting or doing any public speaking, and you're not 100 percent in the zone, you can preface your talk with an excuse. Let the audience know you're nervous, inexperienced, exhausted, hungover, or depressed because you ran over the squirrel that couldn't make a decision in upcoming lesson #45. It will put the audience at ease in case your performance is slightly off, and they'll relate to you more. This also humanizes you. Not to get all new age on you, but people can feel your vibe, and if you feel your vibes are off, you need to let people know, or they won't vibe with you.

# #27

# FIND SOMEONE WHO BELIEVES IN YOU

*"Having someone who believes in you makes a lot of difference. They don't have to make speeches. Just believing is usually enough."*

—STEPHEN KING

If you have a significant other, make sure they're actually significant or they'll make you insignificant over time. The right partner is everything in business, but the right life partner is everything in life, including business. Do not marry someone who doesn't understand your need to work or sees your passion as competition for their attention. This applies to deep friendships as well. Ambition is a condition, and trying to subdue it will make you both miserable. If someone tries to change you for their benefit, they either don't understand you or, worse, they do understand you, and they're being selfish. They will only delay your greatness.

You know the classic horror film, *Carrie*? What you might not know is that the original novel, written by Steven King, fell victim to one of those unavoidable spells of self-doubt we've all experienced. Our inner critic kicks in, and that unwavering self-belief we pride ourselves on suddenly falters. When that happens, it's vital to have someone who believes in you even when you don't. For Steven King, that was his wife, who dutifully rescued the only typewritten copy of his masterpiece from the trash bin. She uncrumpled the coffee-and-cigarette-stained pages, re-instilled her genius hubby's confidence in his abilities, and helped launch the book that would propel King to superstardom. This future kingmaker endured abject, trailer-park poverty because she believed in the legend-to-be. You are a legend-to-be as well. Even if you don't believe it in this moment, you must find someone who does. They can raise you from the temporary depths we all face, to overcome whatever challenge comes your way.

In my case, it's been helpful to have sense beaten into me with harsh words and the occasional physical violence. This has almost without fail been lovingly applied by my saintly-patient business partner and two-decade-long friend, David. I am thankful every day for how curt he is with me and how hard he is on me. Without him keeping my ego, work ethic, and pie-in-the-sky thinking in serious check, I would not be where I am, and neither would he. I haven't exactly been easy to deal with. As you know, I'm stubborn, driven by spite, and ready to go to the ends of the Earth to accomplish or do anything for the simple reason you told me I can't. He's helped shape me into the man I am, and I am eternally grateful. Thank you, David.

I keep him in check too, but I'm way nicer about it and use humor instead of hellraising, which one day I hope he learns. The tough love, though, is something I wouldn't trade for the world. I just don't need it 24/7.

# #28

# FIND THE RIGHT CO-FOUNDER

*"Ford by himself could not have managed a small grocery store, and Cousins could not have assembled a child's kiddy car, yet together they built an organization that astounded the world."*

—EXCERPT FROM *I INVENTED THE MODERN AGE: THE RISE OF HENRY FORD* BY RICHARD SNOW

Having a business partner, creative partner, or co-founder is like a marriage. It takes work. It gets stressful. You fight. Especially when you're broke or on the brink of ruin. You think about saying fuck it and striking out on your own. Keith Richards did solo projects, so did Mick Jagger, George Harrison, and John Lennon, but nothing touches the Rolling Stones or Beatles because when you find the right match, there's sparks, there's fireworks, there's electricity in the air. You want to find someone whose strengths are your weaknesses and vice versa. I got extremely lucky there.

You can't have two leaders at any given time. One of you needs to lead the other, but not permanently. Ideally, whoever's in charge will switch like how the Navy SEALS do it. You follow one leader to breach the building, then when the door is blown, the other takes the lead to clear the first room, shoots a terrorist in the face, and calls "all clear." Then the first one is safe to walk into the second room. When one is scared, the other one gives them strength. When one is tired or being lazy, the other pushes that last ounce of energy out of them. When one is arrogant, the other puts them in check. When one takes a bullet, the other mends them back to health. If one of you is bearing all the stress on their shoulders, the other should be unconditionally supportive.

As corny as it sounds, the key ingredient is communication. When David and I split our roles to run not one company but two simultaneously, I let him know I was there whenever he needed me. When I was running our underwear brand by myself, I tried to shield him from the insurmountable stress and problems I was going through. Big mistake. I needed to be more communicative to let him know what I was going through. Perhaps if I had, he could've offered advice that might have saved me much anguish and not plunged us so deeply into debt. Now we have a daily catch-up and a weekly meeting to let each other know the details of our domains, and things have never been better.

Be open, be transparent, and when you're going through hell, don't just keep going like the Churchill quote. Ask for help. Churchill asked for help too. FDR wussed out in the beginning. Refusing to give any assistance, but the incessant Churchill eventually appealed to FDR with an undeniable approach by saying something to the effect of, "the fate of the free world rests on you giving me some god damn weapons," and thus the Lend-Lease program was born. You need to ask your partners for the same level of support.

You're not on your own. And if you ever feel that way, you're either not asking hard enough, or you're not asking the right person. You might have the wrong partner. If the latter is true, rip that Band-Aid off as fast as you can, and go find a teammate who you can pass the ball to when you don't have a shot.

In my production company, we had a third partner. He was the sweetest, nicest, funniest, and most talented cinematographer I've ever come across. He elevated the quality of our work by an order of magnitude, and we got along great. But he bore too much responsibility without being able to handle it. He rarely kept his word, not in a malicious way; he just forgot. Then he'd make excuses when he didn't do what he told you he would. No matter how talented someone is, if they have these fundamental flaws, you will not be able to work with them long term. David and I had to let him go. It was one of the hardest decisions to make and an even harder conversation to have. He was and still is one of our best friends. As soon as we did it though, we kicked ourselves for not doing it sooner. It was like a ray of sunshine on our business. All the focus on constantly fixing problems created by one team member and all the extra effort to try and get him to change his ways could be redirected.

You need to rely on each other when the going gets impossible. Mutual reliability, belief in each other's abilities, and a balancing of weaknesses with strengths are all you need. You can do everything on your own, but it will take longer, you'll accomplish less, and doesn't that sound lonely and miserable? I do not recommend this.

Fondly reminiscing on his half-a-lifetime partnership with Warren Buffett, Charlie Munger said, "Seek a partner who will never second-guess you nor sulk when you make expensive mistakes. Look also for a generous soul who will put up his own money. Finally, join with someone who will constantly add to the fun as you travel a long road together."

What if you have a fight with your partner? Fights are healthy. They might suck in the moment. You might cry, and you might come to physical blows as David and I have on several occasions. You might storm out of the room and stomp your feet like a child having a tantrum, but once you leave the room, you will reflect, and you will understand they were right, and you were wrong. You'll admit your mistakes like an adult, and you'll move on stronger and better for it. It's called growth. You'll fight more often when things aren't going well. Be prepared for this. Be open to deep-cutting criticism. The more you don't want to hear it, the more you need it. Ben Horowitz credits his success with Mark Andreessen to their daily fights:

People often ask me how we've managed to work effectively across three companies over eighteen years, most business relationships either become too tense to tolerate, or not tense enough to be productive after a while. Either people challenge each other to the point where they don't like each other or they become complacent about each other's feedback and no longer benefit from the relationship. With Mark and me, even after eighteen years, he upsets me almost every day by finding something wrong in my thinking and I do the same for him, it works.

Get ready to hear hard truths, accept your shortcomings, and only promise to do things differently if you're actually prepared to change.

# #29

# BUILD REAL RELATIONSHIPS

*"Business, like life, is all about how you make people feel, it's that simple and that hard."*

—DANNY MEYER, RESTAURATEUR

There's an old adage on film sets: be nice to every crew member and production assistant; they might become a studio executive someday. This happens more than you think. Don't be nice just because there's a chance they'll be above you one day. Be nice because that's the right way to be. Go even further. Genuinely connect with them and get to know them. Use a few minutes of your attention to remember things about them. This goes with every vendor and outside agency you work with. Life is a long game, and who knows, maybe you become such great homies with someone at another company you work with that you end up starting a company together. The result isn't important now; the relationship is.

You're not networking, you're making friends. Tell fucked-up stories, get them to swear, and tell mildly dirty jokes. Be slightly unprofessional. If they respond positively, go farther away from business than you think you should and turn this from a business relationship into a real friendship. Some of my best friends I've met doing business with them. If I stayed in my cautious shell, that wouldn't have happened. Many of those relationships evolved from business to friendship because I took the first step in oversharing. I put myself out on a limb. Sometimes I burned bridges, but those bridges were flimsy anyway and would get washed away in the first storm. Instead, try sticking your neck out a bit, and you'll see the bridges that do get built are way sturdier.

Don't get it twisted, I'm not telling you to share your foot fetish during your first martini together—unless you're meeting Tarantino—I'm just saying to put your professional face back in your briefcase and see what this person is all about. See where your lives intersect. Find the commonalities and the differences. Test a little dark humor. Get to know each other, not just each other's work. The following screenshot is from a text I got while writing this chapter. It's someone who invested in my company, and now we have an opportunity to develop a lasting friendship:

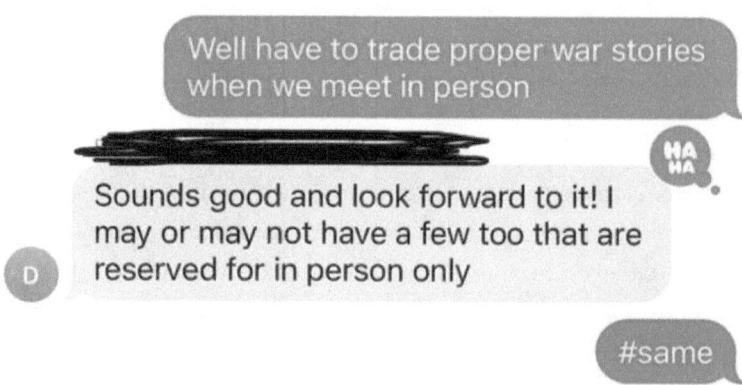

I have yet to meet this person beyond a video call, but rest assured, I will practice what I preached in this chapter, and he will go from investor to probably us being such good friends that he ends up attending my wedding sometime in the next decade.

Don't shrug off someone at an outside agency just because you feel wronged by their company or no longer work with them. When your business is at death's door, you may be saved by a relationship. Money doesn't rule the world. Relationships do. They are worth more than any amount of short-term gain. Life is tragically short, but it's also the longest game in town.

# #30

# INVITE TRUSTED CRITICISM

*"If the criticism is valid and it comes from a point of view of being well thought out, and not just an attack, then I accept it and I get better as a result of it."*

—OPRAH WINFREY

People often criticize because they do not have the mind to create. They can only analyze what you're doing through the lens of what has worked in the past. There should, however, be those in your life you trust to give an honest critique. I'm not telling you to listen if even your most trusted friend says your dream is impossible when you know you can do it. Just know who to go to for no-bullshit notes. Be wary of yes people. It's harder to get an honest answer the more successful you become. For example, if your new project is dogshit and you ask people what they think, they may reply "It's great" because they're afraid to offend you. Bluntly honest opinions are harder to get the more powerful you become. Especially if you're the breadwinner of your inner circle. Find opinions you can trust. When asked what's one piece of advice you'd give to an entrepreneur on their new venture, Elon Musk said, "It's very important to actively seek out and listen very carefully to negative feedback, and this is something people tend to avoid because it's painful." Just don't take criticism from someone you wouldn't take advice from.

When you show someone—whose opinion you trust—your product, service, or exciting new marketing campaign, tell them: "Don't tell me what you like, tell me what you don't like." Actively seek feedback you may dread. It's your decision whether their opinion is valid. But you should know where your target audience stands. Make adjustments before you go through a one-way door.

You can be your own harshest critic. In the 1970s, Arnold Schwarzenegger hired a photographer to take detailed photos of his muscles. He inspected them with a magnifying glass to see where he needed more definition.

Tough love keeps egos in check. It battles lazy thinking and corner cutting. If you have someone honest enough to tell you the truth, consider yourself lucky. Swallow your pride and go out there and make a masterpiece together. Consider it teamwork. Even if they're all business and you're all art, the intersection of the two is what makes something commercially viable. And if your art isn't commercially viable, no one will ever see it. I was in an experimental film program for three years, and all of it was shit. All of it, zero exceptions.

Howard Hughes did not have this. He was surrounded by yes men, people he trusted who didn't want to risk losing their paychecks. They let him succumb to madness, terrible attention-seeking behavior, awful business decisions, worse hygiene—like storing his pee in jars—and paranoia-inducing painkiller addiction. Let the people around you feel comfortable disagreeing with you, saying no to you, and calling you on your inevitable bullshit. Just tell them to follow Dale Carnegie's advice and pull you aside and tell you you're a dickhead privately, lest you lose your stature as a trusted leader in front of your team.

A deleted chapter of this book was called *The Power of Meme*. I showed it to my business partner to get his critique. Here it is.

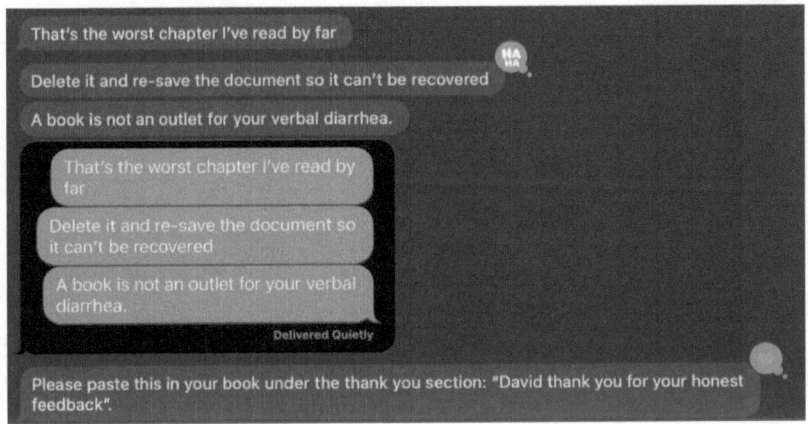

Thankfully, I have someone I trust to tell me honestly—brutally—when I make something subpar. Everyone has off days. Makes another pile of dogshit. No matter how good they are. I was so proud of myself that this chapter was going to explain how powerful memes are and do it in an unforgettable way. All I got was a bruised ego and this T-shirt. But it made *this* chapter better.

# #31

# HARDEST IS EASIEST

*"The bigger the apparent risk, the fewer people that will try to go there. We would surely lose if we had to face serious competition."*

—LARRY ELLISON, FOUNDER OF ORACLE

When the sexy siren of the impossible calls you, and you hesitate because you know it will be a long, bumpy road, remember that in the long run it will be easier than the easy route. Your chances for success will be greater. Why? Because there's less competition.

In the early 2000s, government agencies and the massive, public companies they employed were the only successful game in outer space. Every private space company before had been a several-hundred-million-dollar, extremely public, abject failure. Going up against government-subsidized aerospace juggernauts and NASA itself was borderline impossible. But because it was so hard, no one else was doing it. This ambition was what made Elon Musk's private space startup so alluring. SpaceX was able to pick from the best rocket scientists in the world because it was the only startup of its kind.

Henry Kaiser, the genius who helped us win World War II with lightning speed manufacturing, made his name by winning massive government contracts to build the Hoover Dam and the *even bigger* Grand Coulee Dam because at that level he had almost no competition. But when his company went after smaller contracts, they often lost because everyone else could compete at the lower levels.

When it comes to achieving the impossible, few rival James Cameron. His movies are often so expensive if they don't crack the top five list of most successful movies of all time, they won't break even. He has to invent new camera systems and visual effect techniques on virtually every movie he does. His dedication to pushing the boundaries of what's currently possible lets him achieve visual feats that are so difficult, other directors don't even attempt them. His inventions don't just make movies though, he helped invent the camera that's on the Mars Rover. On seemingly impossible tasks, he has this to say:

> I'm attracted by difficult. Difficult is a fucking magnet for me. I go straight to difficult. And I think it probably goes back to this idea that there are lots of smart, really gifted, really talented filmmakers out there that just can't do the difficult stuff. So that gives me a tactical edge to do something nobody else has ever seen, because the really gifted people don't fucking want to do it.

It's for this reason that of the top four grossing movies of all time, three of them are his. At that level, there's just no other single individual for him to compete with. This makes his impossible job of consistently pushing the dual envelopes of technological breakthroughs and success just that much easier.

# #32

# DARE TO BE DIFFERENT

*"When everyone is going right, look left."*
—SAM ZEMURRAY, IMMIGRANT TURNED BANANA MOGUL WHO CAME FROM NOTHING AND TOOK OVER THE MOST POWERFUL CORPORATION OF HIS DAY, UNITED FRUIT

You can't stand out by looking the same, and you can't get to the top by fitting in. Back when newspapers were hawked by cigarette-smoking twelve-year-old "newsies" shouting, "Extra, Extra, read all about it," every paper looked the same. Joseph Pulitzer knew that not only did the content have to be better, but the appearance had to draw eyeballs, so he would jam his paper, *The World*, full of as many illustrations as possible. To this day, it's the bestselling paper in history.

You don't have to literally reinvent the wheel like James Dyson did with his ball-barrow—a wheelbarrow with a pneumatic sphere instead of a tire that can drive through mud—but you do have to differentiate *dramatically*. When Dyson came out with his next invention, the Cyclone Vacuum Cleaner, it was the first bagless vacuum ever. It never lost power as it filled up and showed the dirt swirling around in a mini-cyclone as it cleaned. It was *revolutionary* 😉. His contemporaries told him no one wanted to see the dirt. They explained he should cover it up and make it look slick...he flatly disagreed. He figured if this thing picks up dirt better than anything else, people will want to see that. So, he made a clear window to see the dirt sucked up by his cyclone. Did it work? How many bag vacuum cleaners do you see these days? None unless you're watching an episode of *Mad Men*. Dyson defends his machine, especially when "competitors say it looks disgusting. Salesmen think it suffers from looking so filthy in a row of gleaming machines. But its aesthetic disadvantage is what gives it its magic. People look at it and say, 'My God, it works!'"

By being different enough, you can "accidentally" become a monopoly. The only way to ethically make monopoly-style profits is with a differentiated product or business. Culprit Underwear does not have a monopoly, but when we first launched LadyBoxers, we were the only game in town. Since then, we've been copied like a drunk guy's ass at the office party's Xerox. What we do differently though, and what's way harder to copy, is how wild we go with our prints. This one is called Comfort Food.

At first, they look cute, but then all of a sudden you notice the details. You think, "Oh God, is that meatball spanking another meatball with spaghetti?" You either laugh or get offended. You're either an instant fan for life, or you'll never wear them. We pride ourselves on the niche we've carved out. Every print tells a story, and we design each one so it could be its own animated show on Adult Swim. We take being silly seriously.

This is an example of a *moat*, a term coined by Warren Buffett, which is a defensive layer around your business that rivals would have a tough time copying. Or in his words, the moat is "a metaphor for the superiorities that a business possesses that makes life difficult for its competitors."

Find what makes you different and lean into it. Being better isn't enough. When Steve Jobs decided to create retail stores for Apple, he didn't say, "How can we make a better store?" He asked, "How can we reinvent the store?" To paraphrase Warren Buffett, build the fucking moat!

# #33

# DON'T GO CHASIN' WATERFALLS

*"In a gold rush, sell pickaxes."*

—UNKNOWN

In the California Gold Rush of 1849, the majority of miners didn't strike it rich. Few made enough to send money home, and many didn't even make enough to cover what they spent getting out there.

Those who really profited were the people who sold the supplies and provided the services the miners needed. Many made money off tools like pickaxes, tents, and clothing. Those who set up restaurants, hotels, saloons, banks, or sold real estate did extremely well. During the gold rush, Levi Strauss saw that miners needed durable clothing. He saw that the tents' fabric held up, so he started making pants out of tent canvas and selling it to miners. This led to the creation of more comfortable *denim* and later, blue jeans. The multibillion-dollar Levi's brand would never have existed if Strauss hadn't decided to sell his version of pickaxes instead of following the herd mining for gold.

When everyone converges on the same industry simultaneously or chases the same risky boom, your odds of success go down. You are not seeking your fortune like you might think; you are simply competing against a growing multitude. In the automobile gold rush of the early 1900s, some 3,000 American auto companies were formed. Of those, most never made money, and now, after bankruptcies and mergers, there are only three left. Instead of competing with Henry Ford, Albert Champion invented better sparkplugs, which led to the founding of AC Delco, a massive car parts company.

Howard Hughes Sr., the famous aviator's dad, made his family wealthy not by drilling for oil, but by inventing highly advanced drills during an oil boom. Instead of selling the drills, he leased them, providing free sharpening and servicing with each lease. After a few months, the drills paid for themselves, and every month after was pure profit.

In the ashes of the dot-com boom, many websites failed, but computer companies like Dell and Apple made a killing. For the smartphone-app boom, the modern pickaxe is Amazon Web Services. They sell server power. It has a higher profit margin than Amazon's normal business, ya know, Amazon.com? And as I write this book with my own dumb, analogue sausage fingers, the current boom is, of course, AI. You know who I see killing it the hardest? Nvidia. Making so many chips, we ran outta salsa.

Instead of following the herd, provide for it. But in a pandemic, don't go buying up all the toilet paper and sanitizer; you're not enterprising, you're just an asshole.

# #34

# BE UNFAIR

*"You might as well send a cow in pursuit of a rabbit."*

—GEORGE WASHINGTON

Our first president was telling his tea-loving overlords, "the Bri-ish," that fighting Native Americans in the French–Indian war with formal, gentlemanly, turn and face your enemy—while wearing a bright red, fancy coat—war tactics were impractical. When you're in your opponent's territory and your "superior technology" musket can fire only three times a minute, while they can silently ambush you with arrows and flee on horseback, who's really got the advantage?

What he would've said in today's business environment is to only compete where you have an edge, or else you're going to get slaughtered by people who know the terrain. He survived having multiple horses shot out from under him to teach you one simple lesson...Find Your Unfair Advantage.

You know when little kids say life isn't fair? You want to be the person they're talking about. I take this so far that I even have an unfair advantage when I shop for a Halloween costume. Most people I know go to costume stores last minute with lines out the door for cheap throwaway outfits that impress no one. The day before Halloween, I go to a Hollywood wardrobe rental warehouse that, in the Google description, specifically calls out that they do not rent for Halloween, "Do not even try." It is not open to the public. You must have a production currently filming (or the illusion of one) to enter its doors. Luckily, I still have my production company's checkbook. I simply say I'm doing a shoot, and I gain access, even though the only shoot I'm doing is iPhone snaps for my post-Halloween photo dump. I'm the only person in the whole warehouse on the day before Halloween. I'm changing clothes in the middle of these racks, trying on costumes, and there isn't even a mirror in the whole building. It's such an unfair advantage, and I routinely kill it every year for Halloween with zero effort. Apply this to your business and make sure you do nothing without that juicy, unfair quality that gives you an edge.

## WHAT'S YOUR UNFAIR ADVANTAGE?
## IS PRICING YOUR UNFAIR ADVANTAGE?

*"Any customer can go online and find the cheapest price for anything anywhere in the world. The strongest thing your company can do is something no one else can do or will do well."*

—YVON CHOUINARD, FOUNDER OF PATAGONIA

Your unfair advantage can come from making a product cheaper than anyone, like SpaceX. Their reusable rockets cost one-third the price to launch. Walmart's prices can't be beat because they buy in such high volume. Standard Oil could undercut any competing refinery because it sat between a river and a railway. That way, they could pit the steamships and railroads against each other on shipping costs.

Once, John D. Rockefeller simply showed Standard Oil's accounting books to a rival. The rival saw that there was no way to compete. Rockefeller was refining oil and transporting it so cheaply that he could still make a profit while his rival lost money at the same price. They would lose unless they sold their refinery to Rockefeller. This led to the "Cleveland Massacre" when Rockefeller gobbled up twenty-two of the twenty-six rival refineries within just two months.

Southwest Airlines could get you to your destination for just a few bucks more than driving or taking a bus. The company realized it wasn't competing with other airlines; its prices were so low that it was actually competing with ground travel. When another Texas airline tried to swoop in and cut prices even lower to drive Southwest out of business, they fought back, not by lowering their price, but by offering a free bottle of liquor with each ticket purchase. The businessmen on these flights paid extra for Southwest because they were expensing the flight, and their boss didn't know they were pocketing a bottle of Johnnie Black.

## IS YOUR UNFAIR ADVANTAGE SUPERIOR TECHNOLOGY OR DESIGN?

*"Just think of all those Ford owners who will one day want an automobile."*

—JOHN DODGE

If you're the iPod publicly whooping the Zune's ass or the iPhone coming for Blackberry, it's going to be an easy fight. If your cyclone vacuum looks like nothing you've ever seen and costs 4x the price, it might be hard to convince stores to carry you, but it's easy to stand out to customers. Even the brokest of the broke folk need a superior vacuum and will shell out the cash—even during a recession—because it's a fantastic investment in keeping your home clean. If you have electricity, you own a vacuum cleaner, and a bagged vacuum costs much more over time. At the time of Dyson's Dual Cyclone launch, vacuum bags were a $500 million business in Britain alone.

The Dodge brothers knew they couldn't compete with Henry Ford on price, so instead, they continuously made improvements and raised their prices a little each time. Dodge cars got better while the Model T stayed the same.

When you hear the words "Walmart," I'll bet you're not thinking about a technological breakthrough. However, when Sam Walton was forty-four years old, he decided he was wasting too much of his precious time left on this Earth on ten-hour commutes between two stores. It was at that moment when he looked up in the sky and heard a heavenly buzzing. It was an angel named Cessna. Sam decided to charter a flight. For a little extra money, his commute was reduced from half a day to ninety minutes. It was then he decided to save his most precious resource, time, and learn to fly a plane. Flying low over traffic patterns, he would not only skip the trip, but he'd also see ideal towns for new stores. Using his unfair advantage in the sky, he could also see how busy his competitors' stores were by checking how many cars were outside. Is there an underutilized technology you can use to carve yourself an extra edge? What other advantages are ripe for the taking?

## IS YOUR UNFAIR ADVANTAGE A NETWORK EFFECT?

*"A telephone, without a connection at the other end of the line, is not even a toy or a scientific instrument. It is one of the most useless things in the world."*

—THEODORE VAIL, CHAIRMAN OF AT&T IN 1908

The term *network effect* comes from when AT&T first dominated the telephone game. In the early 1900s, after striking an agreement with Western Union, which went something like "this game ain't big enough for the two of us, stay off my phone lines and we'll let you have your shitty outdated Morse-code wire that will only increase in irrelevance as daddy-long-lines takes the reins." They then used the existing telegraph poles for rapid expansion and figured that once 20 percent of a town was on the same phone network, the rest were going to follow suit. The value of the network increased the more people joined. If someone was on another network, they couldn't reach their friends and family who were on AT&T, so they'd have to switch. The network's value overtook everything in its path and led to the term "network effect."

Facebook garnered a network effect in a way that MySpace and Friendster couldn't. While its technology was superior, you joined because your friends were on it or someone you thought was hot "poked" you.

## IS YOUR UNFAIR ADVANTAGE THE QUALITY OF YOUR PRODUCT OR SERVICE?

*"If quality is your edge, you can't compromise it."*
—ISADORE SHARP, FOUNDER OF THE FOUR SEASONS HOTEL

When it comes to quality, you know your Levi's won't tear, your Toyota won't leave you stranded, and your Rolex will tell time. And tell people you're rich.

Amazon's service is unparalleled. They offer free, same-day delivery. In fact, it's so good, it hurts my underwear company because people expect orders to arrive tomorrow. Amazon focuses on customer obsession. They make it really easy to return anything. If you've ever had a bad experience with a product, they'll make it right. When you're that obsessed with customer satisfaction, no one else can compete.

Patagonia's product quality is its number-one focus. No other climbing or outdoor clothing compares. You know it will last, and if you ever have an issue, you can simply bring in your ripped jacket or broken zipper, and they'll fix it for you. That's how you make customers for life and make sure they tell everyone they know about how great your company is.

With McDonald's, it's not that their quality is so amazing, it's just so consistent. You can roll into a McDonald's in Madagascar and have the same meal you can in Manhattan. The quality is always the same, so if you're on a road trip, you can go to McDonald's and know what you're going to get instead of risking a sketchy diner.

## IS YOUR UNFAIR ADVANTAGE SUPERB BRANDING?

*"Products are made in a factory, but brands are created in the mind."*
—WALTER LANDOR, ACCLAIMED DESIGNER

Charlie Munger said, "A brand is a promise." Is the chord your brand strikes strong enough to promise your customer something? Building a strong brand is no easy task. You have to have a strong why. Liquid Death works so well, not just because of their noble mission, "Death to Plastic," but because before them, there was no cool water. You don't want to be seen drinking a bottle of Dasani in a photo. Drinking Liquid Death promises you look cool while being healthy. It also works so well because the heavy metal music culture is universal; it's the same in virtually every country.

Ian Blair, founder of Laundry Sauce, asks, "How can you apply brand to get outsized margins?" He's done a great job of branding, scent creation, and using all-natural ingredients. They charge three times the price of a Tide Pod. When you can't compete on price, this might be the answer. This is how luxury goods work; it's all about the prestige of the brand. Yes, the quality is great, but it's only marginally better than a premium or even mid-range brand. Unless it's precious metals, the materials don't cost that much more. Neither does the manufacturing. Just the designer's name. The only way to get luxury margins is with a luxury brand.

## WHAT'S CULPRIT'S UNFAIR ADVANTAGE?

Brand for sure. Specifically, our videos. Yes, we have the quality and the attention to detail, but it's really the branding and content driving the sales. We are known for it. We make people laugh. Funny videos get shared more. People get a positive feeling toward the brand because we made them happy. Our wildly detailed print designs continue this. So does every touch point with our customers. We take things further, figuring you'll either love it or hate it, but you definitely won't be indifferent. With a name like Culprit, we can do insane prints and get downright salacious with our content and jokes. We can do this now because it's who we were at the beginning.

David and I directed commercials for a decade before we launched our first Culprit ad. We're the only underwear company with a full-time,

Pixar-level CGI artist. No other boxer brand has a chance of beating us on content quality. But we use these skills to make the dumbest videos ever. We take not being serious seriously. Other brands have investors to answer to, a company board, and more to lose than to gain by putting balloon animals getting it on on their underwear prints. We have nothing to lose and everything to gain; our niche is for people who never grew up. Adults who are kids at heart, yet love a good R-rated comedy. We don't even call ourselves an underwear brand. We're an entertainment company that happens to make underwear.

That's our unfair advantage. What's yours?

# #35

# LIFETIME VALUE

*"Lifetime Value is the total value of a customer's business over the lifetime of their relationship with your company."*

—JOSH KAUFMAN, AUTHOR

Casper mattresses had hockey stick growth when they launched, but were unable to sustain this growth because how many mattresses are you buying in your life? Unless your spouse is taking your mattress in the divorce and you're getting married like Tom Arnold or having kids like Nick Cannon, you really only need one mattress a decade.

Make sure your product is great, but doesn't have a low ceiling for growth once most of your market purchases one. The lightbulb industry ran into this problem because lightbulb tech got so good that people didn't need to replace them as often. So they introduced "planned obsolescence," essentially products that would wear out quicker on purpose, so you'd buy more. I swear most appliance companies have done this, because anyone who still has a fridge or stove from the 70s, it still works. But anyone who's bought a new one needs a new one every decade. I have a hunch about iPhones too. They made it impossible to replace the battery and something about that software update two years in and my phone gets all glitchy.

I'm not telling you to make shittier products so you can scam your customers. The opposite. Make stuff that lasts, but make a product that people will buy more often than mattresses. I know earlier I said, you have to find something you're passionate about or you won't succeed. Now I'm adding a caveat. Do not be passionate about mattresses. Being passionate about underwear, however, has been great for me because everyone wears underwear except absolute savages. And it's recommended you change your underwear every six months. I have a huge market and a lot of customers who buy twice a year, and many subscribers who buy twelve pairs a year because they don't want to miss the limited-edition prints.

A consumable product that needs to be replenished often is the best for lifetime value. Especially a mildly addictive one. Starbucks is a great example. But beverages are tough outside of retail. They are expensive to ship. I don't recommend that for an online business. Supplements, snacks, soap, and beauty products are excellent for LTV. You're selling to consumers. Make them something special to consume.

# #36

# THE INDIRECT PATH

*"We look to the conifer tree and its logic of growth, and we learn from one of the truly great success stories of natural history. Through its adaptive strategy, which has allowed it to survive for hundreds of millions of years. The patient and persistent conifer teaches us that it is far better to avoid head-on direct competition for scarce resources and instead to pursue the roundabout path toward an intermediate step that leads to its eventual position of advantage."*

—MARK SPITZNAGEL, A PIONEER OF "BLACK SWAN" INVESTING

Author and hedge fund manager Mark Spitznagel, explains the roundabout way of achieving greater success perfectly with the story of Robinson Crusoe. Shipwrecked and stranded on a remote island, Crusoe must catch fish to survive. Catching them with his bare hands takes hours and is wildly inefficient. He decides he must take time off from 'fishing' and go a little hungry, so he can make a fishing net. He starves a little now to realize an advantage in the future. Instead of one or two fish a day, he can catch five or ten. He has more time to build a shelter, figure out a way to salt and store his fish, and so on. He's able to evolve and achieve so much more because he invested time and effort, and was less successful for a while until his investment paid off.

Go slow now so you can go fast later. Be the turtle that morphs into the hare. Build up your strength and gradually accelerate. This is what Henry Ford did when his car cost too much for the everyman to afford. Ford spent time perfecting mass production. He invested in coming up with new techniques to save man-hours. Instead of making a car in two hours, he had one driving out of the factory under its own power every twenty-four seconds. When speed goes up, the price comes down; when the price goes down, the volume goes up. Increased volume equals increased profit. It was this investment in time, manpower, and technique to get things unbelievably efficient that sold fifteen million Model Ts and achieved Ford's goal of a car so cheap his workers could afford it. One thing he didn't account for was space to park them all, because every employee actually bought one, and they routinely had traffic jams in and out of work. The best opportunities are created by the indirect path.

Investing in new technology is a great example of the indirect path. When *The Jazz Singer*, the first feature film with synchronized sound, came out in 1927, Warner Bros. and Fox moved quickly to adapt their studios to sound. They spent a lot more money and took a big financial hit up front, but this paid off as they pulled way ahead of Paramount and MGM, who were too busy making money from the old way of doing things.

Yes, it costs more up front. That's the point. It's called an investment. Take the pain up front. It amortizes over time, and the uphill road ahead flattens out quickly as you pick up speed.

# #37

# CUT THE GORDIAN KNOT

*"The reasonable man adapts himself to the world; the unreasonable one persists in trying to adapt the world to himself. Therefore, all progress depends on the unreasonable man."*

—GEORGE BERNARD SHAW, IRISH PLAYWRIGHT

The Gordian Knot was a complex, intricate, impossible to untie, you guessed it knot that secured the yoke of King Midas's wagon, full of offerings for Zeus, in a temple in Gordium, a city in modern-day Turkey. An oracle had declared that whoever could untie this magical knot would become the ruler of all Asia. People came from far and wide to try to unite this knot. Maybe I'm downplaying how fucking impossible this knot was to untie. This was like when you leave all your necklaces in a drawer with some dental floss, N64 controllers, your ex's hair extensions, and you spill some superglue on the pile, except way worse because it had no visible ends. You couldn't just start with one end and get untying. There was nowhere to start. David Blaine would be like fuck this. Penn & Teller took one look at it and threw up. Everyone failed. For years. It was like a joke to even try. Little kids would point and laugh, "Oh, look at that poor bastard, he thinks he's gonna rule us all!"

But then one day in 333 BC, guess who showed up? Alexander the Mother-Fucking Great. I imagine it was a crisp fall day; it smelled of crunching leaves and rotting apples, and squirrels were getting drunk off the fermented fruit. When the brilliant, tutored by Aristotle (who was tutored by Plato, who was tutored by Socrates) superstar bounded up those steps like the entitled young warrior brat he was, I bet the squirrels were too drunk to care. And I bet Alex didn't stop to film the sloshed squirrels with his iPhone like you would because he was on a mission: a mission to untie that knot!

He fiddled with it, he jiggled with it, he wrestled with it in his mind. But what to do? There were no ends to grab ahold of! People were watching and snickering at each other. He didn't want to think about what brilliant thing he should've done later while he's in the shower. He wanted to become a legend. He wanted to one day be a chapter in this book. He had to act now, but it was impossible!

However, the rules were never specified; in fact, there were no rules. He wasn't gonna let some knot make him not the next ruler of Asia. He drew his sword and, with a single stroke, sliced the knot cleanly in half. Or maybe it wasn't clean. Maybe he hacked the fuck out of the knot so bad, the wagon broke too, and whatever offerings were there for Zeus got smashed, cursing Alex to die at the age of thirty-two. But that isn't the point! The point is, those terrible bully kids stopped laughing, the squirrels sobered up, and Alex the Great became the ruler of Asia.

What's the moral? When a problem is intractable, impossible, insurmountable, or any other big word that starts with "I" and means very fucking hard, traditional approaches and thinking can only carry you so far. Hint: not far at all. So what you need is a bold approach, first principles thinking, and decisive action.

David and I had just won a viral video campaign, beating out a massive agency responsible for the biggest movie, TV, and videogame campaigns of the day, including *The Hunger Games*, the *Tomb Raider* videogame, and every Netflix show. They weren't used to losing jobs, especially to two nobodies. They wanted to know who these arrogant upstarts were and called us in for a meeting. When asked, we told them the insanely low price we were able to shoot the campaign for. Naturally, I quadrupled what we actually spent, which was still half what they were used to paying. They put us to the test with a job for Mattel. We used a friend's house for free and kept the crew low.

Expensive scenes, such as firefighters in front of a firetruck, they thought they'd have to buy stock footage for. Instead, we delivered each scene they had already written off as "stock footage" with original, cinematic content. We drove to several fire stations with a case of beer, asking to shoot in their garage next to the firetrucks. The first two said no; the third one took the beer. David and I donned fire suits. We got the shot. For free. That's how scrappy we were.

Moments after getting that shot.

We submitted the footage, and they were blown away. The following week, they called a meeting and wanted to hire us full time. They asked us for a business plan, so that night I read a book called *How to Make a One-Page Proposal*, and we were off to the races, making more money than we'd ever seen, but way less than we could've asked for.

Over a century ago, advertising pioneer Albert Lasker met with a company that made matchbooks. They were having trouble standing out from their competitors. In the business of mini sticks that can light fires, brand loyalty is apparently rare. He tells them, no one cares about your branding. If I can make people care about the branding on the back of your matches and make customers loyal to your matchbooks, will you give me a million dollars? They said yes. He tells them, instead of putting your branding that no one cares about on the matchbooks, sell that as advertising space to other companies. For the last hundred years—until everyone switched to vaping—almost every classy restaurant and local businesses had their own matchbooks. That way, every time you light up a drunk cig, you think of them. That simple idea was worth millions per year to the company, and Albert got his million.

There are few real shortcuts in life, but sometimes, when everyone else sees an impossible knot to untie, you can pull out your sword.

# #38

# SPECIALIZATION IS FOR BIRDS (AND THOSE BUGS THAT LOOK LIKE STICKS)

*"It's a manner of deep conviction to me that specialization was the death of genius."*
—VANNEVAR BUSH, EARLY COMPUTER ENGINEER AND INITIATOR OF THE MANHATTAN PROJECT

You're not a highly evolved bird of paradise that only knows one elaborate dance to get a mate. You have loads of skills, a variety of knowledge, you're great at a couple things, but maybe not the best in the world at anything. Perfect. You're an entrepreneur, not an athlete. But even if you were, it's more impressive to win a bronze medal in the decathlon than a gold medal in shot put.

You've heard the phrase "Jack of all trades, master of none," which paints being a "generalist" in a bad light, but did you know there's a second half to the quote? The original was "Jack of all trades, master of none, but oftentimes better than a master of one." Being versatile is a blessing. Knowing a little about a lot is more useful than knowing a lot about a little. You don't want to spread yourself thin, but with technology evolving so quickly, if you've poured all your time into mastering one skill, you might get left behind. Being multidisciplinary and having the best ideas from a broad range of subjects helps you deal with the uncertainty of life.

Naval Ravikant famously said, "Become the best in the world at what you do. Keep redefining what you do until this is true. You can only achieve mastery in one or two things. It's usually things you're obsessed about." This is true; however, don't confine yourself to only being a master at one or two things. If you're a great inventor and don't know marketing or basic finance, you're putting your fate in the hands of others. How will you know if the marketing team you hired is doing a good job? If you can't read a financial statement, how will you know if your CFO is worth the money you're paying her? By all means, be the best in the world at your main focus, but pick up other skills so you can have your own back. If you don't learn to be a good judge of character, someday you'll get fucked over.

## FOLLOW YOUR NATURAL DRIFT

If Leonardo Da Vinci was curious about something, he'd just go dissect hundreds of corpses or look at a woodpecker for days until he could draw its tongue from memory. Claude Shannon was a master at not being a master of one thing. His ability to study multiple subjects and combine them led us into the digital age. Even if you're reading this on actual paper like a barbarian and not on some kind of futuristic device, it's because of Claude Shannon. I sure as shit didn't type this on a Selectric Typewriter.

The more diverse skills you have, the more you have to offer to quality people. The more quality people you hang around, the more likely great opportunities will arise, because you've increased your surface area for luck. Luck strikes when preparation and opportunity get it on in the backseat of your car.

Being too specialized in one domain is dangerous. The world is changing faster than ever, and you don't want to hold onto a dying industry like it's the last life vest on the Titanic. The biggest year in history for horse-drawn carriages was 1906. A decade later, those companies were out of business. It's hard to give up on what's working before it's too late, but the best years can come right before a complete and irreversible decline. Warren Buffett says, "Only when the tide goes out do you discover who's been swimming naked."

You could argue Steve Jobs was a specialist at one thing: making insanely great products. In reality, he knew a lot about design, user experience, simplification, presentation, marketing, and storytelling. Without his vast array of knowledge, he wouldn't have been able to simultaneously helm Pixar and Apple. His greatest skill set was recognizing talent, knowing how to inspire greatness in his team, and organization building. There's a reason "Apple is Steve Jobs with 10,000 lives."

Steve Jobs's idol, Edwin Land, was a specialist in light. He read every book on light available in the New York City library. When he founded Polaroid, it was to make polarized lenses for car headlights and windshields to prevent glare and save lives. When the car companies cheaped out on his technology, he went into eyewear and made "the best damn goggles in the world" for the war effort. Here's General Patton wearing them on the cover of *Newsweek*:

Without also having a deep understanding of chemistry, physics, and photography to combine with everything he knew about light, Edwin Land couldn't have gone on to invent the Polaroid instant camera.

For the sports fans, let's talk about NFL all-star Deion Sanders. He didn't just specialize in being a cornerback. He's the only athlete to play in an NFL football game and a Major League baseball game in the same twenty-four-hour period. Yes, I know the private jet helped get him to the other game on time, but he wouldn't have been able to afford the jet if he didn't also know how to put on a show for the crowd. Even with all the money and fame, his career would've been over as he aged out of professional sports. Luckily for us, he did not specialize. These days, he's proven himself yet again as a great leader and legendary coach of my alma mater, CU Boulder.

Now, don't get me wrong, letting your brain ping-pong around too much won't accomplish anything. No one gets to greatness without focus. Edwin Land said, "Intense concentration for hour after hour can bring out in people resources they didn't know they had." Focus is vital. Even when you have multiple pursuits, focus on one thing at a time.

# #39

# WHAT DOESN'T CHANGE

*"I don't think the internet is going to change how people chew gum."*

—WARREN BUFFETT

With the pace of the world, it's impossible to predict exactly what will change. Sure, you can say soon AI will be the biggest evolution in human history. Okay, how? When? What jobs are going away, and what new ones are coming? Will people turn into Bohemian artists living in utopian abundance, or live just above basic survival, never able to own their own home? Is everyone going to be supersmart with Neuralink and have all the answers? Or will we be dumber than ever from widespread misinformation? Will we finally realize we're living in a simulation and have to start civilization from scratch when the smokescreen comes down? The truth is, no one has any idea. Instead of worrying about everything that's going to change, focus on what won't.

When automobiles first came out, people clung to horses like hay dingleberries. Cars were noisy, slow, unreliable, dirty, smelly, and gasoline wasn't around the corner because gas stations didn't fucking exist. Grass and hay, on the other hand, were everywhere. And unlike automobiles, horses started up every time. All you needed was water, hay, and a swift kick to the ribs with your spurs. Cars were only for rich enthusiasts, kind of like horses today. Funny how the stables turn.

When Bezos thought about the future of his company, he didn't focus on what was going to change, because that's impossible to predict. He focused on what *wouldn't* change. People will always want the lowest prices, the most selection, and the fastest shipping, so he focused on that. Maybe now he has more data, though on what will change based on the hockey-puck-sized wire taps everyone, including me, has allowed into their house.

# #40

# LET THE CRITICS THINK YOU'RE CRAZY

*"It never ceases to amaze me: we all love ourselves more than other people, but care more about their opinion than our own."*

—MARCUS AURELIUS

You'll have to be a crazy sonuvabitch to take your idea *all the way* while facing a typhoon of criticism, adversity, "advice", and valid-sounding reasons why it won't work. Here are some examples of things people stuck to their guns about that, at the time, everyone thought was absolutely bonkers:

- Sony's board thought founder, Akio Morita, was crazy for wanting to make a tape player that couldn't record and could only play back: the Walkman went on to sell 400,000,000 units.
- When Sam Walton was working for JCPenney, his manager told him he was just not cut out for retail.

- Steve Jobs was criticized like crazy for getting rid of the floppy disk on the iMac, then getting rid of the CD Drive, then losing the keyboard altogether for the iPhone, but Steve trusted his gut.

While on the subject of Apple, let's discuss their retail stores. Pretty cool and visionary, right? That's not what Apple's former CFO, John Graziano, thought when he said, "Apple's problem is it still believes the way to grow is serving caviar in a world that seems pretty content with cheese and crackers." Expert retail consultant, David Goldstein, said on the subject, "I give them two years before they're turning out the lights on a very painful and expensive mistake." I must say, *Businessweek* takes the cake though:

Long story short, Apple winds up being the most successful retail brand in history. *mic drop*

*Barron's* had a similar glimpse into the wrong timeline when they published this article about Amazon's impending doom on their cover:

In the 1920s, Robert Goddard, a pioneer of modern rocketry, wrote many papers on the subject, and he patented many techniques we still use for liquid-fueled rockets today, including using multi-stage rockets to escape Earth's gravitational pull. *The New York Times* got wind of his crazy idea and wrote an article detailing how "a rocket could not work in the vacuum of space." Goddard replied, "Every vision is a joke until the first man accomplishes it." Many years later, The Times retracted its statement and issued an apology.

So, what's the moral of the story? Most critics don't know shit. Joe Rogan said, "The people that are tossing shit your way, they're doing it to distract themselves from the fact that they're not contributing anything." Just listen to your gut and drive the train forward. If you're pioneering something new, criticism is a good sign. May the voices of my critics grow ever louder. What I fear is the chirp of the crickets; the deafening boom of indifference.

# #41

# BET ON YOURSELF

*"You can fail at what you don't want, so you might as well take a chance on doing what you love."*

—JIM CAREY

Sometimes you need to gamble on your idea and your ability to execute that idea better than anyone else alive. It's a gamble to quit your cushy Wall Street job like Jeff Bezos. It's a gamble to sell your only possessions like Wozniak and Jobs did when founding Apple, and it's a gamble to go against the advice of experts who might be right for once after all. But if you want to be successful, there will come a time when you'll need to bet on yourself. This is what George Lucas did when he took a minuscule salary on Star Wars in exchange for something the studio considered to be worthless: merchandising rights of the franchise.

After every well-respected academic told him it's impossible to predictably win at Blackjack, Ed Thorpe bet on himself that he could figure it out. He came up with a formula, literally invented card counting, and painstakingly programmed a gigantic mainframe computer using punch cards to give him every possible scenario. He carried tiny index cards with him to reference his strategy. When no one else would fund him, he raised money from a small-time gangster to go up against big-time gangsters back when Vegas was controlled by the mob. When he started winning, the mob casinos cheated to counter his success, but he *still* managed to beat them. He caught them cheating blatantly and reported them to the Nevada Gaming Commission. But they, too, were controlled by the mob. For safety, he would go to different casinos every time in disguise. When he went to the same casino twice, they poisoned him. He came back the next day and was extra careful, but still got drugged again. The drug made him sick for days, even after only a small sip. The entire drink would've killed him. On his way home, he barely avoided an accident that would've killed him and his wife. They had sabotaged his car.

After doing the impossible twice, beating both Roulette and Blackjack, Thorpe bet on himself again and wrote *Beat the Dealer*. The book detailed his card-counting strategy and some of his exploits so readers could tell when casinos were cheating them. It became so successful, he went from broke teacher to rich author. It changed the face of Blackjack forever, with single-deck blackjack all but disappearing. Card counting became such a problem from the popularity of his book, they had to train dealers to look for it and kick people out when they were caught.

After his Vegas glory days, Thorpe decided his efforts to beat the odds and achieve the impossible would be better served—and his family would be safer—in a bigger, more lucrative, *slightly* more regulated casino: the stock market. Instead of hundreds of thousands, he made hundreds of millions. He founded a market-neutral hedge fund, never had a losing year, and then wrote another bestseller called *Beat the Market*.

Once Ed had proven the bets he had placed on himself, proved everyone else wrong, and made more money than he could ever spend, he retired to get the maximum out of his remaining time. If there's one person to model your life after, it's probably this guy. He looks young for his age, he's active, has all the time in the world for his family, and he does whatever he wants. He realized there's no point in spending time to make money when he has more money than he'll need for the rest of time.

On the subject of betting...only bet when you have an edge...including betting on yourself. Never make a bet that can clean you out to zero. Unless you're Fred Smith, founder of FedEx, who didn't have an edge and bet his company on gambling for real. Faced with insolvency, needing $27,000 by Monday to keep his business alive, Fred did what any desperate man exhausted of options might do. He went to Vegas with a few hundred bucks and sat down at the Blackjack table. He walked away with over $30,000 and the future of FedEx in his hands. FedEx was saved at a Blackjack table. Ask yourself...are you playing to win? Or playing just not to lose?

# PART TWO

# THE PARTY

# #42

# THE SECRET TO BEATING THE ODDS

*"May the odds be ever in your favor."*

—THE HUNGER GAMES

In *The Hunger Games*, everyone dies except one final survivor. The real world of business is harder and more cutthroat because you're not facing other teenagers with zero combat experience, you're facing seasoned veterans—the venerable gatekeepers of capitalism. If you found a startup, you're going against everyone who's ever been successful in your field. You might be going against giant multinational, publicly traded corporations with government protection and other entrenched adversaries that want nothing more than to annihilate ambitious upstarts by any means. These include, but are not limited to, sabotage, imitation, idea theft, and price undercutting that you can't compete with. But you have something they don't: a disruptive idea and the ignorance to blindly execute it, no matter the odds. Because you don't know the odds in the first place and haven't thought about how insane this undertaking truly is.

The real secret to beating the odds is not knowing them. Nothing gives you confidence like ignorance. If you know how insanely hard and rare it is to achieve success in your field, how difficult it will be to avoid embarrassing, public failure, how impossible it will be to do things that haven't been done, you wouldn't begin your journey. So, imagine pre-Oscar-slap Will Smith has just flashed you with the *Men in Black* memory eraser to zap any remnants of this and go full steam into what you know in your bones will be certain success. Belief comes before ability.

Too many people try to wait for the right time, till they feel confident enough, get in the right headspace, or build up the right skills. That's horseshit. Stop waiting. As podcaster Chris Williamson says, "Perfectionism is procrastination masquerading as control." You develop skills by doing, and you get confidence by learning as you go. You don't need to resolve your issues or process your trauma first. Just start building your empire, brick by brick. Now is the perfect time. Get moving today, buddy.

# #43

# THE AUDACITY!

*"I tried to be nonchalant as I signed the papers and placed an order for 5,000 more shoes which would cost $20,000 I didn't have. They said they'd ship 'em to my East coast office...which I also didn't have."*

—PHIL KNIGHT, FOUNDER OF NIKE

In 1841, when future Barnum & Bailey's circus founder and oddities exhibitionist P.T. Barnum wanted to buy Scudder's American Museum in New York, he looked in his pockets and found nothing but lint. This deterred him about as much as meeting a lady with a beard. He dug deeper and came up with an idea. His friend, knowing how little he had to his name, asked how on Earth he was going to purchase such a monumental building. He replied, "With brass. For silver and gold, I have none."

Through a winning combo of skills at the negotiation table, financial gymnastics, and the aforementioned tonnage of brass in his balls, he convinced the owners to let him take over the museum and run it, paying them out of the future profits he would generate. And profits there would be! What followed was a masterclass in marketing, showmanship, and questionable ethics. He unveiled the FeeJee Mermaid, a supposed mermaid skeleton, and in national newspaper ads, he invited naturalists to come and see the genuine article for themselves. He did have several "experts" attest to its authenticity in person. Although if you've read lesson #14 on not trusting experts, you'd know there was something fishy going on here.

The FeeJee Mermaid on exhibit in 1842

Turns out the experts were right, and the bones were authentic; they were just from two different animals glued together. Fish + Monkey Torso = Mermaid. But he wouldn't stop there; he'd host public debates on whether it was real. He'd parade his oddities through town, give free tickets to drum up word-of-mouth, use mysterious headlines to get people intrigued, and he created a sense of urgency around his exhibits, touting them as once-in-a-lifetime opportunities. He knew how to instill FOMO two hundred years ago.

He had an intuitive understanding of human psychology, like advertising greats David Ogilvy and Claude Hopkins. He took things even further because in the lawless 1840s, you could do whatever the hell you wanted—like glue a monkey to a fish and claim you found a mermaid. He knew how to tickle your disbelief, leave you awed, and wasn't afraid to make you morally outraged. His skills paid the bills, and he became the proud owner of Barnum's American Museum. He ran it successfully for a quarter century until it was destroyed by a fire in 1865. When he tried to rebuild it, it burned down again, and that, my friends, was the universe telling him to clean up his act and get into the circus business, which is why you know his name today. If you have the vision, the skills, and most importantly, the audacity, the money takes care of itself.

In 1976, when Steve Jobs famously stormed in shoeless to The Byte Shop, an early Silicon Valley computer store, to sell the Apple I, it was merely a hobbyist kit. For $40, you got the circuit board, and you'd have to build the computer yourself.

The store owner knew that for every hobbyist, there were one thousand people who wanted a computer but couldn't build one. He told Steve he'd take fifty of them, but only if they were completed machines. Steve was about to say something like, "We don't make completed machines," when the owner said, "And instead of $40, I'll give you $500 each."

Steve "No Job" Jobs wasn't about to turn down $25,000, so he simply said something like, "easy-peasy-lemon-squeezy," even though it was more like "difficult-difficult-lemon-difficult" because neither he nor co-founder Steve Wozniak had ever assembled complete computers before and didn't have thousands of dollars for parts. I won't bore you with what happens next. Let's just say I'm writing this book on an Apple, and you might be listening to it on one. I could've written this book in half the time were it not for my Apple phone distracting me. But I would've had half the knowledge without Apple Podcasts. To borrow author Rich Cohen's words, Steve's "calculation based on arrogance" paid off to the tune of being the world's first trillion-dollar company.

At college one day in the 1970s, Paul Allen found out about a new microcomputer kit, the Altair 880, that could rival commercial models. Paul raced back to Bill Gates' dorm, saying, "Here's our opportunity." He knew this was their moment to ride that rare, lifetime-defining wave of success. The two kids called up the inventor of the Altair 880 and said they could provide the software, a "BASIC," that worked with the 880 Intel chip. The inventor asked when they could have it completed. They said it already was. They hadn't started yet.

They brokered a deal to license their software with the sale of each

Altair machine, provided the software worked. They had two months till their meeting to show off their software. They worked incessantly to develop a high-level computer language for the 880 chip—something experts at Intel said could not be done. After just eight weeks, they flew out to the meeting, and the program worked perfectly! This resulted in executives from tech companies flying in to make million-dollar deals with Paul Allen and Bill Gates before they were legally old enough to drink. This was back when the idea that you could "own your own computer was about as wild as the idea today of owning your own nuclear submarine."

In 1999, the Italian founder of Luxottica, Leonardo Del Vecchio, met with the American owners of Ray Ban and tried to talk them into a friendly merger. Those uncouth Americans made fun of his accent to each other, and while he couldn't speak great English, he could understand it. This pissed him off. So what did this man, born a poor orphan in the Dolemite mountains, do? Well, he might not've spoken English, but he did speak the universal language of math. He plunked down an offer of $500 million to skip all the bullshit, buy their company outright, and take complete control. Pretty baller move, right?

The only issue was, he had less than 10 percent of the $500 million. So, he went to the bank with *le palle d'acciaio* (Italian for Balls of Steel), touting his track record and takeover bid, and secured the missing 90 percent. Then he did something truly genius. He removed Ray-Bans from the market completely. Literally stopped making them. He let them all sell out and didn't put them back on the shelves for three years until the supply had dwindled to nothing and demand had grown to a fever pitch. Then he put them back on the shelf. Except now, instead of being $40 and sold at gas stations without a logo, they'd be $100 and have the now iconic logo.

He then launched a prescription lens business, doubling their sales overnight. He decided he wouldn't just sell wholesale and make a 50 percent cut; he would sell them in his own stores. A little place you may have heard of called The Sunglass Hut. Next time someone makes fun of your accent, you can laugh too…all the way to the fucking bank.

Moral of the story: when presented with an opportunity to level up, say yes and figure out the details later. As Rich Cohen writes in *The Fish that Ate the Whale:* "There are times when certain cards sit unclaimed in the common pile, when certain properties become available that will never be available again. A good businessman feels these moments like a fall in the barometric pressure. A great businessman is dumb enough to act on them even when he cannot afford to."

# #44

# COMFORT IS A FALSE GOD

*"Comfort is the worst addiction."*

—MARCUS AURELIUS

If you're comfortable where you're at in life right now, let this book be the pea in your mattress, princess, because *complacency is death*. Not only should you *Embrace The Suck* as they say in the army, but you should actively seek discomfort. Seeking difficulty makes you stronger.

Arnold Schwarzenegger said, "Only through pain can you actually grow." Sure, he was talking about muscles, but this applies to anything in life. As a bodybuilder, the whole point is failure. You need to get to failure in order to build your body. You're doing reps until literal failure. If you don't push muscles to the point they *fail*, you don't get massive muscles. What does this mean for non-bodybuilders? If you're not failing at something, you're not trying hard enough. You are nowhere near the upper bounds of your power. Instead of running away from failure toward a comfortable life, run toward potential failure, as far from your comfort zone as you can. There's no growth in the comfort zone and no comfort in the growth zone. Treat discomfort not as a nuisance, but as a calling for your next stage of greatness.

At twenty-five years old, David and I were running the entire production department of a three-hundred-person agency. We told them not only would we shoot all their commercials, but we'd also bring in $2 million in clients our first year. Well, we shot great commercials but didn't bring in one dollar in new business for six months.

With no warning, they fired us. We had no money saved, no health insurance, no prospects, and nothing to fall back on. David was extremely depressed walking out of that meeting.

I turned to him in the parking lot and said, "What are you sad about? That was the greatest thing that's ever happened to us."

He looked at me like I was crazy. A few weeks later, he realized I was right. We were getting pulled away from our purpose with a great-paying job. Had we not been fired, every paycheck since would have hammered another nail in the coffin of our dreams.

After walking the gangplank, we didn't know where to turn, but we had a nonrefundable vacation booked. Our friend Greg was driving us to the airport. He looked down and noticed David's shoes, Cheetah print sneakers from legendary streetwear brand, Gourmet Footwear.

Greg said, "Are those Gourmet? I know the owner. His office is right around the corner."

On time to the airport for once in our lives, David said, "Take us there right now."

We stormed into their office at Sunset Plaza with nothing to lose. We said, "We're going to St. Barths. We have all this camera equipment, and we're going to shoot your men's shoes on scantily clad French models on the beach."

The ex-con owner, who earned his street cred and starter capital by reselling other brands that "fell off a truck," told us matter-of-factly, "I don't believe you, but here's four pairs of shoes."

We took the goods, boarded our flight, and found ourselves in the middle of this off-season paradise. We shot cool photos and videos of the shoes while acclimating ourselves to the island. That first night, we bounced around the clubs. At the hottest spot, we noticed *Thais*. All eyes were on Thais. Especially ours. We went right up to her, showed her that day's iPhone 4 photos, and asked her to model for us. For the next week, Thais became our guide. She was a St. Barths local and knew all the secret spots. We braved slippery cliffs with rogue waves almost pulling us into the riptide. To this day, it was the most dangerous shoot I've ever been on. She trusted us to shoot beauty, and we delivered. She even posed wearing nothing but the shoes.

David and I swam past the buoys to the runway of the famous St. Barths airport. We did an homage to Nick Cage in *The Rock* and got a wild shot of the shoes dripping water with a plane flying twenty feet overhead. Then we heard the sirens. An emergency vehicle chased us off the runway. We ran laughing our asses off, hopped on our ATVs, and got outta dodge. We had the footage that would change our lives.

Back in LA, we showed this ex-con-trepreneur what we happily did for free for his brand. In his two-packs-a-day voice, what he said next, I'll never forget.

"Whatever you do, don't change a frame." He was blown away.

At 3:00 a.m. one night, David searched blogs for the perfect song. He found "Royals" by Lorde months before it hit radio. It worked perfectly. The next morning, the video was sent to every male fashion blog. High Snobiety and Hype Beast picked it up, and within forty-eight hours, the video had garnered over two million views. Instead of being paid for our work, we made sure our credits were front and center, because of the tasteful nudity, we wrote them in French to make us look like artists. Not only did the video get tons of views, but we also had offers for interviews.

Shortly after that, we got a cease-and-desist order from Lorde's record label because the video had gotten so big. But that didn't matter because with the press from the video, we now had a calling card. We used its success to reach out to anyone we wanted.

When Beats by Dre asked us, "How much did that video cost?" I put the phone on mute and tried to come up with a sane number.

David took the phone off mute and said, "$50,000."

They said, "Okay, cool. Can we hire you for our next campaign?"

And that's how our production company, Culprit Creative, was born.

Seeking discomfort is equally important once you've reached your next stage of success. Rabbi Twerki says, "If lobsters had doctors, they would never grow, because as soon as they felt uncomfortable, they'd get a Valium and feel fine again." That's because a lobster's shell never grows. The only way lobsters can grow is when they get uncomfortable as hell in their shell. They get literally squeezed by their own armor. The pressure and stress is enormous. But have you ever heard a lobster complain? No. It just goes off under some rock, does the work, and comes back transformed and stronger.

Each stage of its growth requires supreme discomfort. Unlike lobsters, people tend to seek comfort; to get fat and happy. This will happen to you. Your company will become more risk averse over time. You will gradually lose the scrappy, resourceful, and ambitious attitude that made you successful in the first place, and you will expend more effort entrenching yourself in a defensive position than staying on the offensive, continuing to innovate. When you notice this shift, remember this credo: stay scrappy, don't get fat and happy. Be like the lobster. And above all, remember to continue taking risks no matter the discomfort, because in the long run, it's riskier not to. Even if the next thing you do fails, it's still the right move to take that first uncertain leap.

# #45

# BE DECISIVE

*"The road of life is paved with squirrels who couldn't make a decision."*
—UNKNOWN

*Decisio* in Latin means to cut off. Once you've made a decision, you've cut off all other options. In picking the course of action, you've disregarded every other option. If you haven't firmly and resolutely cut off other options and moved forward, you haven't actually made a decision. If you spend too long planning or strategizing, you'll get into analysis paralysis. You'll *never* have all the info. Jeff Bezos says he likes to have 70 percent of the information needed before making a decision. Famed American businessman, Tex Thornton, said, "If all the facts could be known, idiots could make the decisions."

There are two kinds of decisions: two-way door and one-way door. Two-way doors are easy to reverse. One-way doors are expensive and time consuming should you be wrong. Let your team of A-players make two-way door decisions without your input. Do a proper cost-benefit analysis on every one-way door decision yourself. Spend time planning your one-way-door decisions because there's no going back. Most decisions are two-way though. So, stop analyzing and start acting. Here's Jeff Bezos on the subject:

> There are decisions that are irreversible and highly consequential and we call these one-way doors. They need to be made slowly and carefully; I oftentimes find myself at Amazon acting as the Chief Slowdown Officer. "Whoa, I want to see that decision analyzed seventeen more ways because it's highly consequential and irreversible." The problem is that most decisions are not like that. Most decisions are two-way doors; you can make the decision and you step through. If it turns out to have been the wrong decision, you can back up. And what happens in large organizations is that all decisions use the heavyweight process that is really intended for irreversible highly consequential decisions. And that's a disaster. When there's a decision that needs to be made you need to ask, "Is this a one-way door or a two-way door?"

If it's a two-way door, make the decision with a small team or even one high-judgment individual. Make the decision. If it's wrong, it's wrong, and you'll change it. But if it's a one-way door, analyze it five different ways. Be careful, because that is where slow is smooth and smooth is fast. You do not want to make one-way door decisions quickly.

## EMOTIONAL DECISIONS

*"How much more harmful are the consequences of anger than the causes of it?"*
—MARCUS AURELIUS

We've all made bad decisions based on how we felt at the time. They say you should never reply when you're angry, make promises when you're happy, or make decisions when you're sad. I'd like to add never make decisions based on fear. I almost purposefully had a kid with a woman I had just met who lived in another country. Was I inspired by Elon? No. I realized I was about to do it because my mom has cancer, and since I don't know how long she has left, I wanted her to meet her grandchild. That was a decision I almost made based on fear of losing her, but it would change the trajectory of my life, the mother's life, and a new life with who knows what ripple effects into the future, all because I wanted to make my mom happy while I still have her.

All emotions are temporary, some decisions are permanent. Never make decisions when you're in a "hot state." This goes for negotiation as well. You always do your best thinking in a "cold state" where you're not letting emotions steer you. Even if you're not feeling particularly emotional, make sure to sleep on every one-way-door decision.

# #46

# HAVE A BIAS FOR ACTION

*"I've never let planning get in the way of doing."*

—MICHAEL BLOOMBERG

At SpaceX, Gwynn Shotwell wrote up a plan to pitch sales to Elon Musk. Musk took one look at the plan and said, "I don't give a damn about a plan. Just get on with the job." Musk didn't need to see the plan because he trusted Gwynn to get it done. Worst-case scenario, she fails and has to try something else. It's better to give your idea a shot now and get the result. See if your experiment works and iterate from there. Plans are good if you need to hammer things out in your brain or you need a simple roadmap for what you're doing, but you don't need to waste time writing anything out if you know the next three actions to take. Just take them. Why waste time pitching if you can just snap into action instead?

At the beginning of our careers, we were denied a Toyota commercial because we had never shot a car commercial. Um, I'm sorry, how are we supposed to get the required experience if to get that experience you need to already have that experience? Not being the type who sits around for a catch-22 to play out, we decided to make a spec commercial for the Tesla Model S that had just come out. We got our hands on one, talked our way into using a massive studio with a car turntable for free, and then David talked a Tesla-Coil company in Texas to let us rent one for free. Only it had to be overnighted because our shoot was the next day, and the thing was massive. It cost the company $10,000 just to ship it, but they agreed because the owner loved Tesla cars and wanted to be part of this commercial. All we had to do was pay for the technician's hotel room. We owned a camera and used favors to get other needed equipment. My dad agreed to do the lighting if I bought him an In-N-Out Burger. We shot this million-dollar car commercial with only five people, spending only $167 between the budget hotel and burgers for five people.

The technician of the Tesla coil said we had to stay twelve feet away at all times, because that was the "death zone," and if we got too close, it would "liquify our heart." We used a tape measure and marked twelve feet with chalk. The car, unfortunately, was inside the death zone and was hit by lightning repeatedly, making all the electronics go bonkers and the screens turn on.

Having a bias for action and gaining this valuable experience on our own accord helped us book a Mercedes Super Bowl ad later on.

Ideas in the form of action, not action in the form of ideas. If you think too much, you might talk yourself out of it. Just act. Make. Launch. Try. Test. Iterate. Build. Stop thinking and do. Jeff Bezos describes:

There are two ways of building a business, many times you aim, aim, aim, and then shoot. Or you can shoot, shoot, shoot, and then aim a little bit. Don't spend a lot of time on analysis and precision, keep trying stuff.

Once you've fired your shot, it's time to see if you hit the target. Then you can re-aim and fire again. If you've launched or you're selling your product and it starts to do well, you don't need to strike while the iron is hot with everything you've got. Make sure you have enough cash to keep a steady momentum. But by all means, if there's no threat to your company from this one idea failing, what the hell are you waiting for? Go see if it works!

# #47

# THERE IS NO SPEED LIMIT

*"If everything seems under control, you're just not going fast enough."*
—MARIO ANDRETTI, FORMULA 1 DRIVER

When it comes to inventing, iterating, innovating, or any other big word that starts with "i" and means making new shit by trial and error, you'll want to push your team to make new versions at a rate they currently deem impossible. New technology, new ideas, new versions of ads, whatever it is. If it's completely new, and you're thinking from first principles, just make decisions and try things. Come up with an idea that might work. Build it, test it, get the result. There's nothing to lose. Every second you burn in the planning phase is burning cash or worse: time.

## HAVE A MANIACAL SENSE OF URGENCY

You need to instill in your team an almost unhealthy urgency until the task is complete. When something isn't working, work together like white blood cells killing the disease. When you're iterating, only test one variable at a time, but all the time, to make sure it takes weeks or months, not years. At the Boring Company, when told by engineers that something will take longer than expected, the leadership says something like, "Are you telling me if there was an asteroid barreling toward earth right now, you couldn't get it done with more time or more money?" The engineer will say, "Well, I could technically do this..." The leader will say, "Then technically do that." The things they get done with this system, being under-resourced, would blow your mind.

Yes, that's a man getting a speeding ticket 'cause his ostrich is too fast.

Parkinson's Principle states that a task takes as long as you give it. I wrote the first draft of this book in three months because I had to have it done by the time I met with David Senra in New York. Would it have been better if I had given myself six months? Even better, a year? Probably. Marginally. Doesn't matter. I can edit it later if it sucks. I spent six years writing a screenplay that didn't sell, so I'm going to shoot my shot at being an author quickly. Remember, fire, fire, fire, then aim.

The same applies to every task you give your team. If you have a one-hour call with your marketing team, you could say, "We need copy for five marketing emails done in thirty minutes," and they will get it done. Then you can jump on the call for the second half and polish them. If you say, "We need our Black Friday/Cyber Monday plan done by Friday," it will get done.

When the founder of Southwest Airlines, Herb Kelleher, needed a TV campaign, the ad agency said, "We can have concepts by March, scripts by April, casting in June, preproduction in July, shoot in August, and editing done by November. It was a nine-month timeline. Herb replied, "We're shooting Wednesday."

When Southwest heard a rumor that their competitor, Midway Airlines, had gone bankrupt in Chicago, Herb and his executive team were at a nearby hotel watching the news for confirmation of the rumor. As soon as it was announced, they pounced.

By the end of that day, they had brokered a deal with the airport and city for control of Midway's gates and planes. When speaking at a press conference the next day, a reporter asked Herb when to expect Southwest's operation of the gates, planes, and routes.

Herb said, "Go to the airport."

They were already operational and had crudely changed the signage to read *Southwest Airlines*. It's no wonder they were the most consistently profitable airline. They didn't dawdle. They jetted ahead because they knew there was no speed limit. Let me repeat that: "There is not a single fucking speed limit sign posted anywhere on the road to success."

Pick The Speed You Can Afford (hint: go faster)

Especially if you are doing something completely new, you might fail repeatedly. This is something to appreciate. It's how you know you're moving in the right direction. If you're not failing, you're not tap dancing on the edge of possibility. So fail splendidly, fail spectacularly, fail with unexplained glee, and most importantly, *FAIL FAST*.

When Google's experimental department, Google X, made smart

glasses with a camera, Google Glass, they sent several super-nerds out into the field. These Google geeks went to bars, sporting events, and concerts. They found out quickly that these smart glasses felt like spy glasses. People were creeped out, thinking they were constantly being filmed. If I remember my conversation with a Google X Exec correctly, some of these nerdy guys got beaten up by "Alpha" males while out on the town. That was when they said, Okay, pull the plug on this multimillion-dollar program. They could've spent years perfecting them, but they knew it would just delay the inevitable. If you're going to fail, fail as fast as you can. Every time you fail, you become smarter. When you fail fast, you learn fast.

To speed up innovation, find the person responsible for the results you want to achieve. If they're already in your company, go work directly with them like Steve Jobs did with iPhone designer, Jony Ive. If they're not in your company, go recruit them.

There was one superstar Elon wanted to hire for SpaceX in Los Angeles, but the guy's wife had a job at Google.

During the meeting, he said, "Sorry, I'd love to take the position, but my wife can't leave San Fran because she works at Google."

Musk came prepared, telling him that he had already gotten Google to agree to let his wife take a position in Los Angeles. Who could argue with that? He took the job at SpaceX on the spot. Talent makes all the difference when you want to go fast.

# #48

# BURN THE BOATS

*"Plan B is to Make Plan A Work."*

—JEFF BEZOS

When Alexander the Great landed on Persian shores in 334 BC, ready to take over an empire, he instructed his men to burn the boats. There was no option except to conquer. And conquer they did.

In 1519, after landing in Veracruz, Hernán Cortés gave his men the same speech (this time in Spanish). Who do you think won, the Aztecs or the conquistadors? They're not called conquistadors because they're bad at conquering. His small army decimated the most populous city in all of the Americas. Granted, they had guns and smallpox, but they fought like the ruthless Spaniards they were, and that's why it's called Mexico City and not Tenochtitlan.

During the 1993 NBA championships, when the Chicago Bulls played the Phoenix Suns, they were up three games to two. Had they lost the next game, they would stay in Phoenix another day for game seven. Michael Jordan told his teammates to pack only one suit. There would be no game seven. With no change of clothes for another day in Phoenix, the team had no option but to win. So they did.

When you don't have anything to fall back on, your chances of success *increase*. When backed into a corner, an animal will do anything to survive.

# #49

# READY, SET, FAIL

*"I've not failed, I've just found 10,000 ways that didn't work."*
—THOMAS EDISON

SpaceX had just enough money to build three rockets in case the first two blew up. Spoiler Alert: the first two exploded. Not only did each rocket explosion cost tens of millions of dollars, but each failure was worldwide news. Musk said, "I thought that if we couldn't get this thing to orbit in three failures, we deserved to die. That was my going-in proposition." Then the third one exploded.

What did Elon do? He inventoried the last of his company's resources. He realized there were just enough parts to scrape together a fourth launch, but only enough money to pay everyone for six weeks. To get their last chance, they'd have to build and launch a final rocket in just over a month. He made a bet on himself, his vision, and his team. Can you guess what happened on the fourth launch? Let's just say SpaceX is now flying missions for fucking NASA and handling resupply trips for the space station. With sweet lucrative space contracts, and depending on when you're reading this, maybe they've landed people on Mars!

One of the biggest achievements in human history happened because the team *expected to fail*. When their failure went beyond their worst expectations, they worked together beyond their best expectations.

Ask yourself, are you willing to have several catastrophic, expensive, public failures with no guarantee of success?

# #50

# YOU CAN LAUNCH MORE THAN ONCE

*"It's hard to beat a person who never gives up."*

—BABE RUTH

If you launch your product publicly in front of all your friends, family, and colleagues and you aren't successful, guess what? You can launch again later. Launch as many times as it takes. Call it your soft launch or your friends and family launch. Who cares?

With Culprit, we launched four times. First, we did what we do best—we made a video. We spent ten grand on a beautiful, wild, high-fashion video with a risqué moment at the end to get people talking. It had famous models in it, and we made sure to do posts from their accounts while on set. We got multiple reposts, including a big magazine, and gained a sizable following just from that day's shoot. The video was edited to perfection and is one of my favorite videos we've made.

It was, however, not made for a broad audience and aimed entirely at the young male, *Maxim* magazine crowd. This would've been a decent strategy and demographic to go after, but then the world started to change. It was the beginning of the #MeToo Movement and the worst moment since the Victorian Era to feature scantily clad women, wearing nothing but reflective, disco ball-style squares of tape, with a video aimed squarely at horny men. We put the video out and got praise from its intended audience, garnering 100,000 views, but didn't get the intended viral splash. So, we simply removed it from the internet. Back to the drawing board!

Our entire company (four of us) sent an email to friends, family, and the 5,000 people in our Gmail accounts. Here's mine:

**Subj:** A New Chapter // CULPRIT UNDERWEAR

Dear Family, Friends, Highschool Sweethearts, Secret Admirers, Secret Haters that want to keep up appearances, People I Haven't Spoken To In Years, Anyone With a Pulse that has at least one iota of respect for me,

Many of you may have been wondering why I take my pants off and pose for pictures so often, well one of those reasons is that for three years I've been working on Culprit Underwear and I would appreciate TF out of your support right now. If you buy a pair of underwear, I give you my word, that if you support me now, I will quite literally support you when the package arrives. But don't buy these if you hate comfort, want your cock to look like a shrink-wrapped bobcat tail, or don't want durability that's tested up to 1000 boners. Or you can try the best pair you've ever owned.

So grow a pair, try a pair, and **use promo-code: trussell at checkout for 20% off** *and* **free shipping**. www.culpritunderwear.com.

And for visual representation of our cock-flattering-comfort, here's a vain rooster:

Ladies, we'll be launching women's soon enough, so for now, buy it for your dads, your brothers, your crushes you're trying to turn into boyfriends, your boyfriends you're trying to turn into husbands, but not your EX's. They didn't deserve you in the first place and they certainly don't deserve a fresh pair of Culprits.

PS I personally guarantee every pair you buy. If it gets eaten by moths that have evolved to eat Culprit Underwear instead of sweaters, you can send me the tattered remains, and I'll Venmo you. But if that DOESN'T happen, go ahead and enjoy the world's most cock-flattering comfort and subscribe so you don't miss out on limited-editions and get to keep that cock flattered all summer long.

And if you have yet to see it, check out our Launch Video.

Thank you for always supporting me!

That got us about $5k in sales. Not bad for one email, but there was no other strategy after. So, we kept trying, and we kept calling it our "official launch."

Never get discouraged if your first public launch is a failure. People aren't paying as much attention as you think. They have their own problems and won't remember it. If you're that worried about failing publicly, just get it right the first time. Duh.

Twitter launched at a music festival in San Francisco. They got fewer than one hundred signups, and Jack Dorsey got so bored and drunk, he fell on his face and had to get rushed to the emergency room. Then they launched at SXSW with a real plan, and the rest was history.

# #51

# TEST THE MARKET

*"Only a fool tests the depth of the water with both feet."*

—AFRICAN PROVERB

Before spending all your cash, test your product with some marketing dollars and see how people respond. Find out just how big and who your market is. The results may surprise you. Finding the right market is more important to your success than a great product or team.

When Liquid Death unveiled their canned water that looks like a craft beer banged an energy drink, they didn't actually launch it. Before starting something as inventory intensive and expensive as a beverage brand, they smartly made a rendering of the can, made a Facebook page, and spent a little on ads to see how people responded.

The response was insane. Within days, they had over 80,000 Facebook likes, and 7/11 reached out to ask how they could get their hands on it for their stores.

Don't get your hopes up. Your first test probably won't go that well. That was years ago, so things have changed a bit. Come up with a test of your own better suited for today's landscape.

The point is you want to see how your audience reacts. Make a simple ad and then decide on a call to action, such as email signup, following your account, or purchasing, and then refund their money. Whatever it is, make it traceable to your ad and measurable. Take it seriously. A successful test is all you need to raise money.

If there's no way to test your product or service with an ad, do an Instagram poll or a survey. For example, I'm currently doing post-purchase surveys to see what new products we should make. Even if you're building a space hotel, you could say it will be ready in three years and already has a waiting list to see how many signups you get.

I wish I had known this lesson when I made swimwear, gym shorts, and other "genius" ideas like socks that came in threes instead of pairs. We still have those in stock if you'd like to take any off our hands. Test before you invest.

# #52

# EXPERIMENT

*"The challenge in a startup is that you almost have to spread your wings pretty far to see what will work, so the faster you do the experimentation and get rid of things that don't work, and keep doing things that do work, the faster you get to the winning business model."*

—MICHAEL DELL, FOUNDER OF DELL COMPUTERS

Everything works in your head until you try it. The best way to experiment is to change one variable at a time. This works with marketing campaigns, intro offers, landing pages, brand positioning, and new product categories.

James Dyson made 5,126 cyclone vacuum prototypes before achieving perfection on his 5,127th. The process took him fourteen years. He forged ahead with his idea after engineers and mathematicians told him that for a cyclone to work, it needs to be thirty feet high. This was after advisors and friends told him if there was a better vacuum cleaner to be made, Hoover would've made it already. Dyson knew it would work because he saw it in his mind. Every time he changed something and learned empirically, he made progress. He says of that time, "Invention is not about being brilliant, it's about being logical and persistent."

Advertising pioneer, Claude Hopkins, was having trouble selling carpet sweepers for a client. He had a thought. He told customers they could customize them and choose from twelve different wood finishes. Sales exploded. You never know exactly which line of copy, feature, or promotion will make the difference. The key is to try every idea, no matter how stupid some may seem. With Facebook ads, you can test hundreds of ideas cheaper and more accurately than ever before. Technology is on your side in a way Hopkins could've only dreamed of.

If you try three, five, or twenty things at once, you'll never know which detail made the difference, and you'll have to backtrack. Don't get lazy on your experiments. Test one variable at a time.

Once you find the winning formula, you can run the same ad for years. David Ogilvy had one ad in a wedding magazine that ran for over three decades. He never changed it because it was working. As Ogilvy puts it, "You aren't advertising to a standing army; you are advertising to a moving parade."

With many products, people who are familiar with your brand will continue to buy, and those who aren't are being exposed to your brand for the first time. If your ad works, don't change anything. Other times, your product might be for a certain age group. In those cases, you have even less reason to change an ad that's working. People grow into your niche. If they've never seen your ad before, it's new to them. Just because you're sick of it doesn't mean you need to spend thousands on a new campaign. If you ain't broke, don't fix it.

# #53

# TRACE YOUR SUCCESS

*"Always have traced results."*

—CLAUDE HOPKINS

If you're Coca-Cola, Doritos, or Taco Bell, or if you're selling Doritos Locos Tacos at Taco Bell, you can ignore this advice. When you have cash to burn and you're a household name, you can drop dough on brand recognition. You already own that real estate in your customer's mind. They know what you do and what your brand stands for.

But if you have next to zero brand recognition, don't you dare buy a billboard or TV ad unless you're adding a way to trace your results. If you buy a billboard, include a promo code localized to that billboard. If you do a TV ad, have a promo code for that region. Make sure anytime you experiment with new advertising, you can trace your results. Never spend $1 on an ad you can't trace sales back to.

We used to be really dumb. We still are, but we used to be also. We paid $10,000 for a billboard on Sunset. It was supposed to be up for one week. We had no way of tracing our results. We failed to include a discount code on the billboard so we could track sales. I doubt that one vain week of having our billboard tower over traffic on the Sunset Strip made us a single sale. Luckily for us, it was the height of COVID, and brands were slashing their marketing budgets. Our billboard stayed up for ten months! Even though we couldn't trace results, having it up for that long was great for our brand, and we'd often overhear people talking about it. We would never do that again, but sometimes, no matter how dumb you are, you get lucky. Here's what it looked like:

Here we are, prematurely popping the champagne—more on that later

# #54

# YOUR MORAL OBLIGATION

*"If you make something, sell it yourself."*

—JAMES DYSON

Great ideas are not rare, great execution of ideas is. On top of great execution, however, your idea still might be dead in the water without impeccable salesmanship.

You've probably heard this Emerson attributed quote, "Build a better mousetrap, and the world will beat a path to your door." It's horseshit. No one is beating a path to your door because no one knows what your product is. What problem it solves, how it benefits them, who you are, or where your door is. Emerson clearly never heard of SEO.

When I created the most breathable underwear since fig leaves, no one knew, cared, or purchased. We sold only to our immediate network. Word of mouth over two years did nothing. Unmatched quality and innovation in the products you create rank at number three on your road to success.

The first is having a great market in the first place, and the second is having the skill to sell whatever the hell you create. To sell someone your idea, all you really need is enough passion to infect them. But if you don't know how to sell, be prepared for hell.

Sales and marketing are two birds of a feather. You need to sell your idea to investors. You need to sell your product to retailers. If you're a retailer, you sell to customers. And when you sell directly to your customers, it's called marketing. As they say in Thailand, "same-same, but different."

If you believe your product will make your customers' lives better, then it is *your moral obligation* to get your product into your customers' hands fast. Ogilvy says, "You can't save souls in an empty church." So, who's the best person to actually market your product or service? Some fancy agency? Ogilvy brought back from the dead? No, dummy, it's you.

Marketing your product is just as important as making a great product. This is why Steve Jobs stressed it as a moral obligation and why he made sure he was in every high-level marketing meeting. He personally signed off on every concept. Everything that was ever released to the public while he was CEO went through him. From the global campaigns to the regional billboards in Missouri. He made sure the quality of the marketing was on par with Apple's "insanely great products." It's tantamount to the product itself. You need to advertise the hell out of what you're doing because no one else cares as much as you do. The best way to get them to care is to *project* your passion into them via marketing. Your passion makes all the difference. Don't know how? Many founders say they don't, but the truth is, no one can pump people up about your product as well as you can. You might currently know zero about marketing or sales, and that's okay. We all start somewhere. And if you're starting at zero, by the end of this chapter, you'll have an edge.

There's no one better to sell something than the person who forged it from the void. You care more and have thought longer and harder about it than anyone. You know more than anybody on this planet about your creation. You can sell it. Out of the trunk of your car or door to door if you must.

No one else was going to get Estée Lauder's cosmetic products into London's prestigious department store, Harrods. She flew there to do it herself and struck out two years in a row. Finally, she got enough press about her products that they couldn't ignore her anymore. When they gave her a hard-to-find section of the store, she told everyone she met in London to go into Harrods and ask where to find her products. This manufactured buzz and led to premier positioning in the store, which turned Estée Lauder into Harrods' top-selling cosmetic line.

When Sid Meier and Bill Stealey—the team who would create the Civilization computer game series—founded their company in 1982, Bill called up stores to try and sell their first game, Hellcat Ace. He had a wild idea. He called, pretending to want to buy Hellcat Ace. The owner of the store said they didn't have it. He called the next week, using a different voice, asking to buy the game. They didn't have it. He called the week after, new voice, same question. The fourth week, he called in his professional voice, representing the game company that created it. He sold the game. Now they were in business.

Don't get me wrong, if you get the right ad agency, they can perform miracles, but no one will care as much as you do. No one else can communicate your passion. And most agencies don't have the right incentives. When I directed commercials for Mercedes, no matter how great a job I did, or if my work sold an extra 100,000 SUVs, I never saw another cent. So instead of trying to sell more cars, I was just coming up with shots that would look great on my directing reel. I didn't care about Mercedes. I cared what future clients would think. Our goals were not aligned.

Now that I'm creating every commercial for my own brand, our goals are fully aligned. It's become a flywheel of passion, attention to detail, and success. The more I care, the more our customers care. The more work I put into the commercial, the funnier it is, the more underwear we sell. The more fans we gain, the bigger the brand grows, giving me more revenue to do even crazier shoots, like spending over $100,000 on an ad called *Cool Sperm*, starring, well, you guessed it...a cool sperm. Here's a screengrab of our Fonzie-inspired sperm waterskiing in a leather jacket. Fun fact: he's played by our actor-turned-COO, Tim Fox.

# #55

# BRAND STORYTELLING

*"We must treat people in advertising like we treat them in person. Center on their desires."*

—CLAUDE HOPKINS

Steve Jobs refers to the storyteller as the most powerful person in the world. He stresses the importance of storytelling in marketing. This can be done with great copywriting. Your ability to stir desires and weave words into a "web which clings to the memory," will dictate your success.

Can you use AI tools for writing copy? Sure, but your competitors are using it too. It's better to get inspired by it if you're stuck than to rely on it. If you don't have a fundamental understanding of what good copy is, what inspiring writing is, and how to make an image stick in someone's brain, you're not yet a master storyteller. Words are a weapon. Arm yourself to the fucking teeth. Instead of using AI to write your brand story, find other brand stories you like. Find words that resonate with you from twenty other brands. Copy the format and tone of each until you've made a style that's uniquely your own. Then you can build your voice from there. Maybe that's why they call it copywriting.

If you're ready to stop telling yourself you suck at marketing and are ready to learn from the best who have ever lived, take a seat and get ready to take notes. Kids, today we're going to learn from David Ogilvy and the master he learned from, Claude Hopkins. Hopkins's book, *Scientific Advertising*, was full of advertising gold. To make sure their competitors didn't learn the secret sauce, Hopkins's boss, Albert Lasker, made him store it in a safe and not release it for as long as he worked at his firm.

Let's start with the truest of all human truths: people don't care about you or what you're offering them. They only care about how it can benefit them. Center on their desires and explain how this product will solve their problems or make their dreams reality. Satisfy their needs, cater to their wants, and they will buy from you.

Focus not on the masses, or your entire niche all at once, but on your ideal customer. Write out what they're like. What age are they? What tax bracket? What level of education? What movies, shows, and music do they like? Really build them out.

Here's a writing exercise I did on our ideal Underwear customer: *She's not immature, yet inside she feels like she's still a kid, though she likes adult jokes, strong language, and stronger drinks. She makes her own money and, though not rich yet, knows one day she will be. She's not content, but she's comfortable in her own skin, especially when wearing Culprits. Her self-belief and coolness under pressure breed the confidence to take no shit, the compassion to do no harm, and the wisdom to know the difference.*

When Hopkins visited a struggling brewery, he was amazed by their process. It was truly a technological extravaganza to mash hops—boil 'em, distill 'em, ferment 'em, run 'em through purification pipes... I don't know, I'm making it up at this point, but it sounded complex and impressive.

Hopkins said something like, "This is fantastic, you need to tell people about every step you take to make your amazing beer, they'll want to know!" And the brewer responded meekly, "But this is how all beer is made." Hopkins replied, "Yes, but the public doesn't know that.

Show them how hard it is, how much work goes into it...*tell the pains you take to excel.*"

Talk about how many failed prototypes you had to make before you got it right. Talk about how many fabric samples you tried, or terrible scents you had to endure to find the right formula for your perfume, or how you have twenty-six kids now because you were trying to make the world's thinnest condom. Whatever your product or service, the point is, show the pain you endured to make it perfect. Show your customers each excruciating detail that goes into making your product. They'll appreciate it more.

Ogilvy says to read Hopkins' book, *Scientific Advertising*, six times before you write your first ad. Great advice. Here's more advice for writing great copy.

## EMBRACE BREVITY

*"I would have written a shorter letter, but I did not have the time."*

—BLAISE PASCAL, FAMED FRENCH PHYSICIST

Our boy, Blaise, wrote those words in 1657, so like maybe you should internalize this already and trim the fat. It may seem hypocritical that I wrote a really long book and am telling you to compress your thoughts. I also spent a year making it shorter. If I didn't expend my valuable time to save yours, you'd have an incomprehensible encyclopedia of self-aggrandizing bullshit instead of a decent read.

Do the same for others. Whether it's a cold reach out to someone you want to recruit, a potential investor, or an internal email to your team, make sure you put the receiver's time before your own. Make it concise. This is especially helpful in mission statements and pitch meetings. As Gen Z says, "Say less."

## DON'T BE THE BEST

*"Everybody stands for quality...as a result nobody does."*

This excerpt from *The 22 Immutable Laws of Marketing* relates to how, in the 1980s, Ford, GM, and Chrysler all claimed they made the best automobiles. Not only did three similar companies claiming the same thing dilute the message for all, but have you ever seen an '80s Ford, Chrysler, or Chevy? Eye sores on wheels. They refer to this period of American car design as "the malaise era" for a reason. Even if you really are the best—which they weren't—come up with something more original.

How many times have you driven by a burger joint claiming 'world's best burger,' tried the world's best beer, or been to the best Italian restaurant in town? Have you tried the world's most comfortable sneakers? All one needs to get away with being the best is being a solid 7/10. No one will protest or give that bad of an online review if you say you're the best and you're pretty good. But everyone sees past this, and you lose credibility simply by making this claim.

Instead of superlatives, just clearly explain the attributes that make your product great. It's better to focus on one clear message so your customer doesn't get confused. Ideally, your brand messaging is so strong, you can own real estate in your customer's head. If you can do that, you will not have any direct competition. Charlie Munger and Warren Buffett refer to these as "consumer monopolies." You will not get there by claiming you're the greatest.

Don't try to be the best. Instead, own an adjective. Ours is breathable. Our undies are more breathable than what you're wearing now. And if anyone else claims this, I will bring them to arbitration in a fucking wind tunnel. But even with that, we still don't say we're the most breathable because that's still a superlative. We simply say, "keeps you cool where it counts (your balls)."

# #56

# THE PEAK-END RESULT

*"The ending is everything. Plan all the way to it, take it into account, let it shape the thing."*

—ROBERT GREENE, AMERICAN AUTHOR

People don't usually remember every detail of a movie they saw, a trip they went on, a DJ's set, an event they went to, a book they read, or their conversation with you...but they will remember how it made them feel. This is because of a tenet of behavioral psychology called *The Peak-End Result*. Instead of remembering the average of an experience, people remember the peak: the most intense part, whether positive or negative. And they'll remember the end.

There are so many fantastic movies that suck. They start strong, have great characters, some wild mystery or twist you can't wait to find out about, and then it ends in confusion, without resolution, or with such a lame climax, it ruins the movie. You will never recommend that movie to a friend. You might watch a YouTube clip of a scene you liked, but you'll never rewatch the whole thing. It's unfulfilling. It can be an hour and twenty minutes of perfection, but if the last ten minutes don't fulfill the first eighty, you will be disappointed. You'll say it was good, not great, even if the first two acts were the best movie ever made. We need a good ending to truly enjoy something. *Game of Thrones* was incredible until they rushed that last season so they could go off and make Star Wars. Or maybe because they had no final book to go on. Either way, anytime I hear a friend talk about that show, they warn other friends, "Whatever you do, do not watch the final season; it completely ruins the show." The creators spent over a decade on the show, but in rushing through that many unresolved storylines so quickly, and to such an anticlimax, it just left a bad taste in everyone's mouth. *Breaking Bad*, on the other hand, had one of the greatest final episodes in TV history. It was beyond satisfaction. You need to put more effort into your ending than anything else.

This goes for public speeches, comedy specials, and conversations with people you've just met. You have to leave on a high note. It cannot feel like it's dragging on. Build to that energetic crescendo, hit your last line, and drop the fucking mic. When you're writing comedy, you always want to end your sentence on the power word. In a social situation, don't tell your whole life story. Get to a great part in the conversation, make them laugh, exchange contact, and excuse yourself. You can run into each other again later in the night or another time.

> HACK: You can always judge from someone's feet whether they're trying to leave a conversation. If their feet are pointed toward you, they're fully engaged. As soon as their feet start to point in another direction slightly, it's time to wrap it up on a high note.

This goes with many careers as well. This is why Tarantino says he's stopping after his tenth film. He cares about his filmography and knows directors in their later years often produce turds. You do not want to pull a Jordan and retire on a championship-winning, buzzer-beating shot, only to come back and play for the Wizards.

When working on a creative project, this goes for your work session too. If what you do is highly creative and takes a lot of brain power, don't work until you're toast. Work until you feel great about what you've accomplished and end your session on a peak as well. You'll be more energized to come back and do it again tomorrow.

End strong in everything you do. This is why DJs usually play a song everyone knows the words to at the end of their sets—some surprise track to wrap it up nicely and leave everyone wanting more.

# #57

# DIRECT RESPONSE VIDEO ADS

*"You don't sell to people. You get them to buy from you. You get people to buy from you. You say to yourself, If I were in their position, why would I want to buy this product? If I was in their position, why would it be to my benefit?"*

—WILLIAM ROSENBERG, FOUNDER OF DUNKIN' DONUTS

Most ads you see don't drive sales directly—for an unknown brand, ads like that can be a fantastic waste of money. If you're starting your own brand, you'll want to drive sales directly. To do that, you'll need to make a direct response ad.

Here's how to write one:

## 1. THE THUMBSTOPPER, A.K.A. THE HOOK

This is the first three seconds of your ad. It grabs the viewer's attention so strongly that they must stop scrolling to see what happens next. When you shoot your ad, shoot five different hooks. When you test different hooks, you may find, surprisingly, that your favorite is the worst performer of the bunch.

Here's an example from our launch video:

A woman torching boring boxers with a flamethrower. Who's not going to stop scrolling to see what happens?

## 2. RELATABLE PROBLEMS

For this section, I always think it's funny to watch old infomercials for inspiration. There's a worthwhile subreddit called r/wheredidthesodago. You want to find funny, yet relatable problems that many of your viewers have experienced. Here's an example:

We showed the visual of a man needing to unstick his nuts from his leg on a hot day using a fake product we invented, the "Scrotula."

## 3. THE SOLUTION: YOUR PRODUCT

Introduce your product and show how it solves relatable problems:

We ripped some clothing off a man during a meeting for an eye-catching scene, revealing our product with some of our selling points on a whiteboard.

## 4. FIRST CALL TO ACTION

Such as, "Click the link and shop now to try for yourself." Be more creative than that. Watch how other ads do it. Don't try to put too many jokes in here; get to the point. You're selling. You want them to take action. Most people won't make it to the end of your ad. This is for those people.

## 5. SOCIAL PROOF!

You need to alleviate your audience's skepticism. They are watching an ad from a brand they've never heard of. Show press and reviews here. Here are some examples:

These days, we say, "over 10,000 five-star reviews," but back then, we only had a couple hundred, so we wrote 99 percent five-star reviews.

## 6. FINAL CALL TO ACTION AND OUTRO

The outro should be semi-boring, semi-entertaining, and drag on a bit. This is to prevent your sales channel from auto-playing the next video too soon, and your audience forgetting to click the link to your website.

Our website and link stay up for thirty seconds in this video while her ex tries to win her back, and she keeps telling you to click the link. Do something more original than confetti here though.

If you follow these steps, add in your own originality, your marketing is good, and your product solves a problem, people will buy. Especially if you're absurd and funny. Humor converts up to five times better, because when you make someone laugh, there's some science thingy happening where they want to open their wallet. They'll also tag or share it with their friends and give you more organic reach. Careful though, nothing will kill buying intent like too many cringey jokes.

# #58

# START A CULT

*"The best startups might be considered slightly less extreme kinds of cults. The biggest difference is that cults tend to be fanatically wrong about something important. People at a successful startup are fanatically right about something those outside of it have missed."*

—PAYPAL FOUNDER, PETER THIEL, IN HIS BOOK *ZERO TO ONE*

Don't just think of starting a brand. What you really want to start is a cheerful cult. Think about how your brand can bring joy to somebody else's life in such a unique and powerful way that they feel the need to tell others about it compulsively.

Apple is a cult. There are other smartphones on the market, yet who's camping out on the street for the next Samsung? Tesla is a cult. When the Model 3 was revealed, 400,000 people preordered it, 100,000 of whom hadn't even seen a photo. There were several electric cars and hybrids on the market, yet how many people preordered a Toyota Prius, Chevy Volt, or Nissan Leaf? Investor Josh Wolfe realized he made a mistake shorting Tesla stock when he saw people were getting Tesla tattoos, saying, "It's very hard to short something when people are tattooing the brand on their body."

None of In-N-Out Burger's competitors have the same cult-like following. Since their burgers are never frozen and come from In-N-Out quality-approved ranches, it took a long time to expand to Texas, but when they finally did, this was the headline from an article in *The Daily Mail*: "Tears and a Two-Mile-Long Line Mark Opening of the First In-N-Out Burger Joints in Texas."

Yes, even the bloody Bri'ish feel the need to comment on In-N-Out's opening in new states.

You know who else's burgers are never frozen? Wendy's. Do they have two-mile lines when opening a new restaurant? Do they have people crying tears of joy?

Tears of delight: Danielle DeInnocentes of The Colony, Texas sheds tears of joy after eight years living away from the chain she had grown to love in California

Source: *Daily Mail*

Harry Snyder, In-N-Out's co-founder, said, "Keep it real simple. Do one thing and do it the best you can." In-N-Out's menu and cooking processes have barely changed in seventy-five years. The only complaint from fans is that there aren't enough locations. In-N-Out is known as "The anti-chain with the cult-like mystique."

How do you turn your brand into a cult? Fulfill the desires and needs of your clientele. People don't care about you or your brand. They care about their own self-interests. You need to connect with them on an emotional level through your brand identity, values, marketing, and product. They become fans of your brand because it resonates with their identity. People don't buy Gucci because the quality or designs are that much better than those of other luxury brands. They go crazy for Gucci because of how it makes them feel when they wear it. It projects an image to the world of how they see themselves. Or at least how they wish to see themselves. Or at least they think it projects that image. People buy rings at Tiffany's for twice the price of an *identical* ring at Costco because of the Tiffany shopping experience and that signature baby-blue box. What does your product or brand allow people to say about themselves?

Apple is great at building its cult because it connects with its customers on a personal level. They make you feel that you, as a creator, can create so much more simply with an Apple device. When they launch a product, it's not merely a new device; it's a cultural milestone. You don't want to miss out on the technological revolution. Apple makes you want to be an early adopter.

Similarly, when you drive a Tesla, you're not getting from A to B. You're saving the world in style. They make you feel cool while you're reducing reliance on big oil, one trip to the store at a time. You feel special when you discover your car can play games and has cult-insider Easter Eggs like its ability to dance, go into crazy Mario-Kart Rainbow Road mode on autopilot, play audio from the famous *SNL* "more cowbell" sketch, and a volume button that goes up to 11 like that famous scene from *This is Spinal Tap*. Tesla cult members love to brag to their friends by showing them how fast their car can go in ludicrous or insane mode. Then once they're done scaring the shit out of their friends, they'll use the car's built-in whoopee cushion to prank them. Tesla gains more cult-like worship when the car's auto-software updates improve features over time, instead of the tech becoming obsolete like other cars. No other car has such fun, gamified attention to detail, which gives each Tesla owner/cult member so many things to brag about to their non-Tesla-cult friends. There are even comedy sketches about this. None of these bonus features are advertised. In fact, Tesla doesn't need to run any ads whatsoever. They can barely keep up with demand as is, letting their cult-members do the marketing for them.

Once your cheerful cult is up and running, make sure you're always true to your fans. Do not try to be everything to everyone; take care of your core audience first. It will grow on its own. Trader Joe's founder, Joe Coulombe, said, "Beware of ever betraying the true believers." You cannot disappoint your fans, or they'll turn on you.

# #59

# TAP INTO FOMO

*"Nothing is more expensive than a missed opportunity."*
—H. JACKSON BROWN, JR, AMERICAN AUTHOR

When Richard Branson launched *Student* magazine in 1966, he had to sell advertising without having his first issue printed. He called Coca-Cola and told them Pepsi had booked an advertisement, but the back page was still free. He then called the *Daily Telegraph* and asked if they wanted to advertise before or after their rival, the *Daily Express*. He sold advertising to major companies in a magazine run by two fifteen-year-olds that didn't yet exist. He said of this experience, "I was too young to contemplate failure."

Put yourself in your prospective client or investor's shoes. How do you get them to feel the fear of missing out on the epic ride you're offering them? How do you combine a sense of urgency, scarcity, and a sense of fear that if they don't act now, their competitors will? People tend to be more risk averse than ready to take a risk. Big companies and wealthy investors are not drawn to quick action unless you make them feel they are risking a big loss by not getting in on your offer immediately.

As 2008 was drawing to a close, both Tesla and SpaceX were facing impending doom. Tesla was going to be bankrupt in a matter of weeks. Elon publicly stated he would put his last $20 million into Tesla himself if he didn't get the funds from investors by the end of the year. This not only showed his personal commitment, it drove his investors crazy with a potent mix of FOMO and greed. They wrote the checks, and Elon didn't have to show his cards. Like the fact that he had already put in the last of his money earlier that year, and he damn sure didn't have $20 mil under his mattress.

# #60

# ABOVE THE INFLUENCE

*"Celebrities are not brands. They're people. If you're a brand, you have to stand for something other than being famous."*

—DONNY DEUTSCH, ADVERTISING EXECUTIVE

You may think the best way to market your brand to the public is by courting celebrities and big influencers. After all, celebrities posting your products used to mean the difference between success and failure for many brands. A celebrity spokesperson can still be great for your brand if it's a good fit, they're properly incentivized, and actually care about your brand. Creative director John Hegarty says, "The use of celebrities in advertising must be a marriage, not a one-night stand." Your celebrity endorser must actually believe in your product, not just hawk it like snake oil. A celebrity endorsement that is not a perfect match to your brand is just a lazy attempt at credibility that no one buys into.

Paying for social media posts doesn't do what it used to and is not a reliable strategy. A world-famous boxing star happened to wear our underwear during two different weigh-ins, which tens of millions of people saw, and we didn't get a spike in sales from either. We spent

$20k on a post from another massive influencer and got $10k back in sales. Without proper research, we sent a bunch of micro influencers underwear with affiliate links so they would get paid for each sale. The resulting sales were less than the value of the free undies we sent. You must be strategic with the influencers you send to; not all are created equal. Use the right tools to find your best fit. For example, on TikTok Shop, you can use a tool called Kalo Data that shows you which influencers are selling which products and how well. You can also use new models that you pay for based on views instead of semi-famous people's going rates.

However, it still might be worth it to send out free samples to influential people in your network. Is your product so good that if you give it out for free, people will buy more? Mine is. But I don't just give it to anyone who asks. I give it out to the most influential and successful people I know. Not only will it show up randomly on their social media where other people will see it, they'll think about me and my company every time they go to sleep, wake up, make love, or go to the bathroom. It's underwear. My logo is always there. It's unavoidable. This has helped me raise money, garnered millions of views on random posts, and is seen organically on everything from boxing matches to paparazzi snapshots. This is great for brand building, but don't expect a spike in sales even if someone famous posts about your product.

Not only do we get free press, these people buy it themselves because they love the product and want more. When someone asks for another free care package, I *send a personalized discount code instead*. I reinforce the behavior that no matter how famous someone might be, they need to support our brand. That first hit is crack, and I am simply the pusherman. Give generously and then demand they support you feverishly.

Some brands still find the right influencer fit, but it's not how it was when any influencer with a big following could hawk your product and get sales. It can be a catastrophic waste of money. There are notable exceptions to this rule, and getting your product out to product reviewers could have an impact, but it's probably not the windfall you want it to be. You're probably better off spending that money on funny direct-response ads or paid User Generated Content (UGC). Few one-off celebrity partnerships will ever be better than a real marketing strategy.

That said, when you have a great opportunity for a celebrity brand ambassador, by all means, go for it. Those are best when they're organic and unpaid to start with. We just received this email from Billie Eilish's styling team:

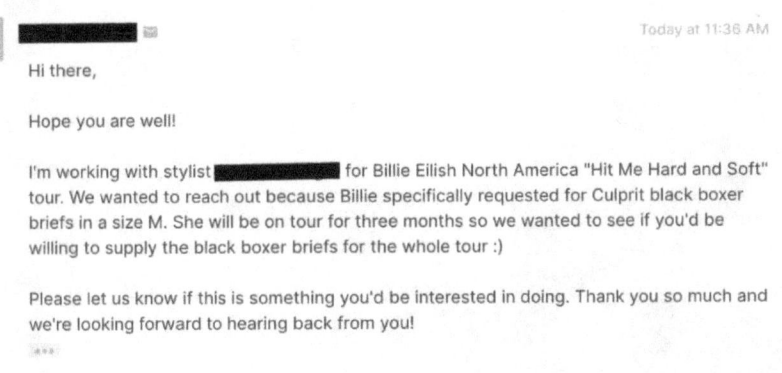

So we took full advantage of the opportunity. We learned she has seventy-one nights of touring, so we gave her seventy-one pairs. We decided to make her a card, but we only had ten minutes to get it done. I wrote a poem:

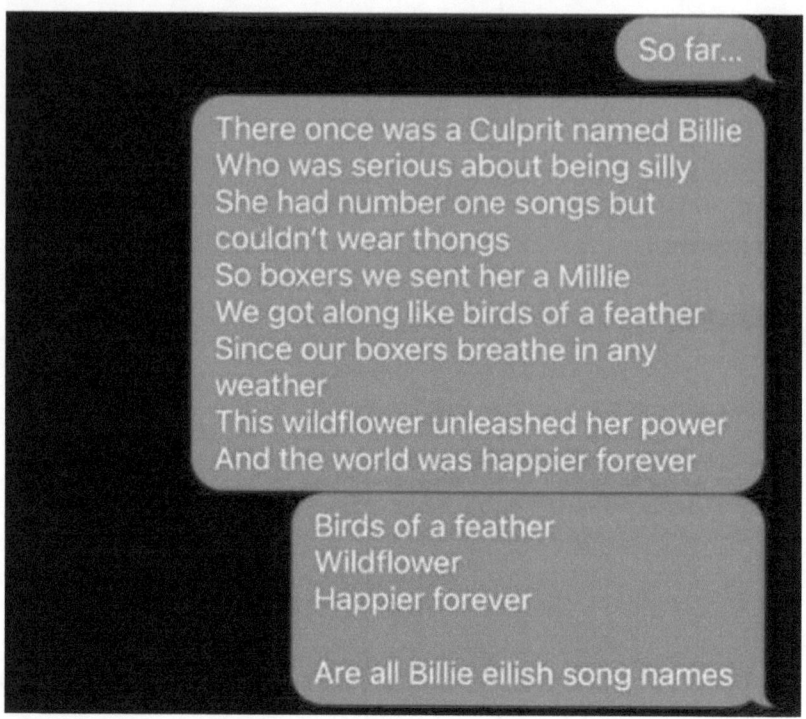

My partner, David's girlfriend, Elena, happens to be a sensational artist and drew her line art on a card. Then she handwrote the poem before the team had to rush off to the warehouse to pick it up before it closed.

The final result

Who knows if anything will happen with that, but it will stand out in her mind and is further explored in upcoming Chapter 63.

# #61

# FULL COURT PRESS

*"One decent editorial counts for a thousand advertisements."*

—JAMES DYSON, *AGAINST THE ODDS*

Oprah listed *Athletic Propulsion Labs* shoes as one of her favorite products, and the Kardashians posted about them organically. APL saw an almost imperceptible spike in sales, followed by zero long-term growth. So, what changed the game for them? One killer article about how the NBA banned their shoes because they gave an unfair performance advantage. Instead of claims that their shoes could make you run faster and jump higher, the NBA was banning them for exactly that reason.

If you can get a good editorial like the article on APL's shoe ban, you have a *moral obligation* (Chapter 54) to milk it for all it's worth. They turned the resulting article into ads, used direct quotes from the NBA, and got it reposted on other sites. Unlike worthless celebrity shoutouts, this moved the needle. This happened in 2010, and they're still using it to their advantage. Look at these articles from 2020, 2021, and 2023:

### Robb Report

STYLE / FOOTWEAR — OCTOBER 19, 2020

**The NBA Banned This Performance-Enhancing Sneaker 10 Years Ago. Now It's Back and Better Than Ever.**

Two new debuts from Athletic Propulsion Labs push the original controversial technology even further.

By KAREEM RASHED

### FAST COMPANY

07-21-2021 | RECOMMENDER

**APL's sneakers were banned by the NBA. Now it's taking on running**

Athletic Propulsion Labs, the sneaker brand once banned by the NBA for giving players an unfair edge, has a new running shoe that promises to boost your speed.

### IN THE KNOW.
by yahoo!

**This brand's sneakers are so bouncy, the NBA banned players from wearing them**

---

Having trouble getting press? Cheat. You can buy press from some decent publications. Wonder how those lists get chosen, like the twenty best gifts to buy your man, the ten presents to make her remember why she loves you this Valentine's Day, our favorite skin products for women over forty-five, and everything in between? Money. Being featured in those lists is affiliate marketing. It might get you direct sales, and it's great for SEO. You can then use the quotes you bought and probably wrote yourself as social proof in your marketing.

American *Vogue* was an expensive feature, so we spent 10 percent of the asking price and got Ukrainian *Vogue* to feature us instead. Now we have quotes on our website and in our ads from *Vogue*. They're real quotes, really from *Vogue*. They're just translated from Ukrainian. And we paid for them. To reiterate, nothing about this was organic. I am giving you the secret sauce here. This kind of press won't actually boost your sales on its own, but the resulting quotes can. We've gotten to the point where the rest of the publications on our site are organic, but that Vogue one is definitely paid for.

To boost your sales organically with real press, you need a reason for people to write about you. I've never had good luck with PR teams. They're expensive and don't guarantee sales, so if you're boot-strapped like us, I don't recommend that route. You're better off creating a viral moment you can pitch to publications. Reach out to writers. It's a classic example of if you want something done right, do it yourself. These writers are not celebrities. They are not hard to get ahold of. They're all on X, tweeting up a storm. They're looking for stories. Give them a good one.

When Gaston Glock launched his infamous handgun, people heard it had a polymer frame and thought it would be undetectable by metal detectors. This rumor that his guns could pass through security led to widespread media attention. Rather than dispel these rumors because they were untrue, Glock said nothing in return and let the rumors persist, turning a fake story into real sales.

# #62

# DEMONSTRATE GREATNESS

*"No argument in the world can ever compare with one dramatic demonstration."*
—CLAUDE HOPKINS

If your brand is high fashion or luxury, you know the prestige that a runway show brings. But if you're a modern-day inventor, you're better off learning from a ShamWow or Flex-Seal infomercial. If you're pitching a new product, you could learn a thing from Edwin Land, founder of Polaroid. In the early days of his career, he was selling a new product: polarized sunglasses. He booked a hotel room that had the sun's direct glare pour in through the window at the exact time of his meeting. He put a fishbowl with several live goldfish on the windowsill. It was so backlit by the sun, you couldn't see the fish. In walked several executives from American Optics. He turns to them and says, "Sorry about the glare, you can't even see the fish. Put these on." He gave them his polarized glasses, instantly cutting the glare in half and revealing the goldfish. He made the sale on the spot.

When Sony founder Akio Morita was heralding his new transistor radio as "pocket-sized," he realized they were just slightly bigger than the average shirt pocket. Easy fix. He simply made the pockets slightly bigger on his salespeople's shirts. When they showed the radios to buyers, they ended each demonstration by saying, "and they fit right in your pocket," and promptly popped them in their shirt-pockets.

When Tesla was on the brink of collapse in October 2008, Daimler executives had told Elon they were interested in making their Smart Car electric. Instead of making a proposal, Musk told his team to scramble together a prototype before Daimler's upcoming US visit. Unavailable in the States, they drove one across the border from Mexico, ripped out the gas engine, and put in a Tesla electric motor.

When the executives arrived in January, grumpy, they had to meet with a nobody electric car company, Musk said, "They were expecting some lame PowerPoint presentation." Instead, he took them out to the parking lot. While already shocked by seeing a working model so quickly, when the tiny car hit sixty miles per hour four seconds later, they must've been dumbstruck. Daimler not only signed a contract with Tesla for batteries and powertrains, they invested $50 million. This investment secured Tesla's future.

# #63

# BE MEMORABLE

Art by Robbie Williams

Similar to a sales demonstration, making your product stand out, being memorable is about making yourself stand out. Become unforgettable in our noisy world. Here are some ways I've attempted to avoid being forgotten:

While pitching a TV series based on the bank robber who inspired *Point Break*, David and I made a criminal file with an FBI logo on it, complete with a collage of his exploits, photos, fingerprints, his various alter egos, and real FBI files we obtained using the Freedom of Information Act. This is what the inside of the folder looked like:

Inside the folder was the series outline and script. We took this one step further and pulled it out of the light-up briefcase from the movie *Pulp Fiction*. The actual one that was used in the movie, which I happen to have because my dad was the lighting director and designed the briefcase's effect. Executives would be awe-struck, but we never showed the inside of the briefcase, because as Tarantino said to my dad when he asked what's in it, "No one ever knows what's in the fuckin' briefcase." Still never sold that show.

We pitched a sci-fi TV show about the first cryogenically frozen person brought back from the dead. While meeting with JJ Abrams's company, Bad Robot, we carried in a different briefcase. This one was a large, sleek, metal Haliburton case, and it had frozen condensation on the outside. It was hissing from the dry ice inside. We strolled past the security guard who eyed it suspiciously. He asked us to open the briefcase. We said we couldn't because it was frozen. For some reason, when you use the word *because*, people just let you go past them. He definitely shouldn't have. The briefcase was not only making a violent hissing noise, but it was also full of weapons. We met with the executives and pitched our script. At the end, they asked what was in the briefcase. We opened it, revealing a giant block of ice with our script frozen in the middle. And a canvas which we unfurled, revealing big knives, hammers, chisels, ice picks, and a hatchet. We said, "Choose a weapon." One executive did, and she cracked the ice open and pulled out our script. They were amazed. They said it was the best pitch they ever got. Didn't sell that show either. Hollywood is hard.

I met David Senra at his event in Miami. We exchanged contact because he liked the detailed notes I had kept of the best quotes from his podcast, and he asked me to share them. When I found out he was doing a live event in New York two months into writing my book, an idea struck. I would use that date as the deadline for the first draft and have it ready to present to him. Since he inspired me to write the book, I wanted him to write the foreword. This helped me keep up a furious pace of writing, but then, as the deadline approached, I realized no one is recommended or sent more books than him. He's reading a book every week for his podcast, and his reading list is thousands of books long. If I gave him my manuscript, it might take months for him to even open it. An audiobook might be easier, but it's much better to give something tangible.

An idea was brewing. Senra regularly talks about how game changing the Sony Walkman was when it first came out. How it put music in your pocket, sold 400 million units, and inspired the iPod. Boom. I went on eBay. An original blue one with the orange headphones in working condition was $500. With only a week till the event, I decided to buy two in case one didn't work. They were from 1979 after all. Both arrived. Yep. One didn't work. I recorded the first hour of my book the night before my flight to New York. When I showed up to meet Senra and his wife for coffee, I was wearing the orange headphones, and I flashed the Walkman and put it on the table.

**Senra:** "Is that an original Sony Walkman?"

**Dylan:** "Yes, it's a present for you."

David and his wife were blown away by the thoughtful present. She even said, "We were just talking about this yesterday!"

**Senra:** So what was the project you wanted to talk to me about?

**Dylan:** You inspired me to write a book.

**Senra:** Oh, awesome, send it to me when it's done.

**Dylan:** You already have it. Open your Walkman.

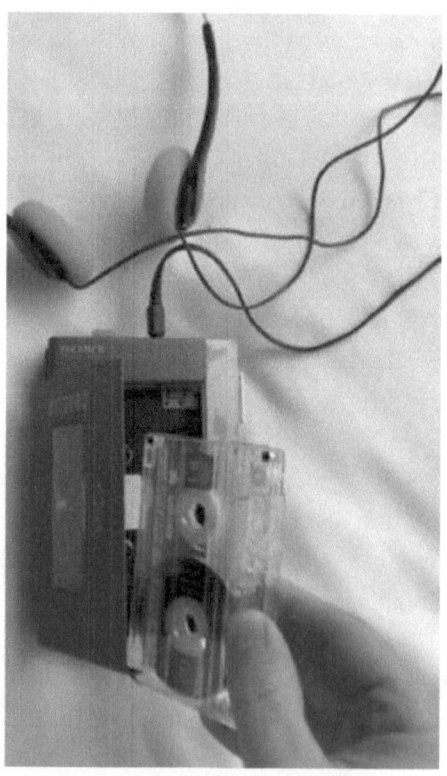

Here's what I gave him. Right before our meeting, I had gone to a vintage audio repair shop in the city and had them put my mp3 onto a cassette tape. At the end of the tape on side B was my request for him to write the foreword of this book with an inside joke from the podcast. He texted me and told me he loved the book, which was an awesome feeling. But he never said anything about the foreword because I don't think he ever flipped the tape to side B! And that, folks, is why in Chapter 57 I say you need multiple Calls to Action 😂.

# #64

# HAVE MAIN-CHARACTER ENERGY

*"Be strong, be confident, be the star of your own life."*

—ESTÉE LAUDER

Imagine the following as a scene in a movie:

INT. WHITE HOUSE LINCOLN BEDROOM—1940—MIDNIGHT

There's a knock at the door. It's a wheelchair-bound President Franklin Delano Roosevelt. The door swings open, revealing Winston Churchill. He's stark naked. Wearing nothing but a cigar in his mouth and a glass of scotch in his hand, he addresses the president:

CHURCHILL

You see, Mr. President, I have nothing to hide.

He motions for FDR to wheel himself into the room. Churchill proceeds to command this meeting for the next hour in his birthday suit, pausing only to pour drinks for himself and the president.

Do you think FDR ever forgot this moment? No, it was seared into his brain. Churchill made a statement, left an impression, and in the end, got exactly what he wanted. You want to be one of one. Follow your own code, live by your own values, stand out in the minds of everyone you meet, and have a style uniquely yours. Your brand must stand out amongst all the noise, but it all starts at the top. You must be a standout personality. It's not enough to just have character; you must be a character.

You already have unique traits that make you YOU. All I'm asking is that you lean into those. Embrace them. Amplify them. Shout from the fucking rooftops who you are, not in a pompous way, just in a self-assured way. Be authentically yourself. Make no apologies when you offend someone for being you.

I was on a trip in Kenya, and with no one else stepping up, I became the group's leader. I made decisions on where we went and when, I directed elaborate group photos that would take a few minutes of everyone's time to nail, but ended up being incredible. I had a nagging feeling I was being overbearing—that I was trying to direct people's lives like a film. I knew if everyone listened to me, we'd get killer photos and have a time to remember, but I couldn't shake the paranoia that I was being too much. I communicated this fear of being overbearing to a woman on the trip. She said four words I'll never forget: "Be overbearing, take space." Your whole life, you've given space to other people. You need space for yourself too. It's okay to take space and be the truest version of who you are. To have main character energy. Not everyone will like you. In fact, when you try to get everyone to like you, you shroud the best parts of yourself. To some people, your honey will taste like vinegar. That's fine. Some people don't like garlic. They're called vampires.

While you're at it, have a motto.

Theodore Roosevelt's was "Get Action," Stan Lee's "Excelsior" (Latin for "Ever Upward"), Jeff Bezos's Blue Origin's motto is *Gradatim Feroc-*

*iter*, which translates to "Step by Step, Ferociously," and means steady progress toward seemingly impossible goals will win the day. Ernest Shackleton's motto was "By Endurance We Conquer," and Isambard Kingdom Brunel's was "Never Despair." A favorite saying of Patton's was, "Always do your damndest."

Like much in this book, my motto is not original. But it does speak to me, and I repeat it whenever things seem impossible. I do not know who said it originally. What's important are the words. My motto is: "If it was easy, everyone would do it." In the next twenty-four hours, have a think about what your motto is and why. Write it out. Live by it. It's okay if someone else said it first.

During WWII, another motto of Patton's was, "Always take the offensive. Never dig in." To illustrate this point, while being shown the defensive foxholes at a battlefield in Tunisia, he asked the unit's commanding officer where his foxhole was. Patton walked over and urinated in it. They would not be taking a defensive position.

# #65

# YOUR GOALS ARE DUMB

*"Seeing your goal in your mind helps you see it in person."*

—PAUL GRAHAM

**Me:** How do I stop grinding my teeth when I sleep?

**My Dentist:** First, make fifteen billion dollars. Then buy your own island.

You need S.M.A.R.T. goals. Your goal needs to be Specific, Measurable, Achievable, Relevant, and Time-Bound. Your goal could be to make a lot of money, but it's not specific or measurable. Wishing to be rich is not enough. There needs to be meaning behind why you wish this; otherwise, you won't get there, and if you do, you won't stay there. Let's thank George T. Doran back in 1981 for S.M.A.R.T. goals.

When my dentist told me to make fifteen billion, it was both specific and measurable. It's lofty as hell, but nonetheless, it's been done by people no smarter than me. It's relevant to my values because I want to be fully financially autonomous, help the world, and stop wearing a mouth guard when I sleep. I firmly believe that with fifteen billion and an island to myself, I will no longer carry invisible stress that makes itself known only in my dreams. And to make it time based, let's say I have exactly two decades. With hard work, luck I'll create myself, vivid visualization, and a little help from inflation, making fifteen billion by 2045 is possible. The limits on what you can do were put there by you. And you, like me, my friend, have not begun to scratch the surface of what's possible during your one-way trip to the grave. Remember, shoot for the stars, and at least you'll die in space.

When setting your goal, you want to be as specific as possible. If your goal is to get fit, instead of saying I want to be fit say, "I want to lower my body fat to 12 percent." Write it down on paper. This engages your neurocircuitry better than typing it on your phone. Make sure to home in on one specific goal instead of many. You can write down all of them, but then cross each one out until you're left with the one you want to focus on now.

## THE POWER OF VISUALIZATION

Now picture yourself achieving your goal. When Shaun White visualized himself on the cover of *GQ* after winning the X Games, he was wearing a specific pair of American flag pants he already owned. He achieved exactly that. Arnold visualized the specifics of winning his first Mr. Universe contest. Later, he used this technique during the recall election that got him elected as governor of California. You can achieve what you can see. Start visualizing not just the goal, but every painstaking detail. Each time you visualize, add detail, color, and depth to your vision. Imagine who's there with you, imagine what you and everyone are wearing, what music is playing, and even what the temperature feels like. Visualize for thirty seconds at first, then a minute, and see if you can go longer. Your visualization power is a muscle. It gets stronger the more you use it.

# #66

# RAISING MONEY AND THE ART OF CLOSING DEALS

*"If you cannot bear the thought of prostrating yourself to earn the seedcorn, then you will almost certainly never own the farm."*

—FELIX DENNIS

Raising money sucks. Hopefully, you have an extroverted, charismatic co-founder who can keep up with you during the endless song and dance, so you don't have to do it alone. This perpetual roadshow has brought me to countless pitches, lunches, cocktail hours, offices, flights, Zoom calls, nights out, roundtables, hikes, weekend trips, hosting on our film sets, and attending kids' birthday parties. I've recently become above average at it. Not because of any innate skill, but because I've put in ten thousand hours doing it. If I got paid hourly for every pitch I've done, I'd never need to actually close one.

Two years ago, people wanted to throw money at us. We didn't really need it that badly, and we wanted to retain both control and 75 percent of our company. We walked away from a good deal—great by today's standard, because the landscape has changed. The mood shifted away from high-growth, unprofitable e-com brands. A competitor of ours, Parade, burned a lot of investors in the DTC underwear space. I've met with investors who wouldn't spare five minutes of their time for an undies brand because of what happened to a friend of theirs on Parade. Now, everyone wants to invest in AI instead of inventory-heavy brands that only exist on Shopify. Your category can go from hot to not, overnight.

If you're in a position where people want to give you money, make sure you retain control. Just don't get so hung up on equity. As long as the deal is decent, take it. Get some cash in the bank and don't spend it on trying to grow too fast or expand into new categories. In the investment world, things can change rapidly; a dollar now is worth two theoretical dollars later.

So put on your ruby red slippers and get ready to do the song and dance. Start with some lower-hanging fruit and build your confidence in a room. Your numbers are less important than your passion. Most smart investors invest in the person, not the idea. If you can show that you're the type of person who will eventually be successful no matter what obstacle gets in the way, you'll find money. Just get ready to let go of your pride for a while.

I always send investors our underwear to have them understand they're not just investing in our financials, they're investing in a great company and a fantastic product. Once their undies arrive, to be memorable (Chapter 63), I follow up with a handwritten note. Here's an example:

Now that you're gearing up to meet investors, let me tell you what will kill the deal.

1. **Time:** The #1 killer of deals is the #1 killer of us all, *time*. Make sure everything your investors ask for, like updated numbers, is delivered within twenty-four to forty-eight hrs. If you have trouble making a revised deck to their standards, ask for someone in their office who can help you "in the interest of efficiency; so you get it how they like it without any back and forth.
2. **Lack of transparency:** If you're not hitting a projection for any reason, get in front of it. Let them know why and how you're going to fix it. You can never hide anything number related from your investors. It will all come out in the wash. If you've had a worse quarter or year, you can tell the story of where you're going and how. Just be honest. For example, we did almost $9 million last year, and this year we did $6 million. We paid off $2 million in debt and have better margins than ever, but our ad spend efficiency was down. Instead of glossing over it, I drew attention to it. Why it happened, how we

fixed it, and how we're already doing better in the first part of this year than last year. Bad news is better than no news and a surprise later. Focus on the positive changes you made without shying away from the negative. Hype them next year.

3. **Perpetual negotiations:** Don't get stuck on any one point. If you go back and forth more than a few times, you're about to kill the deal. Let them know what's nonnegotiable from the get-go and don't torpedo a deal over a minor point or a few percent.

4. **Communication:** Get in a cadence with your investors. Ask them every Monday how their weekend was, or ask about specific details like how their kid's Little League game was. Get involved and legitimately care what they're up to. Take an interest in their lives, text them when something good happens in your business, and make sure you let them know. If you're too busy with work and not in constant contact updating them, they will forget about you as you did them. As busy as you are, they're busier, so you have to put in the work to stay top of mind.

5. **Lack of process:** Not all legal teams are created equal. Make sure yours is moving forward, and what needs to be done is being done. Also, make sure your legal team is properly updated regularly. I recently had my lawyer join a call with our investors to answer some technical questions, but I had not spoken to him in months. Our lawyer was so in the dark about recent money that had come in and recent changes to the cap table, it sounded like we were correcting each other on the call. It looked extremely unprofessional, and it's all because I hadn't prepped my team or kept them properly informed. In trying to keep their billable hours down by limiting how often we spoke, I might've just killed a deal.

6. **Lack of oversight:** Your soon-to-be investors need to know the company is properly managed and that funds will be used appropriately. Make sure the right systems are in place, and you have a well-thought-out plan for how the cash will be used. Give them confidence that there are checks and balances in place to ensure the company is managed in their best interests.

Make sure to raise more than you need now and more than you think you'll need later. Being underfunded is the #1 killer of new businesses. If you suck at raising money, crowdfund. Then you can show off your successful crowdfunding to future investors if you even need them by then. If you can't crowdfund, you either didn't do a good enough job, didn't ask the right people for help, your product sucks, or you don't have enough of a market, and you should pivot. If you can't raise a dollar, and you're still hellbent on this idea, sell your most prized possession and go make it a reality.

# #67

# PITCHING YOUR PRODUCT

*"Everyone has something at stake. If you address that predicament, you can move anyone from no to yes."*

—HERB COHEN, FAMED NEGOTIATOR

As a founder, you will constantly have to be selling not only your product, but yourself. You need to always be ready. To prepare for every possible scenario and have a flexible strategy for each. To be ready for every situation and to speak in a way that feels natural every time. You'll face phone calls, video calls, in-person pitches, and chance encounters. Here's how to maximize each.

## PREPPING FOR AN IMPORTANT CALL OR MEETING

*"Overprepare, then go with the flow."*
—CULPRIT CREATIVE, MY PRODUCTION COMPANY'S MOTTO ON SHOOTS

When you have an important call, ten out of ten times, you are selling something. If you're raising money, you're selling the investor confidence in yourself. If you're calling a retailer, you're selling the buyer confidence in your product's ability to sell. If you're calling to negotiate with your manufacturer, you're selling the fact that your future volume will scale. If you're meeting with your board, you're selling an idea. Treat every important call or meeting like you're about to make a sale.

It's not just about mentally preparing; it's about physically writing out *every possible scenario* and what you will say for each into a *roadmap*. This roadmap is how your call or meeting is going to go. If they try to steer the conversation that way, you have it typed out in your notes on how to steer it back this way. If they ask for "x" percent or dollar amount, you're ready and have reasons why it needs to be "y." By making a detailed roadmap, you're over preparing. You want to overprepare, then go with the flow.

By having it in writing, you can easily refer to your ceiling or floor or worst-case scenario. You can bring up every bullet point that makes your idea sound killer and craft a story that strategically deflects everything that hurts you. Your whole map is in writing. You have every answer in front of you staring you in the face in every meeting.

If you have a business partner or someone you can riff with, take turns playing both roles. Go harder playing the other party than you think they will go in the actual meeting. Practice each call like a soap opera, referring to your roadmap every time you go back and forth. Try to get your partner to shoot holes in every argument you present.

Also, in your roadmap, include any jokes you can tell and any subjects you can switch to, including positive facts you can bring up about your business, should the conversation start going awry.

Have one small concession you're willing to give, and you can even get your partner to act like that's too much when you say it on the call. For example, if the other party wants 20 percent and you told them you're staying firm at 10 percent, you can go up to 12 percent and have your partner get mock angry that you did that. Never split the difference.

Here's something they won't teach you in business school: if the conversation really starts to get off track, pretend you're losing service or your Wi-Fi is cutting out. Pretend you're frozen if you're on video.

Get off the call and jump back on thirty seconds later. Start the conversation at the point you want to take it from. In NLP (neurolinguistic programming), it's called a "pattern interrupt."

## A CONFIDENCE HACK FOR YOUR FIRST BIG PITCH

If you're thinking, "Yeah, but I'm just not great in a room pitching to powerful strangers, I get nervous." Don't worry. As long as you're passionate about what you're doing, you will become exceptional. All you need to do is make your passion infectious. Great speakers and salespeople are not born; they are made.

When I was twenty-four, the night before my first big Hollywood pitch at Fox Studios, we were practicing at a friend's place and drinking white wine. My practice pitch was confident, hilarious, and on point. I wanted to recreate it exactly for the room full of high-powered executives. The white wine made the atmosphere more fun and relaxed. The two glasses I'd had loosened my tongue just the right amount without feeling or appearing intoxicated. I knew what I had to do.

At 8:00 a.m. en route to the meeting, I stopped by Starbucks. I grabbed three to-go cups and split a bottle of white wine evenly between the three of us who were pitching. We brought in our "coffee" and were merrily drinking Chardonnay during our pitch. We slayed it and had the executives cracking up in laughter.

If you're sober, don't fall off the wagon for a pitch. If you pitch a lot, it's not healthy to drink every time. But if you do drink and are nervous to the point where it could affect your performance, I recommend having a glass of wine on the first couple of big pitches to get used to it. Then on your third pitch, when you're more comfortable in a room, you won't need the sauce.

## ELEVATE YOUR ELEVATOR PITCH

When you're at a party, a dinner, a bar, in the steam room, or God forbid, an actual elevator, and there's someone you want to meet, it's time to make a great first impression. This could be your next investor, or maybe they know the perfect person. It could be their network that helps you cut the Gordian Knot. Or maybe this person will become your new best friend.

The most important thing is to *land the plane* quickly and respect their time. You may have thirty minutes, you may only have thirty seconds. Ask about them first if time permits. When the spotlight turns to you, have your curated, canned response ready to go, no matter what mindset you're in.

Think of the best pitch you've ever done. Now boil that down into one to three sentences. Relate to your audience as much as you can with analogies they'll understand. For example, if I was doing a biotech brand that could take small blood samples and give a variety of results, I'd simply say, "Theranos, but it works." When I pitch my R-rated comedy film that's set in a balls-to-the-wall scavenger hunt on wheels during senior year of high school, that's a mouthful to say and hard to mentally digest. So when I meet with studio executives, I say, "It's *Fast and The Furious* meets *Superbad*." They get it immediately and demand to read it. You need to have your elevator pitch seared into your brain and have it practiced so well that you can pitch your biggest idol without stumbling.

When people find out I make underwear, they always ask what's special. I say, "You hate sweating, right?" then I gesture toward my lower body. They unanimously say yes. "Well, Culprit Underwear is so breathable, you don't sweat. Also, you know Care Bears from the 80s?" They do. "Well," I say, pulling out my phone to an easily accessible album of all our prints, "Here's Don't Care Bears." And then I show them our parody:

If what you do can in any way be explained visually, have your visual cue ready to go on your phone in an album or note folder saved at the top. Make sure it can be accessed immediately within ten seconds, whether you have Wi-Fi or not. Loading screens kill momentum.

Don't show too much either. It's better to show one to three images and leave them wanting more. I always show a couple, then say, "There's tons more," and put my phone away. Even if Tarantino himself was showing me the storyboards to *Pulp Fiction 2*, at a certain point, less is still more. After five minutes, I'd rather just wait for the movie. And don't you dare read anything out loud from your phone. Commit it to memory.

Know your audience, respect their time, and as soon as you've shown your best cards, switch the conversation back to them. But before they leave your presence, make sure to say, "Before I leave, let's exchange contact." They could "Irish Goodbye" the event you're at, and you may never get the chance again. Send them some product or whatever link you have as a follow-up, and remember to be memorable!

# #68

# RETAIN CONTROL

*"You're going to develop more. You're going to get a hold of your medium. But to protect your independence, you've got to do as I have done: own every picture you make."*

—CHARLIE CHAPLIN SPEAKING TO WALT DISNEY,
*WALT DISNEY AN AMERICAN ORIGINAL*

Negotiating your term sheet with investors during your seed round or Series A is going to be the most important negotiation of your life. While it's true that time is the world's worst deal killer, you should not rush through this process to the point of overlooking details. Understand what every line means, fight tooth and nail on things that could one day get you kicked out of your own company, or let you lose control of your board. Make sure no one can raise more money, have first rights of refusal, add board seats, remove you as CEO, dictate when you should sell, or threaten you with anything existential without your approval.

It's okay to give a little more equity than you'd like to if it means you keep *total* control. It's far more important to negotiate for control than it is for an extra 5–10 percent. Remember, it's your company, and a single bullet point on a term sheet can mean the difference between you calling the shots for life or taking a hike when you do something the board doesn't like. While it's true that getting fired from Apple was the harsh lesson Steve Jobs needed to become the seasoned leader who'd later save Apple, I doubt you want to spend twelve years of your life with your face pressed against a window watching a feast like a hungry orphan.

Make it so you have the freedom to do whatever you deem necessary. Are there outside projects you want to do that won't take away from your main business? Give yourself the freedom. Want to take time off if you need to? Make sure you can. It should be up to you to call the shots on when to sell the business and have veto power on all major decisions.

Felix Dennis refers to venture capitalists (VC) not as sharks, but as dolphins, because all they want to do is flip. They want to flip your company at the first chance they get, even if it's one-tenth of what you'll eventually be worth. They want to make a quick return because they have forty other companies in their portfolio, and thirty of them will fail. Your profit needs to pay for those failures. These dolphins want to flip your company and then go flip another company to keep the oxygen pumping through those thirsty dolphin blowholes. Also, as Felix says, be wary because "Dolphins can kill sharks."

Control is the most important thing you have. That's right, to every VC reading this, I'm advising the founder to be a power-hungry control freak, making it impossible for the adults in the room to have their way. Why? Because every VC knows power is so much more important than a little extra money. As a founder, you need to internalize that.

Walt Disney had everything taken from him because his distribution partner married a controlling douche. While who a partner marries is out of your control, with the right contract, retaining control will be in your control. After learning this harsh lesson, Disney vowed to retain full rights to everything in the future. Without total control, he wouldn't have been able to make the first full-length animated feature in motion picture history or the happiest place on Earth. Everyone else told him his ideas were too expensive, crazy, and impossible. Experts told him no one would watch a ninety-minute animation and called what would become *Snow White* "Disney's folly." Later, theme park experts told him he didn't have enough of the staple rides like Ferris wheels. They said the original rides and worlds he created at Disneyland were too expensive, and no one would care about his attention to detail. Luckily, he didn't have to listen to anyone else because he had control.

James Dyson lost control of his first company and, after having this lesson seared into his brain, he made sure that to this day he owns 100 percent of his multibillion-dollar empire. He learned from his mistake, and you, you lucky sonovabitch, have the luxury of learning this *the easy way*. You have an opportunity to skip the hell of having your dream stripped from you like a cell phone in a busy subway. Now there's a visual, here's another:

Imagine I'm writing this lesson on the spirals of a gigantic screw, and I'm about to drill it into your head. The spiral of the screw reads "Retain control at all costs," over and over. You can now avoid Disney and Dyson's pain and over a decade of lost work. You are welcome. *Retain control at all costs.* This includes retaining control from investors, VCs, shareholders, and yes, even business partners.

Here are some tricks investors will try to pull on your inexperienced ass:

First of all, they will either move too slow, because they know you're desperate and don't have any other options, gradually making you more desperate and likely to take any bone they give you. Or, they'll move super fast to get you before someone else does with lightning-fast responses, so the momentum is kept, and you don't have time for second thoughts. The key is to always get their requests for more info or data done as quickly as you can—as if you already have what they asked for, even if you secretly are pulling an all-nighter to get it done.

However, when they ask you to make a decision or sign anything, always take your time. If you have to redline something or make changes, do that quickly as well. You can actually do a lot of the overarching changes without a lawyer, and have your legal team do the specific micro stuff like changing language. It's always more professional to have the redlines come from your lawyer, but if you're strapped for cash, you can move things forward on your own. As long as you preface it and say, "In the interest of efficiency, here are the main changes we have. There will be one more round of micro changes from our team once we agree on the following."

It's up to you; there's no "standard" way of doing things. Which brings me to one of the main pulling-the-wool-over-your-eyes techniques that VCs will attempt to do. They will dismiss details on the term sheet *that you question* as "standard." This happened to Evan Spiegel while raising money for Snapchat. He says when he brought up questions, the investors "took refuge in the notion of standard." This led to them having the first right of refusal and ability to lead rounds in the future, even if Evan would rather go with a different investor to not give any one entity too much control.

Remember, the word *standard* means your investor might be pulling a fast one on you, because that is their standard way of doing business. To not get screwed, raise your standards and say no to what's standard.

Now here's a neat party trick you can employ as a founder to retain control. It's called a dual-class stock structure. It's what Google's founders did to retain voting rights no matter what, and it works like this: Class A shares have one vote per share (typical for publicly traded companies), while Class B shares have ten votes per share. This means that even if the founders hold a minority of shares, they can maintain a majority of voting power.

# #69

# DON'T USE YOUR OWN MONEY

*"You're better off being broke and having a good idea and raising money, than spending all your money on your own idea."*

—BARBARA CORCORAN, *SHARK TANK* INVESTOR

Starting a new company, you have a 90 percent chance of failure. I wouldn't bet my own money on those odds. Professional investors expect many investments will go to zero. The ones that succeed carry the debt of the duds. If you don't have other investments, don't invest your own money. If you use your own money, you'll probably still be undercapitalized and will have to raise money anyway when you run out. Better to just raise from day one and keep your savings.

Once our business was proven and had done millions of dollars in revenue, I put my own money in. Originally, to buy back some equity at the original price. More recently, I've had to put more in to keep our team paid during hard times. That's different because we've proven our model. I've known many a previous rich person who went broke funding their startup themselves.

While we're on the subject of not using your own money...don't make any investments in anything else while you're running your company. Invest your time in yourself and your business; don't waste your time following stocks or crypto. By all means, invest in that stuff, but put it on automatic recurring buy and don't divert your attention watching the price. The worst mistake you can make is when friends or family members want you to invest in their companies. Not only does it take you away from your purpose and suck your most valuable resource: time, but it can also make you broke. The number-one way rich people go broke isn't cars, planes, mansions, or tax. It's investments. When your brain hears the word investment, it bypasses your brain's "expense" filter. Because you view it as an investment, it ceases to be an expense in your mind. The same 90 percent chance of failure that applies to your business applies to any other ventures you invest in. If you feel you absolutely must invest in stocks or crypto, then put it on daily or weekly auto-buys and don't even look at it. You'll probably do better than most investors who spend all their time on it because you won't make emotional decisions.

# PART THREE

# THE HOUSE IS ON FIRE

# #70

# IT'S SUPPOSED TO BE HARD

*"The sense of accomplishment from overcoming difficulty is satisfying in a way that a life of leisure and ease will never be."*

—HENRY FORD

Life doesn't happen to you, it happens for you. Each mistake is a lesson, every obstacle contains an opportunity, and every challenge makes you more resilient. If founding a company was easy, everyone would do it.

One of my favorite quotes is "Entrepreneurship is living a few years of your life like most people won't, so you can spend the rest of your life like most people can't." Or as I put it to David the day our sales hit $10k, "Entrepreneurship sucks…until it doesn't." The common misconception is that it's going to be a fun ride the whole time. The truth is, it will be fun in retrospect once you look back and see what you were able to overcome. Then you'll be able to laugh at it.

Happiness is a byproduct of becoming indestructible. Being able to shrug off whatever the universe throws at you like water off a duck's back. The ability to laugh in the face of crisis. You are unshakeable because you've learned from others who've had it worse. You persevere because you're passionate. You will show up every time, no matter how you feel in the moment, because even more than your own well-being, you care about the results. Hardships you've already faced or soon will, seem like major setbacks at the time, but they are simply preparing you for what's next.

What you're doing right now at this very moment is likely not what you'll be known for. However important it seems now, it's just a stepping stone. Similarly, when I was going through hell at the worst job I've ever had, it was my whole world. Looking back, I see it was just a drop in the bucket.

When David and I had just finished college, we had no job or way to pay rent. We heard about this new nightclub opening up and how it had "little people, burlesque dancers, and trained monkeys running around stealing drinks from people." We looked at each other and knew immediately what the other one was thinking: we had to work there. David called up their company and asked for the club owner's phone number. Then David skimmed a book called *Stand Like Lincoln, Speak Like Churchill*, and within an hour, he was ready. He called the owner and left the most confident voicemail ever recorded.

That return call came a month later while we were out on a Saturday night. We left the bar, showed up to the office at midnight, and talked our way into our dream job. We wanted to be big movie directors. Our first weekend on the job, the owner took us to Vegas with a world-famous director and a more famous producer. They asked us to charm some ladies over to their table. Our new boss talked us up to them, saying how we were going to be the next big thing. The two Hollywood legends nodded, pretending to care. It seemed too good to be true...until Monday.

David went to work immediately while I flew to Texas to bury my grandfather. He bequeathed to me a beat-up 1997 Lincoln Town Car. As soon as I got back, this heavenly Vegas experience was replaced by a seven-day-a-week hell. A sixteen-hour workday was average. Sometimes I'd hit morning rush hour twice in one shift, working twenty-two hours straight. Our lives didn't matter anymore because this sociopath was about to launch the next legendary LA nightclub.

The club was an astounding success, but I did not share in the success. The sociopath deviously hired us as "executives" in the company. Since we were executives, our boss used a legal loophole to pay us less than minimum wage. *A lot less*; $250 per week each. His reasoning? He had just fired a little person who made $500 per week and said that if we both wanted to work, "you can split the midget's salary." You can tell by the words he used, he was a man of extraordinary character. This modern-day P.T. Barnum was paying us just over $2 an hour. You might be thinking, *No one gets paid that in twenty-first-century America. You're exaggerating!* I wish.

As a cruel joke/legal requirement, he put the "federal minimum wage sign" right behind our desks. The legal wage was $7.25. We got less than a third of that. We worked in a shitty hallway. Literally. It was next to the bathroom, and his fat ass would blow that thing up every day after lunch. I had to use my nonexistent income to buy scent sticks to cover up the smell.

If given the choice, would you rather smell shit or be treated like shit? Well, I was lucky. I got both. He verbally berated me to the point where I broke out in acne from the stress. He called me a retard on a daily basis, and if I was slow to answer him, he accused me of being on Vicodin—like I could even afford a drug habit! And he'd threaten to fire me in ten seconds if I didn't have a new version of whatever I just showed him. He'd count down from ten loud enough for the whole office to hear, for the windows to shake, and the walls to reverberate to the point where the birds flew off the bamboo outside. If I didn't make it back to his desk with a new version by the time he got to one, I was fired.

I'd go home at 11:30 p.m., and he'd call me back to the office at 1:00 a.m. Or I'd get a call the next day that I was rehired on a temporary basis. My only days off were the couple of times I got fired, but I never even got the whole day. Not even if I got fired on a Saturday. He'd call me back in on Sunday. In the six months I worked there, I couldn't schedule a doctor's appointment or get time for a haircut, let alone afford one. Neither of us had healthcare either. One night, I got so fed up with my hair, I asked David to shave my head over a bathtub. An ex-girlfriend made me watch *The Devil Wears Prada*. "Isn't she horrible?" Uh, no. She seems pretty empathetic and chill, actually.

When it was time to hype the grand opening of the club, I had to design a thirty-page book of all his old exploits with little people and circus acts. I designed it like a giant nine-hundred-page library book with a die-cutout after page thirty, revealing a mini alcohol bottle and a mixtape CD of the club's DJ. I had no experience designing and laying out a book. The only things more impossible than the project were the deadline and the price target; less than half of what every book printer quoted me. Somehow, with that much pressure on me, I got it all done... right before he counted down to one for the final time (Parkinson's law baby, lesson #47).

After the invites were done, he gave me the addresses of every celebrity from the A list to the D list. Once I finished the invites, the real work began. He made me show up to every celeb's house, talent agency, and office of anyone in Hollywood who had even a shred of power. A director's dream, right? Except I wasn't allowed to make friends. Not only was I an uninvited guest, I was there as the chaperone of a troupe of little people dressed in full head-to-toe Oompa Loompa makeup. In a Hollywood fever dream, I hand delivered five hundred invites. This went on for weeks. If Johnny Depp wasn't home, I had to come back, sometimes five times, always on my own dime for gas.

Not only did I have to escort the Oompa Loompas, but there was one named Lil' Kim I had to pick up every day. Except she didn't live in Hollywood or even Los Angeles; she lived in a trailer park eighty-three miles away. Every day, I had to march into the trailer to wake her up, greeted by her mom, who wheezed hello to me through an oxygen tank. I had to wake up at 6:00 a.m. to get there by 9:00 a.m. Did I mention I had to pay for my own gas??? I remember specifically that gas was $4.29 a gallon back then. Each week, gasoline burned through half my salary without making a dent in rent. Needless to say, I fell three months behind on payments to my building and almost got evicted. To make rent, I had to ████████ and ██████████████.

Rent was the least of my worries though. I was sleeping so little, I fell asleep at the wheel and almost died. Sometimes I would pull over and set an alarm for seven minutes. That's how long extra I calculated I could be gone without him noticing. Sometimes I'd nap at red lights and have my Oompa Loompa companion, Kim, wake me up when the light turned green. We became good friends, although I think she wanted more than that. She passed recently. RIP Kim. We'll end this story here. I went through and witnessed crazier things there, but this book is about you avoiding the torture I went through, not me reliving it. For the first time in my life, I'm forgiving all that happened and moving on.

Was all the torture working there worth it?

No. I still have PTSD.

But it was worth my going through it to tell you what I learned:

- **Nothing is impossible:** Things you cannot currently imagine yourself being capable of will become possible with the threat of being fired or your business failing. The key is to channel this superhuman ability when there isn't an existential threat.
- **How not to treat people:** You can be curt, you can be blunt, but a leader is never malicious. You don't have to treat your team like best friends or try to make everyone like you, but you need to inspire them to greatness. And everyone, especially your team, deserves respect.
- **The "Midgets, Monkeys, and Hot Girls" principle:** This was the key to the success of the club. People want to be in a stimulating environment. As long as there are those three elements, our old boss said in those exact words, people will always show up and have a great time.
- **"As Long As I Have This":** Our boss was gesturing toward his landline phone in his office. He said you could take away every dollar he had, leave him marooned on a desert island, but as long as he had his telephone, he would make every dollar back and be on top again. The value wasn't in what he had built; the value was in his ability to sell. And he was the best salesman I have ever met. When you know you can build it all back up again, you're more likely to take bold, decisive action.

In high school, James Dyson wasn't good at anything. Until he discovered running. He learned that running on sand was fantastic for endurance, so he woke up every day at 6:00 a.m. to run on nearby dunes. This gave him an unfair advantage, and he started winning. Winning gave him positive feedback, so he worked harder and got even better. It was being able to run that first led him to develop confidence in his abilities and helped him overcome intense hardships later in life. He faced terrible odds. He invented impossible products and built his companies with no money and the wrong partners. Without the confidence he learned from being able to outrun his athletic competition, he'd never be able to out-invent, out-market, and out-sell his business competition.

# #71

# GIVE UP!

*"I was an overnight success alright, but thirty years is a long, long night."*
—RAY KROC, FOUNDER OF THE MCDONALD'S FRANCHISE

If you give up, we won't be reading about you in the future. What kind of life do you want to live? What kind of legacy do you want to leave behind besides some bones in the ground or some ashes in a Folgers can? Do you want to eke out an unstimulating existence or throw yourself into the gauntlet of greatness?

If getting tax liens from the state of Ohio or having California and Washington use a levy to take money right out of your bank account at a crucial moment, having your other account frozen by the State of Florida, or having your payment processor pause payments to you because a lender put a hold on your business doesn't sound fun to you, maybe entrepreneurship isn't for you. But as long as you keep your sense of humor, you'll be fine. In fact, humor should be your default mode when something goes wrong. As soon as I ripped open the letter that contained the tax lien notice, I put "Lean on Me" by Bill Withers on full blast, then got back to work.

The people training to become Navy SEALS who don't make it through Hell Week are the ones looking ahead and realizing they have several more days of this. They think, *There's no way I can do four more days.* The ones who survive Hell Week and become SEALS stay focused on the task at hand. They think, *I just gotta get through this run.*

If you're going through hell, keep going. Success could be right around the corner. Odds are though, it isn't. Be patient. Don't be fooled by an overnight success story. They don't exist. But that doesn't mean there won't be a monumental shift overnight. I had an early investor lose faith because we had made little progress in two years. He pulled his money out on a Tuesday, and I had to pay him out of my own dwindling pockets. We launched our first successful ad two days later, and by the weekend, we no longer needed his money.

Amazon lost money for the first eleven years straight. When news anchor Tom Brokaw asked Bezos if he could even spell profit, Bezos replied, "Yes, P-R-O-P-H-E-T."

You can't talk shit about Bezos. You just can't. Not even for his laugh.

The guy is relentless. So relentless, in fact, go visit the website relentless.com right now and see where that takes you.

Here's a list of people who were pushed to the brink and almost quit, but didn't, and the world is now a better place due to their tenacity:

- Henry Ford
- Inventor Charles Kettering (because his eyes stopped working)
- Elon Musk
- James Dyson
- Stephen King
- Me
- You

Here's a list of people who couldn't handle the pressure and did quit:

- Neville Chamberlain (but thankfully, he did, or you might be speaking German)
- And ten billion people whose names you'll never know because they gave up on their own greatness

Sometimes running your company will feel like you're playing one of those video games where you're running on a bridge and it's falling down and completely destroyed behind you. You have to stay one step ahead as the ground you're walking on is literally crumbling beneath your feet. Just stay focused on the steps ahead, and no matter what, keep moving forward.

# #72

# SIT SHOTGUN, LET YOUR EGO DRIVE

*"Only the arrogant are self-confident enough to press their creative ideas on others."*
—NOLAN BUSHNELL, FOUNDER OF ATARI...AND CHUCK-E-CHEESE

You don't mistakenly become great. Modesty doesn't equal success. You need ego to push you and drive you. Just do us all a favor and hide it. Henry Ford pretended to be humble but sought the spotlight and would purge people from his company if they got more attention in the press than him. In that regard, you should not be like Henry Ford. Also, the way he raised his kids, how he stuck to one idea so stubbornly, Ford became outdated, and how he started a newspaper supporting Nazi-esque ideals. Other than that, though, he was great. He revolutionized manufacturing, paid his workers well so they too could afford his cars, and hired disabled people and ex-cons.

Ryan Holiday wrote an entire book called *Ego is the Enemy,* and he's right. But sometimes a worthy enemy is what you need to push yourself toward greatness, as long as when the time comes, you can outsmart the enemy within. Legendary coach, Bill Walsh, says, "Don't let anybody tell you that a big ego is a bad thing. Tiger Woods, Bill Gates, Warren Buffett, and Cal Ripken Jr. have lots of ego, and so does anyone anywhere who is dedicated to taking his or her talent as far as it will go."

Much of what you currently consider impossible but still want to achieve will not be possible without ego. Ego drives you to achieve the unachievable and create unparalleled works of art. Ego mandates: fuck what anyone says, fuck even what physics and the laws of thermodynamics say, I'm going to get this done.

Ego is a powerful tool. Use it wisely and discreetly, and do not let anyone know you have it. Don't let people know you're achieving your success because you believe in yourself beyond all comprehension or logic. To be inordinately successful, especially in difficult or unproven fields, you must have vast amounts of ego. You must believe you are the chosen one to get this done. Ego isn't healthy, but it can make you wealthy.

Too inflated an ego can lead to egotism, usually a result of believing your own hype. Bill Walsh says, "Believing your own press clippings, good or bad, is self-defeating" [because] "you are allowing others, oftentimes uninformed others, to tell you who you are." This can bring you crashing back down to Earth. Think of ego like Red Bull: it will give you wings, but it only got Icarus so far; though he may never have taken off without it. While you should definitely let ego drive you, be ready for the day it will drive you off a fucking cliff. It's not an IF, it's a WHEN. Just make sure you learn from it.

One day you'll slip—like you undoubtedly already have—although next time it will be worse if you don't learn this now. Ego doesn't teach you all the valuable lessons it can provide on the first go-round. So, pump the brakes and don't try to swerve from the fast lane to make your exit. Drive the speed limit for a minute. You are not God's gift to entrepreneurship *yet*, and you do not know better than the founders in this book, no matter how loud your hubris is screaming you do. When the confidence is pumping, that's when you need to keep an extra eye on things.

When we launched Culprit Underwear publicly, we did $2 million that year and were growing exponentially. I thought, *Hey, let's go pedal to the metal, let's strike while the iron is hot, and other totally cool clichés.* I thought, *We can easily do $8 million next year.* And guess what? I was RIGHT. Had my ego not been there to guide me beyond what was possible, my company would not have had the insane growth we did.

We bought so much inventory that my fabric supplier was dumbfounded. One week, I bought 3,000 yards of fabric. As soon as that arrived, I ordered 8,000 yards of fabric we could not afford, but we grew so fast it didn't matter. Before that 8,000 yards arrived, I ordered 13,000 more. I was pulling these numbers straight outta my 🍑 and was right on the money too. We needed all that fabric to make enough underwear for the orders we didn't yet have, but I assumed we would. The 13,000 yards proved vital, and we made just enough to supply our demand.

We hit $8 million. I was riding such a euphoric wave. I decided, okay, we 4x'd the company in one year, let's do it again! We planned for a $30 million year. I ordered fabric and started getting new product categories like swimwear, socks, and workout shorts without testing the waters. Well, those waters were fucking shark infested (you'll learn about swimwear in Chapter #85). So did we 4x the company? 3x? 2x? Nope. We stayed right where we were at, except now we had tons of inventory we couldn't sell, too bloated a team, and too many bells and whistles that weren't drawing any extra customer attention. Forget the embarrassment of being so pompously wrong in front of my team; it threatened the existence of our company.

We immediately went into debt. I pulled out a $2 million credit line at 17 percent interest, racked up $1 million in credit cards at 28 percent interest, and had to put in every dollar I had ever personally accumulated just to stay afloat.

From my success as a commercial director, I had bought a house in the hills and a vintage Ferrari, a beautiful F355 Spyder painted in the classic "Rosso Corsa" Ferrari red with only 7k miles. *Luckily,* one night, as it was parked outside my house, my neighbor was texting and driving. Thanks to her unbelievable irresponsibility in driving from only two houses away, my beautiful baby was totaled beyond repair. My neighbor was thankfully unhurt and somehow sober, which was the hardest part to believe. How could she total a car from a hundred feet away? Probably swiping through Hinge matches. Again, *luckily*, I had made friends with a scummy luxury car dealership owner. He gave me great advice to not accept my insurance's first offer to pay me for the totaled vehicle. Instead of $80,000, we went back and forth until I received an offer for $100,000.

For a brief moment, I thought I would finally remember what it's like to have money in my account. David was thrilled. We were able to afford our mortgage on time, and maybe some long-overdue travel. The next day, I got a call from our fabric supplier letting me know we owed them exactly $100,000. This brief windfall was not to be. We needed to pay for the inventory we couldn't sell. The entire $100,000 disappeared into inventory purgatory and hasn't been seen since.

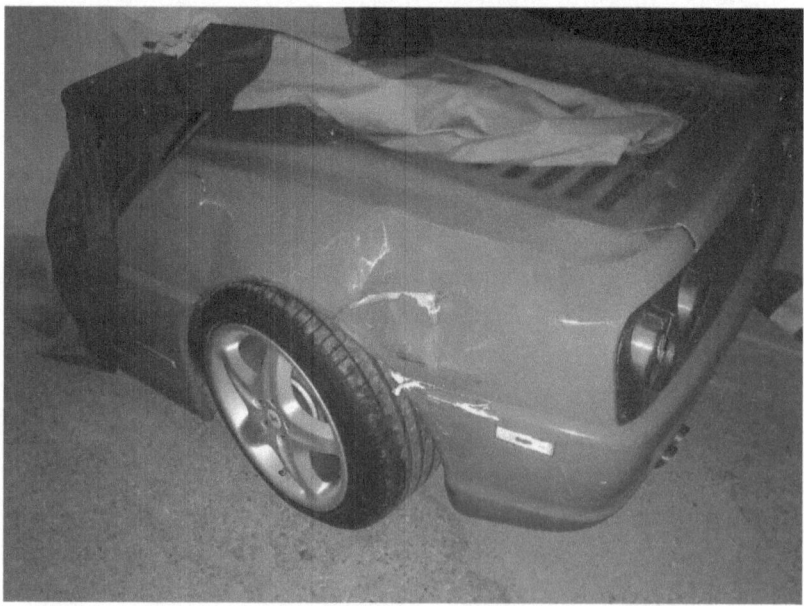

And now for a poem:

When we were all on our own/ with no approvals for loans/

our neighbor threw us a bone/ by driving while on her phone

Had my ego not led us into this quagmire, I could've gotten a new car, had financial stability, or taken a vacation. Instead, I became a slave to my own hubris. At the time of writing this sentence, I'm still paying off that credit line, although it's gone from $2 million to $50,000 thanks to listening to other voices throughout history instead of my own.

Need to distance yourself from your ego? Meditation is a great tool; so is journaling. Ask yourself, "Why am I making this decision? What's causing me to react this way?" Move from self-centered to self-aware. And if all else fails, go into nature, take a pen, a pad, and a handful of mushrooms. Nothing kills ego like mushrooms; the pen lets you remember the revelations.

# #73

# DON'T SNIFF YOUR OWN FARTS

*"Believing your own bullshit is always a perilous activity, but never more fatal than for the owner of a startup venture."*

—FELIX DENNIS

Circa 2000, at the peak of the dot-com bubble, just before it burst, Larry Ellison, the founder of Oracle, received a call from Yahoo executive Farzad Nazem. It went like this:

> **Farzad:** Disney wants to merge with us. Why would we ever want to do something like that? What have they got?
>
> **Larry:** Gee, let me think. They have the most valuable film library in the world, the most valuable TV channels in the world, and successful theme parks everywhere. Disney makes tons of money and they're probably the most beloved brand on the planet. Now, what have you got? A web page with news on it and free e-mail. Has everyone gone crazy?

*Excerpt from *The Billionaire and the Mechanic* by Julian Guthrie

The internet was the hottest thing since electricity. Yahoo was the big swinging thing in the locker room. In Farzad's dopamine-addled brain, Disney was a cartoon mouse with an overpriced playground for kids.

That's what happens when everyone is telling you how great you are, your valuation is shooting up like a hockey stick, and you can do no wrong. But remember, never trust the dopamine. It literally changes the chemistry of your brain and makes you enjoy the smell of your own farts. Or something like that; I didn't major in biology.

Shortly after, the bubble burst. Yahoo went from a market cap of $67 billion to a $5 billion valuation today. Disney went from $47 billion to nearly $180 billion in the same time. Yahoo's value crashed, Disney's value cashed.

## #74

# BE UNREALISTICALLY OPTIMISTIC

*"View things not as they were or currently are, but as they ought to be."*
—DEE HOCK, FOUNDER OF VISA

If something awful happens in my business, I don't think about how stressful the problem is. I immediately start thinking of solutions. I've gotten through everything else in life so far. What makes this any different? Instead of, "Wow, this is a disaster," I say, "Wow, could be way worse." Then I get to work. Every single time, without fail, after the catastrophe, my company is better, more successful, stronger, my team is more cohesive, and I've got one more enemy-marking to add to the outside of my fighter plane.

I'm not telling you to excuse your own behavior. I'm saying it's more productive to make up for it instead of punishing yourself when you make a mistake. If you fuck up, tell yourself, "Well, that was a mistake. I'm going to learn from this, and never do that again." Then make it up to yourself or make amends to the person you wronged. Treat each transgression as a learning opportunity and never look down on yourself for making a mistake.

The following excerpt is from *Walt Disney: An American Original* by Bob Thomas:

"We are in debt to the bank for four and a half million dollars!"

Roy expected his brother to be shocked and concerned.

Instead, Walt began to grin, and then burst out laughing.

"What the hell are you laughing at?" Roy demanded.

"I was just thinking back," Walt said between fits of laughter.

"Do you remember when we couldn't borrow a thousand dollars?"

Roy, too, began to laugh, "Yeah, remember how hard it was to get that first twenty-thousand-dollar credit?" he recalled.

They regaled each other with memories of when they had to plead for loans to meet the weekly payroll. "And now we owe four and a half million dollars!" Walt remarked, "I think that's pretty damn good."

When you start to get on a roll, your morale goes up, both external and internal doubts get quieter, and staying positive gets easier. But keep flexing that muscle, because this cycle also works the opposite way too, and just as every failure is temporary, so is every win. It ebbs and flows, and as quickly as the tide of success comes, it can leave you beached like a whale. If you find yourself unable to take the pains of your business, find somewhere else to draw your strength from. If you accomplish something challenging like a rigorous workout routine, building a new habit of deeply focused meditation, or taking cold showers, you may find a new source of inner power. When things get hard, overcome something else that's also hard—but a little easier—and apply that new-found resilience to your work. Doing bad work or no work at all can demoralize you. Founder of Y-Combinator, Paul Graham, suggests that if you get stuck, switch to easier work for a bit to get something done and turn your morale around before tackling the more challenging stuff. He explains that morale has a compounding effect. "High morale helps you do good work, which increases your morale and helps you do even better work."

When Elon Musk first decided to found SpaceX, he faced intense criticism and external doubt from an unexpected place: his best friends. Everyone tried to talk him out of it. To scare him, one friend even went so far as to make a video compilation of rockets exploding.

If you're doing anything worth doing, you're going to face criticism. First, you'll need to make the loudest critic shut up: yourself. It's hard enough building something out of nothing. Your resolve and self-belief need to be unwavering. For that to happen, you need to be unblinkingly positive. You can't block out all shreds of self-doubt, but you can use positive self-talk to make the hero within louder and stronger than the doubter.

Nip negativity in the bud. As Musk puts it, "If you were negative or thought something couldn't be done, you were not invited to the next meeting." To foster a positive environment to maximize both creativity and productivity, you must make sure the mix of people is just right. There are some talented, brilliant people who will fit in awfully with your company culture. It's not about their resume or experience. Yes, they must be determined and passionate. They must also fit the vibe of your company. All it takes is one Negative Nancy who sounds like they're making a good point for doubt to spread like COVID at the water cooler. You must kill negativity before it multiplies. Either get through to that person or fire them.

Luckily, positive thinking is contagious too. If you are infectiously positive even in the worst of storms, your team will gradually recondition themselves to your unshakeable spirit. Whatever attitude you carry is contagious. Hell, even yawns are contagious.

# #75

# PLAYING BY THE RULES

*"There wasn't a rule ever invented that couldn't be bent."*
—CHUCK YEAGER, PILOT WHO BROKE THE SOUND BARRIER

In the early twentieth century, "fair-trade laws" stated that a retailer could not offer a specific product to the public lower than a set price. This hurt consumers. However, there was a nonprofit called Fed-Co that let sailors store their uniforms and purchase civilian clothing at prices below fair-trade limits. Sol Price saw an opportunity to get around this unfair law. He could exploit this membership program for civilian shoppers. And so, a decade before the first Walmart, Sol *"I'll-set-whatever-the-hell-price-I-want"* Price founded FedMart and changed the face of retail forever. People traveled hundreds of miles for lower prices to shop at FedMart, and it quickly grew. Sol Price left his company after a dispute with a dickhead German retailer who bought a controlling interest, but he wasn't out of the game yet. He would have his sweet revenge.

He started a spite store called Price Club, which was so successful that it crushed FedMart out of existence. His new membership business model was so pioneering, Sam Walton would walk around Price Club with a tape recorder, taking notes. One day, he got caught. His tape recorder was confiscated by security. Sol Price was such a stand-up guy; when he heard of the incident, he mailed it back to Sam Walton. Maybe he shouldn't have though, because Walton created a direct competitor, Sam's Club. To beat Sam's Club, Sol merged with his protégé's company and became Costco. To this day, Costco makes most of its money from its memberships, invented as a loophole to that unfair law.

If there's an unfair rule, regulation, law, or practice in your industry, don't let it hamper your dreams. A good loophole can be your wormhole to success. Exploit any ethical loophole you can. But not the unethical ones. They will always come back to bite you.

In the early 1970s, when Fred Smith founded FedEx, there were too many carrier regulations in his way as a trucking company. There was no way he could deal with all these annoying rules. So, what did he do? He founded FedEx as an airline instead. Even still, he ran face first into a brick wall. He needed approval from the Civil Aeronautics Board under air taxi regulations, which would permit FedEx to fly unrestricted. Good plan. Except that anything flying as an "air taxi" at the time was limited to a takeoff weight of 12,500 pounds. The jets he had already mortgaged weighed 15,000 pounds empty. Others would've given up at this insurmountable obstacle, but Fred Smith had survived three years of combat in Vietnam and wasn't about to let some horseshit law clip his wings before he could fly. For absolutely no other reason than possessing unwavering self-belief, he believed he could get the law modernized and permit greater takeoff weight. He did just that.

Up until 1992, it was illegal to connect a commercial service to the internet. Why was it legal after 1992? Because Steve Case, founder of America Online, said screw that and got the law changed.

Were any of these law-unabiding founders connected to the movers and shakers in Washington to call shots like that? Absolutely not. They just refused to take the brick wall in front of them seriously.

When anything, and I do mean anything, gets in your way, whether it's a guideline, a regulation, a rule, a federal law, or a literal brick wall, if you know your mission is sacred, it is your duty to go around it, over it, under it, or bulldoze right fucking through it. Question everything that is not defined by the laws of physics. In fact, question physics if you must. Quantum physics is a new field and, therefore, subject to change. Yes, I'm telling you to even question the fundamental laws of the universe if it serves your purpose. We still don't know anything about dark matter. Until then, the world as you know it is yet to be determined. Be the change you want to see in the world. It's safer to change laws than break them; just never get discouraged by a silly little rule.

## #76

# THE BORING ROAD TO SUCCESS

*"Boredom can be more dangerous than failure."*
—JAMES CLEAR, AUTHOR OF *ATOMIC HABITS*

You will be tempted by golden new opportunities. There will be enticing, lucrative revenue streams and *shiny new objects,* no matter what field you're in. Your mostly useless business plan that you first wrote, hopefully, contains enough of your original vision to steer you away from worshipping these false idols.

How do you know you're on the right track? When you start feeling bored. Founder of Four Seasons, Isador Sharpe, says, "Excellence is the capacity to take pain." True. It's also the capacity to take boredom. As I write this, I'm bored with my brand. It's the same thing every day. We're not growing at the moment, just barely surviving, in fact. I love designing new prints and directing our videos. But we don't have the money to design new stuff or shoot fun new ads. It's just stressful purgatory every day. I've paid off a good chunk of debt, there's no existential crisis the week I'm writing this chapter, but even if there was, I'd just yawn it off.

I'm looking for something to reinvigorate me. My passion has become a dormant volcano.

The best athletes in the world go through this. They do the same lifts over and over. Run around the same track. It's boring to train every day. You can't act bored when you lose motivation or your business gets stuck in stasis. Really successful people feel this same lack of motivation. This boredom borders on burnout. The difference is, they keep showing up no matter how they feel. And I know I'll soon have my opportunity to mastermind the next evolution of my business. And I'll get excited again. So, I continue to force a smile and keep everyone motivated, waiting for my time to strike with a jaguar's ferocity while my passion takes a cat nap. And I stay away from enticing opportunities that are not my core business, no matter how shiny they seem.

The flip side of this is when you just get tired and don't want to do it anymore. This happened to Frank Sinatra. He wanted to quit performing. His friend and promoter at the time, Jerry Weintraub, said, "You don't need a rest, you need a new hill to climb." He explained to Sinatra that he's not tired, he's bored and needs a challenge. He pitched him a live show in a boxing ring at Madison Square Garden called *The Main Event*. The challenge of this live show, set in that iconic venue with zero rehearsal, reinvigorated him.

# #77

# IF YOU DON'T ASK, YOU DON'T RECEIVE

*"The squeaky wheel gets the grease."*

—AMERICAN APHORISM

This phrase is so true. Asking for things all the time ensures you get unexpected, amazing things sometimes.

My friend worked for YouTube Originals and was about to quit. I told him, "Before you quit, ask them to double your salary." Threatened with the thought of losing one of their most valuable employees, they doubled his salary.

In a store, as I'm checking out, I'll ask if they have any discounts available or promos running. Sometimes they just give me a discount, sometimes they say there's a local's discount if you show your ID, sometimes they give you one if you sign up for their email list. I was in a store yesterday doing holiday shopping and asked what discounts they had. They said new customers get 15 percent off. I saved $150 just by asking.

When I check into a hotel, I always ask if they can give me a free upgrade. Usually it doesn't work, but it never hurts to ask, and it happens more often than you'd think.

To make this tool even more powerful, you can add the magic word *because*. There was a study done where people would ask to cut the line to make photocopies. They had marginal success asking to cut, but almost everyone said yes when they added a reason. Something like, "Can I cut you in line because I'm in a rush?" is so simple and worked almost every time. They dumbed it down further to see how human psychology worked and simply said, "Can I cut you in line because I need to make copies." It worked just as effectively. It didn't matter the reason, even if there was none, the simple magic word *because* just works. Why? Because it does.

## #78

# YOUR MOST SACRED BOND

*"All I have in this world is my balls and my word and I don't break 'em for no one."*
—AL PACINO IN *SCARFACE*

Is your most sacred bond with your parents? Your significant other? Your children? Absolutely not.

It's your word when you give it out. No matter who you give it to, always keep your word. *Especially to yourself.* If something goes on a to-do list and you don't do it, your brain teaches you it's okay to lie to yourself. You're training yourself that it's fine if you don't finish something, procrastinate, or take the easy way out. YOUR BRAIN CARES. Keep your word as your sacred bond to yourself. Don't go to sleep until you finish what you told yourself you would.

I wasn't always this perfect **cue sitcom laugh track.** Sometimes I'd falter on my word, telling someone I'd do something, then forget. You're not allowed to forget. It's your word.

> **HACK:** Set calendar reminders. You know when you're at a party and you talk to someone and they're like "Yeah, let's grab lunch this week," or "I'll send you that thing," and it never happens? Don't be that person.
>
> Every time I give my word to anyone for any reason, I put it in my calendar. It's now set in stone for the next day or week and for anyone I share my calendar with to see. Anytime I give my word to anyone, even if I'm at a party and everyone's drunk, I pop it in my calendar with two reminders set. Every single time. Sometimes I won't even remember I told someone I'd do something. Then bang, the calendar notification goes off, and I just do whatever it says to do.

Be the person who surprises the other, equally drunk person with what you said you'd do. The number of times people are amazed when the underwear I promised to send them at 3:00 a.m. shows up at their doorstep is incredible. People don't expect you to come through, because most people don't. It makes magic in your life when you keep your word in even the most surprising cases. You become dependable. You become the real deal Holyfield of a friend who has a flawless follow-up game that always does what they say they're going to. People will respect you on another level, and your life will change dramatically.

## STOP GIVING OUT YOUR WORD SO EASILY

Your word is not to be passed out like a flyer for a struggling car wash. It is sacrosanct. Don't make a single promise to anyone about anything if you aren't 1,000 percent sure you'll keep it. You can't break your word if you never gave it.

When I don't feel like that level of commitment, I simply tell someone, "I don't know if I'll remember," "Not sure if I'll be able to," "It's unlikely, but I'll try," "I can't because... (or just 'I can't' without a reason)," "We'll see," or any other vague or direct no you can think of. It's saying yes to everything that really screws you out of keeping your word.

# #79

# SUNLIGHT IS THE BEST DISINFECTANT

*"The best way to maintain trust is to be as transparent as possible."*

—ELON MUSK

This idea came from Louis Brandeis, the first Jewish Supreme Court Justice. His goal was to make things like government payroll public knowledge to prevent corruption. You can apply his lesson to prevent resentment and internal conflict in your company, which is a major killer of startups. As Paul Graham says, "Startups are more likely to die from suicide than homicide."

We all go through rough patches; the best thing you can do is be transparent.

When you have issues with people in your company, it can be uncomfortable to talk to them about it. But when done right, it can be more efficient and a lot cheaper than hiring extra HR. Using this concept in your company comes from my friend, Jeff Gendelman, co-founder of

Daring Foods. He uses it to create greater efficiency in his company by openly addressing the problem at hand. He does this both internally and in external negotiations. Having problems with a manufacturer? Call them on it. Bring the problem out into the open and use it as a negotiating tool to get better terms. Problem with a customer? Be proactive. Expose the issue, address it, and provide a solution for it. An uncomfortable conversation can be the difference between success and failure.

Until recently, I was awful at this. I would tell a vendor we could pay them, and then have to push the payment into next week because sales went down. When next week rolled around, Florida would pull sales tax from our account, and we'd be out of cash again. So instead of sending the promised $50,000, I'd send an insulting $1,000. I'd set another date with another promised payment and another excuse. On and on this cycle would go, the goalposts constantly shifting and the trust built over years evaporating in weeks.

Companies are composed of people. If you're going through a rough spot, let them know. It's better to tell them sooner. Better to let them know how bad it is than to try to sweep it under the rug and cross your fingers for sales to pick up or for an investor to actually wire the money they promised. You must assume everything will go wrong. Let them know you don't have cash now and you don't know exactly when you will. It's better to promise a smaller amount by a further date than to continuously break your word. They might not like it, but they'll understand. They're human. Appeal to their humanity and stop treating them like a corporation. Then, when you magically have more money sooner, they're happy. And congrats, you've built trust because you were transparent. You under-promised and overdelivered, which is the best thing you can do.

Don't give exact dates and payment amounts if there's even a 1 percent chance you'll miss them. Vendors don't want to hear "things are a little fucked right now and we can't pay you till at least next month." But it's better to piss them off a little now than to break your word and piss them off forever. Vague language is great because no promise has been made. Be vague yet transparent. Be kind while being realistic. Keeping a vendor happy short term does nothing; sometimes you need to upset them with news they don't want to hear, so you can keep them happy long term.

Apply this to life as well. If you're "off" because you're going through something, having financial woes, grieving, or just got dumped, let the people around you know. They will sympathize, and your "off" behavior will be justified.

Surprise, surprise. I've made another mistake since writing the words above. We found a much cheaper manufacturer and started up production with them. We had built a great and trusting relationship with our old factory. I put off telling them we were moving most of our production to the new factory, because I was worried they would stop caring and be late delivering, as they had previously. I put it off for too long. They found out in the worst way possible: from an Instagram post. Our new print, which they clearly didn't produce, was staring them in the face. They told us that if we had just been up front with them, it would've been fine. People change factories all the time.

Don't know what I was so scared of. It wouldn't have delayed production if I was up front. How easy would it have been to say, "Guys, we're going to pause on new production for now. We have a factory that's making things cheaper and need to switch for the health of the business." Instead, they thought what we did was a sketchy move. They halted our credit line with them, and it destroyed our relationship. It's a difficult line to toe. I just wish I hadn't acted so middle school. Honesty is the best policy. Be up front, and it will be a smoother transition.

# #80

# NEVER LOSE A SINGLE CUSTOMER

*"There's only one boss. The customer. And they can fire us any time they want by spending their money elsewhere."*

—SAM WALTON

Banks spend upward of $300 to acquire a single customer, and once those customers are acquired, they don't spend a single dollar to keep them. If a customer costs you $40 to acquire, be willing to spend up to $39 to make sure they have a fantastic experience and come back. Value their time above all else, be willing to replace products, and if they want a refund or to send their order back, come up with an alternative solution that's win-win. Make them happy, make them feel important, and if you can, make them laugh.

> **HACK:** Solve customer service complaints by giving your customers cash in your rewards program for them to spend in your store.

In the early days of Culprit, I was the only employee because David was still running the production company. I was driving 1,000 yards of fabric downtown myself in a topless Jeep Wrangler stuffed to the gills; I couldn't even see the mirrors. I was printing each shipping label, packing each order, and handling every customer service request myself.

If you think I enjoy the occasional drink now, you should've seen me then. After a full day of grinding labor and packing up the last order I could physically handle in my garage, and making my last trip to the post office, I would come home, and the only way I could bring myself to continue working was to drink an entire bottle of wine while I did one hundred-plus customer service emails until I passed out from exhaustion at the kitchen table, mid-email. This was extra stressful because it was peak COVID. People were yelling obscenities at me and legitimately sending death threats because they didn't get their underwear fast enough. For the first time ever, I am sharing one of the death threats sent to us. Here it is in all its unedited glory:

---

**Re: A shipment from order #18513 has been delivered**

Tue, Sep 22, 2020, 3:58 PM
to Culprit

Wheres my mother fucking boxers at you cunt faggots you rob me , you just robbed a chicago gangster and realize I dont fear anything and will come fuck you up and everyone there if I dont get what I paid for mother fuckers your cunts your bitches and you going to have my dick in your ass by the time I'm done with you I'll put you on your knees and make you pray before you someone else snatches the soul out of you for robbing me you cunt mother fuckers. How dare you you just started and guess now now your fucking done for !!!

He had ordered two pairs. One had been delivered, but he didn't see it. Then he found it and tried it on:

We told him the missing pair was still being completed and would ship in a few weeks. We got this response when it hadn't arrived yet nearly a month later:

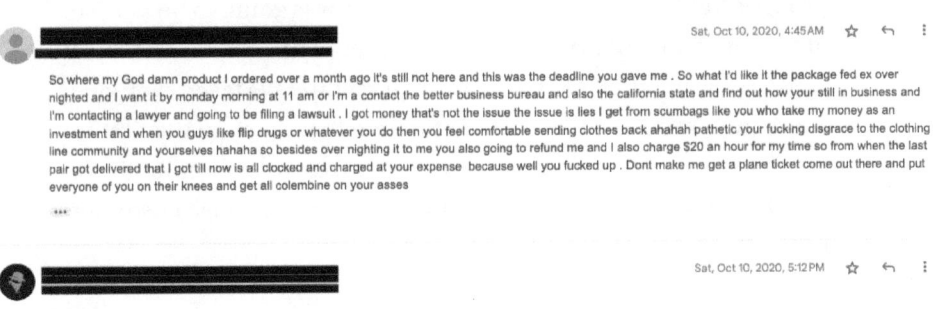

I'd love to say *never* lose a customer. But it's okay to let the crazy ones go. You're running a business, not an insane asylum.

Quick reminder: be nice to customer service folks. They deal with a lot, and it's not them you're actually mad at. No customer service agent actually wants you to have a bad experience—except at certain airlines; for some reason, I feel like they secretly relish when your flight gets delayed.

But something interesting happened. Because my customers were swearing at me, and because I was five glasses of wine deep, I started swearing back. I started sending unprofessional GIFs and Memes in the support emails and made customers laugh out loud. I was treating them like a human instead of reading from a script.

I realized, wow, no brand is doing this. We can have an entirely unique style of customer service where the customer isn't always right. Sometimes the customer needs context. Sometimes the customer is not only wrong but being a total dick. It's way easier to win them over with memes and jokes than it is to cry about how you're a small business. They don't care; they want their order. Make them laugh. Luckily, our brand is Culprit, so we can send R-rated memes, dark humor, GIFs of people doing epic fails, and say, This is us trying to get you your underwear.

This style of "when you can't please the customer, make them laugh" can go a long way. It's super personalized. One woman bought some Culprits for her husband's anniversary, and it was going to be late, so I sent flowers and a hilarious handwritten note as well. I taught this method to our first hire and every subsequent hire. We teach everyone on our team how to reply to customers when they start, so they get to know what our customers are like and can take over on replies if we get a sudden influx. We routinely get told we have the best customer service in the world.

> Book recommendation: *Never Lose a Customer Again* by Joey Coleman.

# #81

# LIVE AND DIE BY WORD-OF-MOUTH

*"Being detached from the customer is the ultimate death."*
—MICHAEL DELL, FOUNDER OF DELL COMPUTERS

The best way to understand your customers is to talk to them. That's what we used to do in the early days. David and I made a pledge to call ten customers every Friday on the car's Bluetooth while driving to our factory downtown. When I was doing the customer service alone by myself, after midnight, wrapped around a bottle of wine, I was getting to know their thoughts.

Paul Graham has a great essay titled "Do Things That Don't Scale." A great example is when Estée Lauder would give individual makeovers to women while traveling on a bus, who would in turn become lifelong customers. The founders of Stripe, the online payment system, would meet other founders in Silicon Valley and tell them, "Give us your laptop for five minutes, and we'll get you accepting payments immediately."

That strategy not only gets you your first customers, it lets you learn how they feel about your product. However, as the title of the essay suggests, it's not scalable…BUT *surveys* are!

Once you grow an order of magnitude, you'll need a new weapon in your arsenal: The *survey*. It will tell you everything you ask it to ask. From how customers feel about your price point to what products to make next. I'm no survey expert, but I do happen to know the most important one of all. And, boy, do I wish I knew this five years ago.

## NET PROMOTER SCORE

Your NPS score is the most important metric you have when it comes to your customers. It's not just how your customers feel about your brand; it's your reputation as a company made measurable. It's one simple question that predicts your most important growth metric: word-of-mouth.

I'm in London right now. I just got off the phone with a friend who's visiting, and she said we *have* to go to this coffee shop in Richmond Park. I asked, "Why? Do they serve that coffee from Indonesia where it has to get shat out by that weird Civet cat first?" "No," she said, "there's deer walking by that come right up to you while you drink your coffee." So obviously I'm going there this week. That's someone raving about a business right there. Obviously, you don't have the luxury of wild deer, but what can you do that makes your customers feel so special they will risk their reputation by raving about it? That's what you need to have a killer NPS score so you can spend less on ads and grow by word-of-mouth. If you win at NPS, you win at growth. It should be called the Net Profit Score. The following passage may contain more swear words than usual because it is my cheap hack to make simple, boring, yet important shit entertaining.

Simply send a survey with this one question on it and don't fucking alter the question one word:

"On a scale of 0 to 10, how likely are you to recommend [Company/Product] to a friend or colleague?"

What they score your brand out of ten puts them in three groups:

- Promoters (9–10): Rabid fans who had the best experience of their lives, who'll recommend you without being asked.
- Passives (7–8): Happy, but not passionate. They might shop again, but they won't fight for you.
- Detractors (0–6): When asked by their friends what they think of your brand, they might say, "meh" or MUCH WORSE. I doubt you'll be getting death threats like we did; however, these customers can actively damage your reputation not only through word-of-mouth, but also on social media.

## THE SIMPLE MATH OF YOUR NPS SCORE

Percentage of Promoters minus Percentage of Detractors.

Ideally, you want an NPS score of 60 or above. Ours is currently 55, and we were still successful at 49, so don't jump off a bridge if you're not there yet.

If 70 percent of your customers are Promoters and 10 percent are Detractors, your NPS is 60. (Passives don't count toward your score, but you can still learn from them.)

## WHERE IT GETS REALLY POWERFUL

A high NPS doesn't just mean people like your product or service; it means they're so happy, they'll stake their own good name to tell friends about you. Boom! Your customers have now turned into an unpaid sales force, promoting credibility and trust that ads can't buy.

Can you guess what a low NPS score means? It means you need to fix things immediately. It's a warning that customers are talking shit behind your back. Detractors don't just quietly stop shopping with you—they actively steer potential customers away.

Think of businesses you love. What did they do right? How did they treat you? Companies thrive on word-of-mouth. Brands like Apple or

Tesla don't just have cult followings; they obsess over every negative comment or complaint. Give every reason for your customers to tell their friends how great your company is. Monitor your NPS score like a hospital monitors your pulse, because at the end of the day, it's the same thing. And if your score gets too low, you will flatline.

# #82

# THE TALL GRASS GETS MOWED

*"There's no point in bragging in the good times. Your friends don't need to hear it, and your enemies won't believe it anyway."*

—PAUL ORFALEA, FOUNDER OF KINKOS

Do you want a target on your back? Do you want people to know you're worth robbing? Do you want a swarm of money-hungry people seeking you out for something other than your personality and charm? Do you want competitors to know your secret sauce and make it their life's work to hammer nails into your coffin? Do you want the government to invent laws to affect your business?

All this and more is possible for the low, low price of not keeping your mouth shut. Fly under the radar unless you like the idea of getting shot down. There's a reason Notorious B.I.G. said bad boys move in silence.

The easiest way to fly under the radar is to avoid interviews about how your business works and how much money you make. Obviously, you should do interviews that promote your product or business. Just don't give too much away. If, like James Dyson or Gustav Glock, you have a unique product that requires media attention to build intrigue, get all the press you can. But make sure it's for your product. Not for yourself. And if your business is easily imitated, keep your trap shut. If you haven't built that deep of a *moat*, don't *gloat*, or they'll come for your *throat*. And keep exciting, upcoming news and achievements to yourself so they happen. Do not tell people about your upcoming good fortune, or it could dilute the energy propelling it forward.

# #83

# THE ROOT CAUSE

*"If you don't change the underlying condition that created the problem, expect the problem to recur."*

—JEFF BEZOS

The Japanese word *Kaizen* means to continuously improve all functions and involve all employees. In a factory or warehouse, if an area continuously gets dirty, don't just endlessly clean it. Find out what's causing it and stop it in its tracks. Bezos famously implemented this philosophy at Amazon in everything from customer service to warehouse management. Don't just fix the problem; fix what caused the problem.

Toyota's techniques for manufacturing are world renowned; any employee on the line can shut down an entire factory when there's an issue at the press of a button. When they find the issue, they ask "Why?" five times: When a piece of machinery breaks, they say, "Why did it break?" Because it ran out of oil. "Why did it run out of oil?" Because it hadn't been oiled in a week. "Why hadn't it been oiled in a week when it's supposed to be oiled every three days?" Because the worker didn't know that. "Why didn't he know that?" Because it wasn't covered thoroughly in training. "Boom, train 'em better."

See how powerful that is? Get to the deepest possible root cause of any problem, and you can fix it for good.

In my company, it's like this: "Why don't we have any money?" "Because you launched swimwear at the end of summer like a dumbass." See? I only had to ask it once.

# #84

# THE NO-ASSHOLES RULE

*"You can't do a good deal with a bad person."*

—WARREN BUFFETT

If you consider someone a scumbag, no matter how good the short-term proposition is, stay away. It will come back to bite you. How they talk about others in business is how they'll talk about you someday. If you work closely with someone, you'll know within a few months. If you deal with them less closely, it might take a few years, but if you pick up a stone and there are maggots underneath, don't put the stone back; get rid of the maggots.

Have a zero-tolerance policy for assholes. You don't want to be associated with one for even a single short-term business deal. It's not worth it. If they're your best salesperson, it will still come back to bite you. Ditch the short-term gain and prevent the long-term problem. I heard a great tip that if you play golf with someone and they cheat, don't do business with them. But I don't golf. So, I look for other cues like how they treat the waitstaff at a restaurant.

However, even if you avoid assholes, there's a high likelihood that someone will try to mess with your livelihood. Generally, people don't *want* to fuck you over; they are just looking out for their own self-interest. Not yours. It is business; you should not take it personally.

Scratch that. *Absolutely* take it personally. I take business disrespect more personally than personal disrespect. We're talking about your livelihood here. Your family's. Never let that fly.

Now, here's how to spot it and prevent it. This lesson is written by guest author David Dinetz, my beloved business partner.

Hey, David here. You've probably heard of me by now. I've scolded Dylan more than his mom. Which is easy because she only scolded him once ever. In eleventh grade, when she went into his closet to get his sister a blanket, she found six mature weed plants. Back when that was a felony. Anyway, Dylan asked me to provide a chapter with an anecdote from our formative years in business.

*Don't work with assholes*. Easier said than done. One day, you'll end up working with one. Here's an example of what happened to us and how common sense—and a sense of humor—saved the day:

A client hired us to create a commercial for his battery-charging phone case company. He had a beautiful office and invited us to come check out the prototype. In between fits of berating his assistant (red flag ⚑). He was an asshole, but we justified it because we needed to pay for Coachella (**back when it was cool**). So, we took the job, shot the commercial, edited it, made it perfect. As we prepared to deliver it, I noticed he had not paid the first 50 percent (⚑). I called and asked him to pay. He told me he would pay all at once instead once we delivered (⚑). I told him that was not acceptable. He told me how much money he has (⚑). How many more commercials we'll do together (⚑). How I was fucking this up by being petty (⚑). Then he hung up on me and called our other partner, asking if he could send him the completed video because *I* was "an idiot who was ruining our company's reputation in LA." He told me to deliver the video. I flatly refused and called the client. I calmly explained I would not deliver the video unless I was paid in full. He explained he needed to show it to his Chinese investors first (⚑). Then he would pay us, and I could watermark the video with our logo. I said no. He called me a "cheap fuck" and said to come to the office and pick up a check (🏳) for the full amount and deliver the video he needed for the investors.

Dylan asked me what the plan was. We weren't going to pick up the check and deliver the video, were we? He trusted my gut, but also desperately needed the cash to flaunt his finest sequin vest at Coachella. I told him my plan. It went like this:

**David:** I'm going to call his assistant and find out if he's going to rip us off.

**Dylan:** She works for him. She'll just cover for him.

**David:** Remember when ▮▮▮▮ treated us like shit? Would you have covered for him?

**Dylan:** Fuck no.

**David:** Watch this.

I called his office, and before his assistant transferred me, I asked her to stay on the phone. I said, "Hey Ashley, you're really sweet, but your boss is a fucking asshole." She laughed. It was that kind of laugh, where you know you're speaking the same language.

"Can I ask you something?" I said.

"Hold on, lemme go outside...okay, what's up?"

"Your boss said he's going to pay me by check. Is he trying to fuck me over in some way?"

She paused for a moment.

"I've gotten five calls today from people screaming about checks he's bounced. He's definitely going to fuck you over. If I were you, I would ask for cash."

"Thank you, that's all I needed to hear. You have my word, this conversation never happened."

"I'm just happy to see someone actually getting under his skin. He's been screaming about you all morning."

In short, his goal was to impress investors with zero risks to him by getting a free "concept" video, and fuck over our little creative agency.

The video was amazing and would've no doubt impressed the client. It was better than the Mophie ads at the time, which were being sold in

Apple stores. Our logo was cool, and if we simply watermarked the video, he would just make something up to the investors about how it was a work in progress and still have the dynamite pitch he wanted. Insert *DickButt*. Not familiar with DickButt? Don't worry, let me educate you.

As you can now thankfully imagine, it's a dick with another dick with a butt as its butt. Colloquially known as *DickButt*, created by cartoonist Jeffrey McQuirk. He is the patron saint of not getting screwed. Read on.

Some people love Mickey Mouse, but I find *DickButt* to be one of the cleverest and most iconic works in cartoon history. This hybrid-dick-butt sparks joy in cool people and outrage in people attempting to show investors a video. Especially when they're expecting to play off the simple Culprit watermark to their Chinese investor.

I told the client I would not accept a check, and he would have to pay cash.

"I haven't even seen the video yet. You're so fucking paranoid. Send me the video with the watermark, and if I like it, you can come pick up the cash from my house."

I said, "No problem. You're going to love it."

I asked Dylan to watermark the video with *Dick Butt* at 90 percent opacity. We were told this was going to ruin our reputation in LA. I explained to the doubters that this will help our reputation. Anyone who likes this guy, we don't want to work with.

Dylan exported the video and sent it.

The client called me back, seething.

"Did you like the video?" I asked.

"Are you fucking kidding me, you <insert every expletive you can imagine>. I can't show this to the investors, you <more expletives>."

Dylan and I laughed.

"You think this is funny? You're never going to work in this town again."

More laughs. "I thought you weren't showing the investor till after you approved the video and paid us."

Silence.

"Well, if you don't want the video, that's fine with us. This was a lot of fun."

"Come pick up the cash from my assistant. I never want to see either of you as long as you live. You will never work in this town again."

"Great, we'll send the video once we have the cash."

"And you'll remove the watermark."

"It's called Dick Butt."

"What?"

Here's what the watermarked video looked like:

At the end of the day, we got the cash, sent the video, went to Coachella, and spent all of the cash like we'd won it in Vegas. And we get to tell the *Dick Butt* story. As for the asshole client, his C-list celebrity business partner sued him for stealing money from the clothing line they co-owned. He never got around to launching that charging case company. Or making sure we never worked in this town again. Although I haven't heard that he's been working in this town. Funny how that works. All thanks to a little help from our good friend, *Dick Butt*.

Thank you, David, for preaching a lesson we learned from The Beatles and got by with some help from our friends. In this case, our friend was *Dick Butt*. You don't have to use *Dick Butt*; just know he's now a new weapon in your arsenal. If enough red flags ⚑ materialize, who you gonna call? We're gonna call *Dick Butt*.

This lesson alone netted us $10,000 in cash from an asshole's safe that we would've gotten screwed out of.

# #85

# STAY IN YOUR LANE

*"You simply cannot mix your messages when selling something new., A consumer can barely handle one great new idea, let alone two, or...several."*

—JAMES DYSON

Fun fact: you can use your Dyson vacuum as an extremely effective dry cleaner. They don't advertise this because it would confuse the customer. They focus on its primary use and don't get into the weeds on what else it can do. When being introduced to your product, your customer's brain can only process so much.

When Louis Chevrolet and *Billy Durant*—the often overlooked, visionary founder of General Motors—founded Chevrolet, they decided to fill the void left by Henry Ford's world's cheapest cars. Ford's cars all looked the same and famously came in the "any color you like as long as it's black," rejection of individualism known as the Model T. After making fifteen million of these hand-crank-to-start slight improvements over a horse-drawn carriage, there was a gap in the market.

Namely, people who had more than $260 ($3,900 in 2025) to spend on a car. People wanted something to show up the Joneses. For slightly more than the cheapest car ever made, you could really have any color you wanted, four doors or two, six cylinders instead of four, and whatever else they had back then, I don't know, rumble seats?

The point is, while Ford was stuck in the same two-millimeter zone of: *make a car my workers can afford,* Chevrolet decided to occupy the giant empty space just above Ford—the space that a lot of people could afford. Back when America had a robust middle class, one minimum wage worker could support a family of four. Chevrolet didn't try to compete with Ford on price, nor try to compete with Packard on luxury; they simply found their niche, saw it was working, then drove a wedge into that niche and widened it.

Don't try to be everything to everyone. Just find your niche, stay loyal to it, and grow your brand to everyone in and around it. Not only did Chevy become the best-selling faction of GM, they outpaced Ford's sales in 1927, sparking a rivalry that continues to this day with many a Chevy truck emblazoned with a sticker of Calvin & Hobbes pissing on a Ford logo.

Bob Marley says, "You can fool some people sometimes, but you can't fool all the people all the time." Well, the same goes with pleasing people. Stick to your goddamn niche, you fool. You want ardent supporters. People who eat, breathe, sleep, and get tattoos of your brand's logo. That won't happen if you try to appeal to the entire world, but don't resonate with a chosen niche. When you hire people to your team, you want missionaries, not mercenaries...the same applies to your fans.

# #86

# DON'T MAKE SWIMWEAR

*"Keep your own image straight in your mind. From the beginning, I knew I wanted to sell the top-of-the-line, finest-quality products through the best outlets rather than through drugstores and discount stores. And so we have. We don't do dungarees, we don't do tablecloths. We do the best skin products available today, the best makeup and fragrance products."*

—ESTÉE LAUDER

Horst Dassler, the son of the founder of Adidas, was instrumental in expanding his father, Adi's, brand internationally. However, he went too far chasing the horizons beyond his father's mission to make specialized sport-specific shoes. Before Adi, all athletic shoes were the same. He revolutionized the making of shoes for specific sports. As far back as 1928, Olympians were winning gold medals because of Adi's shoes. The now infamous three leather stripes were originally for structural support and added strength but were the same color as the shoe. When some doubted whether gold medal athletes were actually wearing Adi's normal-looking shoes, he decided to change the color of the stripes, so they'd stand out, leading to today's triple-striped logo. He also famously made shoes for Jesse Owens for the 1936 Olympics, much to the chagrin of a micro-penised man named Adolph.

Adi had built a legacy and was adamant that Adidas would stay in its lane and live up to its original vision, providing athletes with sport-specific performance shoes. When Horst wanted to make swimwear, Adi told his son, "Swimmers don't wear shoes." In other words, swimwear was a distraction. He was right...maybe he wasn't right when he disowned his son though. Although, I think there was more to that story than swimwear. If your vision isn't to make swimwear, don't try to make a couple extra bucks making swimwear...like I did.

I thought new product categories would attract new, previously unreachable customers. I thought our existing customers would want anything we made. What else can we put our *amazing* designs on? Swimwear was the obvious answer. The next category we'd easily dominate. We made two *genius* innovations: men's swim-trunks for women, brilliantly named the BAEthing suit, with sexy side zippers and a functional pocket. And a hybrid between swim trunks and board shorts for men with a patented removable liner. Men's swim trunk liners get itchy post pool. What if you could insert the liner when you want support and could take it out when it chafes? Here's what they looked like:

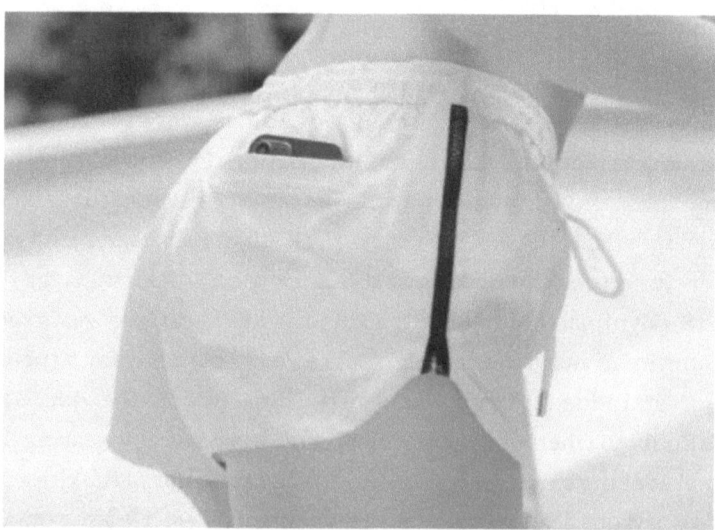

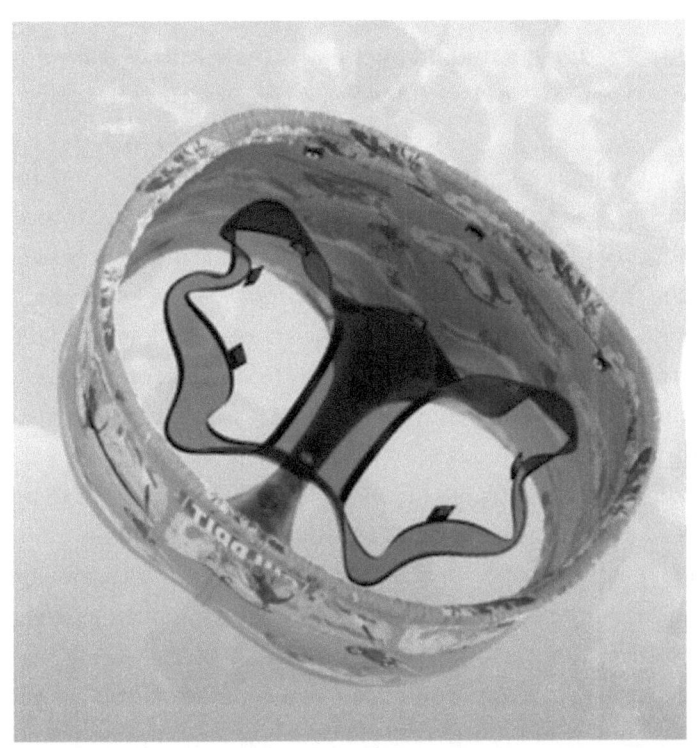

Women's Swim Trunks, Men's Swim Suit w/ Removable Liner

We ordered half a million bucks' worth of swimwear because we knew it was seasonal and had to capitalize. We took on a million in debt to make and market these. The swimwear wasn't ready till July. We didn't know that swim season starts in January and ends in June. At $99 per suit, we were one-third the cost of Vilebrequin. It was a bulletproof plan. Especially because we made the funniest ad in the history of swimwear.

While that last bit was true, no one cared. We had jumped into the deep end with no floaties, wearing the weight of unfathomable debt. Our women's swimwear sold well for two months, then sat on the shelves for eight months till we could move them again. Our men's swim trunks are still sitting in the warehouse two years later. By trying to appeal to men who liked both swim trunks and board shorts, we appealed to no one. Our ad was so funny, I cried…all the way to the empty bank.

You'll probably gloss over this bit and think your idea for category expansion is different. But if you've gotten this far in your journey, and you're successful so far, take it from me, DO NOT EXPAND YOUR PRODUCT LINE.* If you're Apple and you make computers, you can make a tablet computer and one that fits in your pocket; that's on brand. But there's a reason Apple doesn't make printers anymore. We had no business making swimwear, and it nearly drowned us. If you're a fashion brand, you can do little drops, collabs, and limited collections, but don't make a million-dollar bet on an entirely new category, especially if it's seasonal.

[*One caveat: you can do a post-purchase survey and ask your existing customers what they want to see next from you. If there's a clear winner, you can do a small run and test it. It could increase LTV (Lifetime Value) from your existing customers if you launch another successful product that's in line with what you're already doing. Expand slowly. Remember the mantra: slow is smooth, smooth is fast.]

This is of course a bigger lesson, namely, to *keep the main thing the main thing*. I could further extend my product line, but after this lesson, I'm not going to make dress shirts or pants. I'm going to make comfy clothes you wear at home. Maybe some sweats, maybe some undershirts you can wear out, but it's all going to stay within the realm of underwear.

Your customer has space occupied in their minds for the perception of your brand. When you do too many things, you start to cloud your customer's brain.

Become established before you go thinking you can do anything. Nike, as we know it, was founded in 1971; they waited eleven years before introducing apparel. To this day, shoes are their main source of revenue. Apple launched in 1976, their first massively successful product that wasn't a computer was the iPod in 2001.

If Southwest had tried to get into intercontinental or even just intercoastal travel, they wouldn't have been the only airline to be profitable for forty consecutive years. If they tried their hands at luxury travel or flying any airplane besides the 737, they wouldn't have the record they do. By having only one kind of airplane, maintenance crews and staff only had to be trained on one plane, and parts only ordered for one plane. They knew what they were the best in the world at and didn't deviate.

The dopamine receptors in your brain are at this very moment disagreeing, telling you you're different and special and can do anything you set your mind to. They're right about all of the above with one caveat: you can do anything you set your mind on as long as you don't water down your brand's hard-built equity into any product you can fit your logo on; and trust me on the swimwear.

Focus only on the essential and ignore the rest. Sol Price noticed that whenever he opened a new Price Club store, the value of the surrounding real estate shot up. So, he convinced his board to get into real estate development in the surrounding areas to take advantage of the increased value. Was it a good idea? No. Walmart, KMART, Costco, and Sam's Club all outpaced them. They were opening stores far faster because they were focused on keeping the main thing the main thing, not ramping up the adjacent thing. Sol Price wanted it all, and because he wanted everything, he lost his advantage.

In summary: don't get into swimwear. It brought us to the brink of ruin. Do not expand your category and distract your company from the main thing. Even if your dream is to make swimwear. Don't do it. Get another dream. You can do more in life than marginally improve how people look at the beach.

> Book Recommendation: *Essentialism* by Greg McKeown.

# #87

# HOW TO HANDLE YOUR COMPETITORS

*"You should wake up worried, terrified every morning. But don't be worried about our competitors, because they're never going to send us any money anyway. Let's be worried about our customers and stay head-down focused."*

—JEFF BEZOS

Bankruptcy attorneys asked the founder of Vans, Paul Van Doren, "Who's your competition?" He replied, "Sir, it is my opinion that we don't have any."

Whether you believe you have competitors or not, here's how to deal with them.

## OPTION #1: IGNORE THEM

*"Consciously avoid your peers."*

—HENRY SINGLETON, FOUNDER OF TELEDYNE

Your indifference should depend on your degree of difference. If you have a stronger brand, better quality, provide better service to your customers, or superior technology, you should flat-out ignore your competitors and focus solely on your mission. Continue excelling, experimenting, and through successful experiments: innovating. Don't react to what the competition is doing. Focus only on your customers; what's best for them is what's best for your business. Keep in mind that your customers can fire you anytime they like, simply by shopping elsewhere.

Racehorses wear blinders so they can't see the horses to their right or left. The best way to effectively put your blinders on is to be so different and on such another level than your competitors that you widen your moat. Make yourself into something they can't become because it's too risky, edgy, technologically advanced, or simply because you're working harder or thinking more creatively than they are. Then you never have to worry about them.

## OPTION #2: FIGHT THEM FOR SPORT

*"Our competitors have honed and sharpened us to an edge we wouldn't have without them."*

—SAM WALTON

If your competitors are hot on your heels, this will only motivate you to push harder, work smarter, and invent new methods of beating the pants off them. If you keep your eye on the ball, you can one day thank your competitors for pushing you past what you and your team are currently capable of. If it wasn't for Yuri Gagarin, we wouldn't have moonwalked till Michael Jackson. But because one brass-balled Russian braved Space for humanity's first time, we suddenly snapped to attention. JFK riled us up, and we spent the next eight years working toward the most impressive thing humanity has ever achieved. We left our size twelve Air Jordan footprints on the lunar surface, planted the flag on New America, and made the Soviets eat the Parmesan flakes out of our moon dust. After we did that, and sprayed some champagne in zero gravity, we then won the space race so hard we drove a fucking car on the moon. "Veni, Vidi, Vici." We saw there was no more worthy competition. So, we got bored, then lazy, then fat. We stopped progressing. We stopped thinking big, and we haven't been back to The Big Cheese since 1972.

C'mon, China, step your game up and try to beat us to Mars. We need the competition more than ever.

## OPTION #3: COPY THEM

*"Watch your rivals closely and never be ashamed to emulate a winning strategy."*
—FELIX DENNIS

If the competition stumbles across something that can change the game, you'd be an idiot not to emulate it. When Lyft launched its short-distance service that was essentially "your friend with a car," Uber's more luxurious idea of "your own private driver" had to scramble to launch UberX or be left in Lyft's peel-out marks.

I run into friends at parties, and if they're wearing any other underwear brand, I say, "Why the fuck aren't you wearing Culprits?" and they say, "Because you don't have a separate pouch for my nuts like…" and then name any one of our competitors because they all already copied each other. So, are we going to launch our own version? You're goddamned right we are. But they're all currently suing each other over this exact thing, so as they say in Thailand, we'll be "same same, but different."

You can also study them to do what they aren't doing so you can be different and stand out. Advertising ace, David Ogilvy, says, "In general, study the methods of your competitors and do the exact opposite."

## OPTION #4: ANNIHILATE THEM

*"If my competitor was drowning, I'd put a hose in his mouth."*
—RAY KROC, FOUNDER OF THE MCDONALD'S FRANCHISE

In the 1860s, there was a tough, young, not-afraid-of-a-gun-fight Wall Street impresario named Jay Gould. Later on, Rockefeller unflinchingly called Gould the smartest, most formidable business mind he'd ever come across. But at the time, this young upstart was battling Cornelius "The Commodore" Vanderbilt in a series of corporate battles for control of the Erie Railway known as *The Erie War*. The Erie was a significant railroad because it connected New York with the Great Lakes. The Commodore wanted it to expand his rail empire. The 'road's director wanted to resist the Commodore, so he enlisted wealthy cutthroats, Jay Gould and Jim Fisk, who began the battle by issuing watered-down stock in The Erie to prevent Vanderbilt from taking control.

It turned into an all-out price war over transporting cattle from the West to the East. Vanderbilt cut the price from $100 to $50 per cattle car. Gould countered with $25, so Vanderbilt cut his price to a profit-destroying $1 because he had more capital and could hold out longer. This, he knew, would force Gould and Fisk to give up.

But Gould was not the type. He was more the type that said something like "Fuck it, you want beef? I got beef." Then he secretly got into the beef business, buying trainloads of cattle in the West and transporting them to the East—happily paying Vanderbilt his dollar a boxcar. The Commodore was unknowingly subsidizing Gould's cattle business, making Gould and Fisk a healthy profit in the process and the Commodore more poor. Gould emerged as the winner, forcing Vanderbilt to give up his nearly controlling stake in the Erie Railroad.

## OPTION #5: SWALLOW THEM WHOLE

Rockefeller was so cost conscious, he personally measured the amount of solder used to seal his oil barrels. Once, he asked a worker, "Why are you using forty drops of solder? Have you tried thirty-eight?" They tried thirty-eight, and some barrels leaked, so they went with thirty-nine. One less drop of solder on a barrel of oil might not sound like much, but on millions of barrels, it sure adds up. Those cost savings compound over time.

How does one compete with a man like that? They didn't have to; Rockefeller bought them all out. But what if you won't sell? He'd buy one of your other competitors first. Then give you an offer from that competitor's company. When he buys you, you think you're being bought by one of your friends. You think you're joining a band of rebellious "little guys" to fight the nine-headed hydra, when it's actually one of the nine heads disguised as a lovable puppy.

The only thing you can do in this situation is take the stock. Swallow your pride and take the stock. Do not cash out your paltry chips. Everyone who took Rockefeller's stock instead of cash and held it became generationally wealthy. Everyone who took the cash spent the cash or tried their hand at oil again and failed.

## OPTION #6: JOIN THEM

*"Business is not a battle to be waged, it's a puzzle to be solved."*

—SAM ZELLE

If y'all are similar enough, it may make sense to join forces to stand back-to-back, guns blazing, attacking the wider industry instead of fighting each other while also battling bigger, more entrenched players as well. PayPal and X were fighting a pitched battle while the digital payments industry was heating up as a whole. They decided to join forces to prevent losing any ground and became such a powerful group together that, later in their careers, they were known as the *PayPal Mafia*. Had they not joined forces, they would've had to battle the traditional, too-big-to-fail banks in addition to each other.

My personal thought is that competition is for losers. You can get inspired by your competitors, but don't compete head-to-head, especially with an undifferentiated product. When Steve Jobs showed Jeff Bezos the iPod, Bezos had the foresight not to compete even though music was one of his biggest money makers...even though the iPod was about to decimate his gigantic CD business. He brilliantly thought, instead, how do I apply this to books? Boom, the Kindle was born.

# #88

# AVOID PROBLEMS DUH

*"After twenty-five years...Charlie and I have not learned to solve difficult business problems. What we have learned is to avoid them."*

—WARREN BUFFETT

You're better off avoiding problems than solving them, although doing so gets you zero credit. Take preventative measures and listen to people smarter than you. Ask people in your industry what problems they've faced, how they avoided other problems, and how they got out of problems they couldn't avoid. Be prepared for things to go sideways in everything from marketing to manufacturing. Because what can go wrong, will go wrong. Make it so that the most amount of things cannot go wrong and be ready when the most amount of things do.

While problems can lead to greater opportunities down the line, you're better off avoiding them in the first place. Here are a few questions to think about before it's too late, and there is no more time left to think:

- Do you have enough money to grow your business or at least to

stay alive for the next year? If not, do you have a plan for how to get emergency funding while you figure out how to raise more or increase sales?
- Do you have a plan if your top-selling product has a defect? Or to prevent defects with proper quality control?

We just launched a cool foldover backtag on our undies that makes them look super premium and hides the waistband seam on the inside. Already getting a flood of emails about how scratchy it is and how people will stop buying my product as long as this tag is on there. *Good thing I only made 50,000.* If I had more people test them and didn't just approve them based on a picture from the factory in Guatemala, I could've prevented this. Don't worry though, I'll probably only lose 20,000 customers for life.

- Could there be an issue in your supply chain if there's another pandemic?
- What if a savvy competitor comes out tomorrow and takes half your market share?
- What if Tim Cook unleashes the next IOS update and your Return On Ad Spend (ROAS) goes down by 50 percent and stays there like mine did? What do you do?

That was a serious problem for us that we're still recovering from. I imagine it affected every business that advertises online. We had become too reliant on a single source of revenue: Facebook ads. When that famous IOS update came out and Facebook no longer had access to Apple's data, that channel was no longer able to scale. Neither was our company. To fix this, we had to explore new ways to generate sales, such as affiliate marketing, strategic influencers, other online retailers, as well as physical retailers. Had we had some of these strategies going previously and weren't reliant on just one, we would've been able to avoid the brunt of this problem.

Either way, as an entrepreneur, you're going to have to deal with a lot of shit. Speaking of which, in London, there was an event called *The Great Stink of 1858* that made the city virtually unlivable—the man who solved it was Sir Joseph Bazalgette. While designing the new sewage system, he famously doubled the required pipe diameter. His reasoning? "We're only going to do this once—and there's always the unforeseen." His system is still in use today and, even with London's exponential population growth, it hasn't overflowed since. Ask yourself, where are my future bottlenecks?

# #89

# NEVER HAVE A SINGLE POINT OF FAILURE

*"The idea that everything should be cheap and efficient is a very dangerous one. Stability comes from redundancy, and inefficiency can be beneficial."*
—NASSIM NICHOLAS TALEB, AUTHOR OF *THE BLACK SWAN*

Remember the belts and suspenders principle: If your belt breaks, you still have suspenders holding your pants up. You never want to have a single point of failure in any crucial part of your business. If you're shipping product, have multiple warehouses in case one catches fire. If you're manufacturing, have at least two suppliers for every material you need and for making your final product. Get your second source now when you don't need it. The added benefit is that you may find an even better supplier that's cheaper.

Never be dependent on anyone, anything, or any sales channel. We get our sales from word of mouth via incentivized referrals, Google, and Facebook. We're in the process of adding direct mail, TikTok Shop, affiliate marketing, and good ol' fashioned TV, just in case something happens with Facebook or Google. If your primary sales are on Amazon, what happens if Amazon copies your product and sells it as an Amazon Basic?

If you're the Dodge bros and you realize your main source of revenue, Henry Ford, is about to start making all his parts in house and stop giving you that sweet nectar, what do you do? You decide to put your fate in your own hands and make your own car.

The same way you must break your dependency on any single vendor, warehouse, or client, you must also break your dependency on any one sales channel. When TiVo came out and people started skipping ads, companies that relied too hard on TV ads got screwed. When newspapers died a slow death, same thing. When iOS 14 came out and stopped giving Facebook all that valuable iPhone data, nearly every e-commerce brand's return on ad spend got cut in half overnight. These things will happen; it's not a matter of if, but when. Like a smart rat, you'll want to leave a sinking ship, but you must have another strategy ready to deploy.

Unfortunately, I had to learn this lesson the hard way. The year is 2021. We're at the top of our game. We're about to close our second year of business with $8 million in revenue. Our customers love us, we're riding a wave of euphoria, and our biggest weekend of the year is coming up in a week. What could go wrong?

To answer that question, here's our Chief of Operations, Tim Fox:

> When Dylan and David launched Culprit, I was the first hire. I had met Dylan at a Hollywood party, and he said he was a writer/director. I was a writer/actor. We spoke about writing a comedy project together called "Florida Man." He's one of the few people who actually follow up and call you the next day when they drunkenly said they would. We ended up having a great time writing comedy together, and they ended up selling that project. Cut to: middle of COVID, there's no acting work, and the restaurant I'm working at closes down. I'm shit out of luck, and Dylan calls me out of the blue, figuring that since I'm a comedy writer, I'd be great at emailing customers in his unorthodox style. I became the head of customer service and ended up

hiring a couple of people before moving into the role of running operations. Let me reiterate the fact that not one single person at Culprit, especially me, had any idea what the hell we were doing.

The hard part about running a business when no one knows what they're doing is that you need to rely on getting help from others. The second someone smells that you're remotely successful, they reach out and offer their services. They say they can make your life easier. You don't know any better, and you're from Virginia, so you trust them. Looking for a new third-party logistics company (a 3PL) to do our shipping, we go with this company, Resurge. They were cheap so we liked them. Cheap is not always the best; sometimes cheap is cheap. We were about to find out what the adage, "you get what you pay for," really means. But they were the only company willing to take our products without them being properly polybagged and barcoded. They said they'd do it for free if we went with them. It was the worst decision of my entire one-year-long career. I became an employee of *theirs*. I had to go to Reno all the time to help barcode. I carried inventory into the warehouse myself every time I was there because they were understaffed. I'm an actor turned underwear executive, and in one year, I was better at their logistics job than they were doing it for two decades. Not that it's anything to brag about. A forklift-certified possum could do better.

A year in, they tell us there's a problem. The warehouse wasn't owned by them, and we had one day to move all our stuff out. The next day they said, "Don't worry about it, we bought the building, so it's all good." A couple of days later, right before Thanksgiving and our busiest time of the year, they called and said the doors are locked because the company that owned the warehouse went bankrupt. Every single pair of undies we have to our name, the only assets our company has, is now sitting locked in a single warehouse in Reno during our busiest month.

I immediately flew to Reno and stayed at the most-certainly-not-a-resort, Grand Sierra Resort. I did eight days the first stint. I pretended to be a landlord to do some detective work and find out what the fuck happened. I talked to nearby employees on their smoke breaks. Apparently the owner locked the doors in the middle of the night. I looked through a window and saw all $4 million of our inventory sitting right there on racks. I did a stakeout in a rental car in the cold, waiting to see if someone would open the door.

I flew back to LA. It was upon entering my kitchen and dropping my bags on the floor, I suddenly realized there was a former employee who might have a key. I told her we'd give her $1,000 cash. Well, she had the key and no job. What do you think she said? I grabbed the bags I had just dropped on my kitchen floor and flew back to my new residence at the not-so-Grand Sierra. I made the call, and as I waited, I sat at the bar and drank Campari sodas. I became friends with the bartender. And some homeless people. One of them convinced me to let him refer me to the Chase App to get himself free pizza. I obliged.

I meet up with the employee. Give her $1,000 cash, and we get the door open! Luckily it's peak COVID, so the fact that we're all masked up like bandits is totally kosher. I called a home moving company, and we got 200,000 units out in five hours. Our product was all over the place. I had to climb forty-foot rafters with no ladder like Tarzan. I began tossing fifty-pound boxes down, trying not to hit the movers. It was sketchy. At one point, a security guard runs up with his flashlight. I'm like, we're fucked. We're going to jail. He asked who we were. I said Culprit. He said, "Prove it." I pulled down my pants and showed him my underwear. He said, "Oh, you're the Culprit guys? You need help?"

With the security guard now helping us do crime because I showed him my undies, we needed more trucking capacity. I went out to the parking lot and found a guy with his own pickup truck, but no teeth. He was also named Tim. We bonded. He helped us drive the inventory to our new warehouse. Which was forty-five seconds away. Every other company said no way they could onboard us during Black Friday. Ship Network came through in the clutch. They got us $4 million in inventory onboarded in forty-eight hours. A new world record of ass saving. And when our old 3PL later asked us for the remaining $30,000 we owed them, we threatened to sue them for ten times that, which was the amount of sales and refunds we lost by shipping orders a month late during the holidays.

Thank you for your service, Tim 🫡. I'm sad I didn't get to drink with you and all your new friends at a Reno bar on Thanksgiving, and instead was with my family.

# #90

# THE HIDDEN OPPORTUNITY

"*Problems are just opportunities in work clothes.*"
—HENRY KAISER, KEY FIGURE IN MOBILIZING AMERICAN INDUSTRY DURING WORLD WAR II

In 1963, Phil Knight started selling the Japanese running shoe brand, Onitsuka Tiger, out of the trunk of his car. After several years, his company grew frustrated with Onitsuka over delays, breakdowns in communication, and increasing restrictions on where they could sell. They soon found out why. Knight sat down at his office with a visiting Onitsuka executive. The exec pulled out his briefcase to go over numbers, complaining that Knight's company wasn't selling enough. Knight shot back that his sales had doubled every year since they began working together. The exec looked at the papers in his briefcase again, then said it wasn't enough. He excused himself to the restroom, and Knight took the opportunity to *excuse himself* to look in that briefcase. While the exec was taking a leak, Knight opened the case, pulled out the stack of papers, and hid them in his desk.

Knight's worst fears were confirmed. After seven years of loyalty and even showing them how to design a better shoe, Onitsuka had set up meetings with a dozen retailers who were Knight's direct competitors. Now all the sketchy behavior, delays, and bullshit made sense. He knew the relationship would soon sour. Knight tried to think of what to do next. Then Onitsuka went for the kill. They tried to force Knight to sell them the majority of his company, or else they'd cut him off with no shoes to sell. He bought time and started *taking action*, gearing up for the inevitable day. It came before he was ready. He delivered the news to his team:

> "We've come, folks, to a crossroads. Yesterday, our main supplier, Onitsuka, cut us off."
>
> I let that sink in. I watched everyone's jaw drop...
>
> "We're completely on our own. We're set adrift. We have this new line, Nike... But, well, frankly, that's all we've got..."
>
> I looked down at the table. Everyone was sinking, slumping forward. I looked at Johnson. He was staring at the papers before him, and there was something in his handsome face, some quality I had never seen there before. Surrender. Like everyone else in the room, he was giving up. The nation's economy was in the tank, a recession was underway. Gas lines, political gridlock, rising unemployment, Nixon being Nixon—Vietnam. It seemed like the end times. Everyone in the room had already been worrying about how they were going to make rent, pay the light bill. Now this. I cleared my throat.
>
> "So...in other words...what I'm trying to say is we've got them right where we want them."
>
> Johnson lifted his eyes. Everyone around the table lifted their eyes. They sat up straighter.
>
> "This is—the moment," I said. "This is the moment we've been waiting for.

Our moment. No more selling someone else's brand. No more working for someone else. Onitsuka has been holding us down for years. Their late deliveries, their mixed-up orders, their refusal to hear and implement our design ideas—who among us isn't sick of dealing with all that? It's time we faced facts: If we're going to succeed, or fail, we should do so on our own terms, with our own ideas—our own *brand*. We posted two million in sales last year...none of which had anything to do with Onitsuka. That number was a testament to our own ingenuity and hard work. Let's not look at this as a crisis. Let's look at this as our liberation. Our Independence Day. Yes, it's going to be rough. I won't lie to you. We're definitely going to war, people. But we know the terrain... And that's one reason I feel in my heart this is a war we can win. And if we win it, when we win it, I see great things for us on the other side of victory. We're still alive, people. We are still. Alive."

Excerpt from *Shoe Dog* by Phil Knight

If Phil Knight hadn't been cut off from his Japanese shoe supplier, he wouldn't have been forced to make his own shoes. Getting screwed over ended up being the best thing that ever happened to him. His contract being canceled forced him to go all in on Nike. As of 2023, they're doing $51 billion in revenue. Quite the opportunity hidden in that seemingly existential problem. All business is—at the end of the day—is problem-solving. And every problem you solve gets you closer to your goal. The next time you're facing a crisis, invert it. Look at it from a new angle. Where is the opportunity? The adversity creates the strategy.

# #91

# CONCEPTION VS. EXECUTION

*"All of us have had great ideas from time to time, the follow through, the execution is 1000 times more important than a great idea."*

—FELIX DENNIS

Everyone has good ideas and a few game-changing great ideas. However, an extreme minority of these great ideas ever come to fruition because almost everyone sucks at the most important aspect: execution. You must swim against a mighty current of critics, competitors, and cash flow to turn your dream tangible.

Sol Price, the greatest retailer who's ever lived, had great ideas and shared them generously. He told Bernie Marcus and Arthur Blank to literally copy his model and apply it to what they've learned in home improvement. Voila, Home Depot was born. He also shared his ideas with protégé Jim Senegal, who went on to found Costco. His ideas have inspired KMART, Walmart, and Amazon Prime.

However, as we know from Chapter 85, Sol's focus was flawed, hurting the execution of his main idea. The result: Costco, Sam's Club, and Walmart feverishly outgrew Price Club. Thankfully he was able to merge with Costco and didn't do too shabby, but imagine if he was the best executor of the bunch? He'd be our false-idol lord and savior instead of Bezos.

# #92

# CAUSE NO HARM, BUT TAKE NO SHIT

*"Gentlemen, let's do one more round with them."*

—HERB KELLEHER

Southwest Airlines was almost driven out of business before they ever put a plane in the air. After getting their application approved by the Texas Aeronautics Commission, rival Texas airlines fought a three-year "turf-war" lawsuit to keep Southwest grounded. After running out of money fighting them in court, losing the first case, losing the appeal, and running out of money before they even got a chance to fly, Herb Kelleher uttered those fighting words. Then he took his case for Southwest's right to exist to the Texas Supreme Court. They overturned the court's decision. It didn't hurt that he was a practicing lawyer.

You might not have passed the bar, but that doesn't mean you can just let the existing leviathan in your industry walk all over you. If you're not a lawyer, that's fine. Neither was Elon Musk.

When government agencies, including NASA, threatened SpaceX's very survival, Elon decided to sue NASA. On multiple occasions, they sued government agencies and won almost every case. Let me repeat that. SpaceX sued the government and won. Had they not sued, Boeing, Lockheed Martin, and Northrop Grumman would have eaten them alive. Juicy government contracts were being unfairly awarded to these companies based not on merit, but on personal relationships. People would work at NASA and then leave for more lucrative paydays at one of those companies, using their relationships for private gain.

SpaceX could prove they were being unfairly overlooked in favor of inferior competitors because of crony capitalism. They had superior technology, lower costs, and were actively working to disrupt this overpriced, wasteful industry to benefit humanity. It was because of their mission and singular focus that they let nothing, not even the government of the most powerful nation in the world, stand in their way.

They did not get into this game to cause harm, but they were not about to take even one whiff of shit. When survival is on the line, not just your company's, but potentially one day, humanity's survival, taking shit is not an option. If you're congruent with your mission, you and your team believe in what you're doing, and you're making the world a better place, it doesn't matter who the gatekeeper is. It doesn't matter that your rivals have more resources. With enough chutzpah, you can bulldoze right through them. Remember, you're not building a company; you're on a crusade.

# #93

# SLOW IS FAST

*"Slow is smooth, smooth is fast."*

—MAXIM USED IN NAVY SEALS TRAINING

When you're innovating, finding product market fit, testing and iterating, you need to move as fast as humanly possible. However, when you're growing, buying more inventory, opening new stores, hiring a bigger team, or expanding internationally, it's time to slow it down. Take your time and do it right.

Navy SEALS are trained to make higher-quality decisions during high-stress situations. If you're in a situation where there's a shooting or a fire, panicking and following the crowd could get you killed. In a panic, the crowd will run out of a building the same way they came in. They will fail to notice the fire exits. If you want to survive in this scenario, take three controlled breaths before making a decision. Simply inhale, hold for three seconds, then exhale. Do this three times. Your heart rate will slow down, and you'll be able to make a decision that could save your life. The same principle applies to high-stress, high-risk, high-reward moments in business.

Expanding too quickly is a common mistake. This often happens with retail stores. CEOs want to strike while the iron is hot. The rational thought is to capture as much market share as possible while the brand is having its moment. Fashion brand Nasty Gal made this mistake when they focused on excessive growth instead of a healthy business. Their 2016 bankruptcy filing reads, "The costs associated with managing and controlling Nasty Gal's aggressive growth and the setbacks in international markets have created significant liquidity issues."

I made this mistake when I wanted to 4x our business in a single year. We put purchase orders in to do $20 million in revenue from underwear alone, plus another $10 million from unproven, new products like swimwear and socks. Instead of $30 million in 2022, we did less than $9 million. Thankfully, most of it was unfinished goods, and we didn't have to pay full price for completed undies. But it put us $5 million in debt. Things got scary. If I had focused on *smooth* growth, we would've gotten there faster because we'd have better cash flow. Your cash flow window is everything. Instead of a down year in 2023 due to a cash crunch, we would've had an up year. It's so much faster to keep your growth smooth, sustainable, and slower than you'd like. You'll get there faster when you take time to master.

# #94

# ALWAYS HAVE A PARALLEL

*"Learning from the success and failures of others is the fastest way to get smarter and wiser without a lot of pain."*

—EXCERPT FROM *THE TAO* OF CHARLIE MUNGER

Before he ever saw combat, General Patton studied military history voraciously so no matter what happened during his future campaigns, he would always have a parallel to draw from. Patton wouldn't have to think of the solution to a problem while mortar shells exploded around him, blowing the limbs off his troops. He wouldn't have to calculate his next move over the sound of whistling artillery barrages and agonized screams because this quagmire had already been solved, just not by him. Thankfully another of history's great commanders had already dealt with this situation, so Patton could just draw a parallel and do what's been proven to work. This reinforces why books have the best ROI in the world. They don't just inspire new ideas, they prevent you from making easily avoidable mistakes. I would've paid the $5 million I put us in debt for a copy of this book four years ago.

But, Dylan, don't you always want to think from first principles?

Isn't always having a parallel to draw contradictory? Fuck no. You don't always have time to think from first principles. Especially in the heat of battle. For 99 percent of your decisions, you'll want to emulate a strategy that already works. Think from first principles when you need to. When you feel the current technology or way of doing things isn't sufficient. When you think there can be a better way, break it down to its most basic elements and build a new method from scratch. If you thought about everything from first principles, you'd never get anything done. And you'd wind up in a straitjacket.

To keep up with orders, Tesla needed to produce 5,000 cars per month. They tried everything and were still falling short. Their factory simply didn't have the capacity. They had only one month to figure it out before the company took a major hit. Elon knew his history though. He had studied wartime production during World War II. He knew defense companies like Boeing had set up extra production lines in their parking lots as a necessity. This insight likely came to him from reading the book *Freedom's Forge*. Elon was able to draw this parallel and told the story to his team. They okayed it with their legal team and made the parking lot into a production plant. By the end of the month, they had surpassed 5,000 cars.

## THE HOMEWORK HAS BEEN DONE

An extremely successful friend of mine said, "If you're not copying the homework, you're a fucking idiot. Every billionaire is out there on podcasts telling you how they did it. The work has already been done." The most successful people in the world are out there in books and on podcasts, showing you what they did in detail. All you have to do is copy the homework and draw a parallel to what you're doing. You don't need to come up with the answers; you just need to find them.

# #95

# ORGANIZE YOUR ORGANIZATION

*"Apple is Steve Jobs with 10,000 lives."*
—LEANDER KEANEY, AUTHOR OF *INSIDE STEVE'S BRAIN*

One of Steve Jobs's best skills was the way he organized his company. When he passed away, Apple was still able to thrive because his system architecture was in place. One day, you are going to die. If you want your organization to live on, you must do this right. If you are going to sell your company, the better organized it is, the more valuable it will be. The more systems are in place, the more you can scale without having to oversee every detail.

Ask yourself the question: if my business were to 10x overnight, what would happen?

If your business 10x'd tomorrow, first you'd celebrate, then you'd panic. But if you have the proper systems in place, you can chill the champagne and skip the panic part. By systems, I mean protocols to follow for every scenario: bringing in new customers, scaling your team, manufacturing, customer service, shipping and logistics, supply chain, and everything in between.

Here's a look at one section of our company's system organization:

## How To's

- OPERATIONS
- CUSTOMER SERVICE
- PRODUCT
- TECH
- CREATIVE
- IT

≡ List view +

- How to get Underwear delivered from Miami to McCook
- STEP ONE - LTL Freight Pick Up  4
- STEP TWO - Create an ASN for Ship Network
- How to add New Products to Shopify
- STEP ONE - Add Product information to ALL PRODUCTS SPREADSHEET
- STEP TWO - Shopify - Add product
- How to download inventory sales for a specific time period
- ALL Steps - Shopify & Excel
- How to add/remove to STEALS section
- STEP ONE - Add product to Steals
- STEP TWO- Remove product from Steals
- Theme Templates for Shopify products - PDP
- Templates

+ New

This is an organization app we use called Notion. We have a How-To section on our main page. Inside there are detailed instructions to do anyone's job should anyone fall ill. My life is chaotic, but thanks to the systems my team and I have honed over time, my company is organized. If you are disorganized like I was, it's time to fix that.

> Online Video Course Recommendation: *Building a Second Brain* by Tiago Forte

# #96

# GIVE JUST THE TINIEST 💩 ABOUT THE 🌍

> "I have a little different definition of evil than most people—When you have the opportunity and the ability to do good and you do nothing, that's evil. Evil doesn't always have to be an overt act, it can be merely the absence of good."
>
> —YVON CHOUINARD, FOUNDER OF PATAGONIA

Mormons give 10 percent of all their earnings to their church, and they have the nicest churches in the country! And that's just Mormons. What if everyone gave 10 percent of all their earnings, but instead of building these gaudy, tax-haven fiefdom shrines to a bearded man in the sky that doesn't let you drink tea, they made the actual world a better place?

Well, humans don't usually like to give anonymously, and lots of people don't have enough to reliably make rent. So, instead of giving 10 percent, in a perfect world, could we all just give 1 percent? But, for this to be effective, everyone would have to do it. And for everyone to do it, we'd have to run a marketing campaign to eight billion people, and that would cost more than the 1 percent we'd raise.

So instead of passing out a collection tray to the world, do what Yvon Chouinard does and give 1 percent of your company's profits to the planet. Set the example yourself. You cannot wait around for someone else to make the world a better place. It has to start at the top. Trickle-down economics doesn't work, but trickle-down example setting does. Make your company the shining beacon of hope for us all to emulate. It costs only 1 percent of your net, but the long-term gains for the planet and humanity are incalculable.

Throwing tomato soup on a Van Gogh or setting fire to a parking lot of SUVs accomplishes nothing in the way of real change. I understand the sentiment, as over 70 percent of global emissions are not created by individuals, but by the biggest one hundred corporations. We can shout at consumers all we want to consume less, but that's just herding cats.

At Culprit we're joining *1 Percent for the Planet,* and whether our contribution even registers as a drop in the bucket or not is irrelevant. It feels great to take that first step. And you don't have to do it anonymously. You can put it in your marketing and on your website. You'll likely get more sales from it and inspire other companies to do it as well. You win a little and the planet wins a lot.

# #97

# HOW TO NEGOTIATE

*"Negotiation is not an act of battle; it's a process of discovery."*
—CHRIS VOSS, FORMER FBI HOSTAGE NEGOTIATOR

Negotiation will serve you in every area of business and your life. Even things you don't realize are negotiations, like where your spouse wants to go to dinner or getting your kids to go to bed on time. Here are a few examples of how to negotiate.

## NEGOTIATION ON PRICE

In almost every business, you'll have to negotiate on price with your vendors. Here's how I do it: I like to have a manufacturer price out, say 100,000 units and 10,000 units. My strategy is to find out that lower price for the larger number of units and then come up slightly on the lowest number of units I was suggesting. Usually, I can get them to the price for 100k for anything north of 25k units.

Then, if I'm still not happy with the price, I'll come up with an extremely precise number that it needs to come down. I had bullied prices down on 10,000 bandanas this way, and then after their "lowest possible" price of $1.85 per, I said, "Bring it down another 13 cents to $1.72, and you've got a deal." I made it seem like I had another quote that was maybe $1.75. They knew I would walk away from them as a vendor if they didn't meet my price, so they relented. Where did I pull this number from? My ass, of course.

I know a real estate developer as tough as they come. He will beat you up on price as far as he can without you getting up and storming out or hanging up the phone. When he's got you as low as you'll possibly go, so low you don't want to tell your spouse, he'll bring you back up a little bit. An imperceptible amount that doesn't affect him, but makes you feel better about the deal.

## ALWAYS HAVE LEVERAGE

I call negotiating without leverage NOGOtiation.

With its 1991 deal still intact, Pixar would receive up to 15 percent of profits from its films. Steve Jobs thought this arrangement was embarrassing. Instead, he told his team at Pixar they should go public one week after their worldwide release of Toy Story and should renegotiate afterward with Disney to become even partners. He bet big on himself, his team, and the genre-defining movie they had created. Had the movie not been a success, the public offering would've failed, but because it was even more of a box office smash than expected, they were suddenly flush with cash.

Now they were able to come back to the negotiating table with leverage, offering to risk an equal amount of money on each movie. Disney took the deal. They would now receive 50 percent of the profit instead of *up to* 15 percent. It was the greatest deal in animation history.

This simple renegotiation made Steve Jobs a billionaire way before he came back to Apple. Then in 2006, Jobs outdid himself. When the CEO of Disney, Bob Iger, noticed at a recent Disneyland visit that all the new characters' kids were obsessed with were from Pixar, not Disney, he knew he had to acquire it. He called up Jobs to begin talks.

Steve let Bob know that Pixar had the team, the intellectual property, the characters, the sequels, the vision, and most importantly, the balls to walk away if they weren't given a fair deal. He knew Disney needed Pixar more than they needed Disney and told Bob, with all that in mind, to be a straight shooter and lay his best deal on the table. There would be no back and forth. Jobs agreed to Iger's $7.4 billion all-stock deal and became the single biggest shareholder of Disney stock, earning himself a seat on the board and aligning the future of both companies.

## USE PERSUASION

*"Pay peanuts and you get monkeys."*

—DAVID OGILVY

This is particularly effective if it's talent you want to attract. I don't like to negotiate on price or beat people up when it comes to their salaries. I like to pay people what they're worth because I want happy, driven people working with me. If you're only hiring A-players, you don't want them losing enthusiasm from not being properly compensated and seeking another job. The top people have headhunters constantly bugging them with offers. Pay your people well. If you absolutely cannot afford someone at the salary they're asking, let them know and either offer them stock options to make up for it or tell them you'll increase their salary whenever you can afford to. Hopefully, if they're worth the large salary they're asking, they can help get you there.

Sometimes it's not a bigger salary that will get them to join your company, and even more often, they have a bigger offer somewhere else that you can't afford to match. In that situation, find out what drives them. Do they want equity, time off with family, remote working so they can travel, better work-life balance, or public credit on projects so they feel important? We were tight on cash, and one of my team members asked for a massive raise we couldn't afford. I said, "I just read that the Japanese are moving to four-day work weeks in a lot of their companies. Why don't we move you to a four-day work week?" He's thriving, and

I don't have to work so hard finding work to keep him busy. In fact, I swear he gets everything done faster now.

## APPEAL TO THEIR INTERESTS

*"Everyone has something at stake, if you address that predicament you can move anyone from no to yes."*

—HERB COHEN, AUTHOR OF YOU CAN NEGOTIATE ANYTHING

During prohibition, the founder of Seagram's whiskey, Sam Bronfman, decided that when prohibition ended and everyone was still drinking bathtub gin, he would come to market with the finest aged whiskey around. He sailed to Scotland and met with several distilleries in the Scottish Highlands, including the Chivas brothers (of Chivas Regal fame). He made his offer by appealing to their interests, saying, "We have an opportunity here to make scotch the predominant drink in North America. I don't think you want to pass that up any more than I do. Prohibition cannot last forever, and when it is repealed, you will be established in the market, whereas it might take years for the bourbon people to get back into the business again."

Shortly after prohibition, Bronfman's negotiation for top-quality hooch paid off; he had secured 40 percent of the American liquor market while everyone else was playing catch-up. Not just the whiskey market, by the way, the entire US liquor market. And we are a thirsty bunch, aren't we?

## NEVER BE AFRAID TO WALK AWAY

In fact, walk away at least once if you think they'll still want your business.

```
Book Recommendation: Chris Voss's book Never Split the
Difference and his video series on Masterclass.
```

# #98

# NEVER JUMP INTO A CONTRACT

*"A man who represents himself has a fool for a lawyer."*

—UNKNOWN

Tom Clancy sold *The Hunt for Red October* for $5,000. That's it. He was great at reading everything but contracts. He quickly learned his lesson.

You don't need to pass the bar, but you do need to know a little bit, enough to read any contract you receive. If you have a lawyer on retainer, make them read every contract, even the most mundane. If you can't afford a lawyer, do it with Chat GPT. Even if you can afford Johnny Cochran, it costs nothing to have AI take another look. Read your contracts, understand every clause, and give your artificially intelligent assistant context.

When I was making my movie, my seasoned entertainment lawyer overlooked that any product placement we raised would go to pay back the investors and not go into the movie's budget. We spent six months raising $500,000 in additional funds from advertisers to be able to make the movie the way we wanted to—including a $70,000 check from Squatty Potty 😂. Then, the investors took that money away from us as an early payback. We simply couldn't make a good enough movie with just their $2 million. When you're on a shoestring budget, 25 percent extra goes a long way.

What most people fail to realize is that you can ask any client, agency, investor, or partner to change any clause, no matter how "standard." Change the contract however you deem fit, don't sign anything you're uncomfortable with, unscrew yourself from the beginning, and remember Chapter 68, there's no such thing as standard.

## #99

# CAP YOUR DOWNSIDE, NOT YOUR UPSIDE

*"I had two non-negotiable needs. I wanted to open in an emerging neighborhood and I wanted to have the right to assign my lease to someone else if my restaurant should go out of business. Having experienced my father's bankruptcies and knowing something about how many new restaurants went belly up, I was soberly aware that failure was a real possibility. To this day, getting an assignable lease is the first piece of advice I give any new restaurateur."*

—DANNY MEYER, FOUNDER OF SHAKE SHACK

If you spend every day of your life working for someone else, your upside is capped. You might think your downside is capped because you have a steady job, but times are changing faster than ever, and your job may become irrelevant any day now. To be truly successful, you must never let a cap be put on your future success.

Danny Meyer opened new restaurants in neighborhoods that were just starting to become cool so he could get cheaper rent, a great space, and keep his upside unlimited. If the restaurant worked, more people would start coming to that neighborhood, other cool restaurants and bars would open, resulting in even more people coming to his restaurant. He capped his downside, making sure that if the restaurant failed, he could assign the lease to someone else and wasn't on the hook.

Tire mogul Les Schwab would open a new store with a five-year lease and a five-year option to buy. If the store wasn't successful within five years, he'd close it; if it was, he'd buy the real estate it sat on, further decreasing his costs and increasing the value of his empire.

When Richard Branson started Virgin Airlines, he made a special deal to lease his planes for five years, but he could return the planes after one year if it didn't work. If Virgin Airlines didn't work, he'd still have Virgin Music, but because he capped his downside, he was able to expand fearlessly, and his upside was unlimited. His gamble paid off, turning him into a billionaire without having to bet the farm.

Make sure whatever gamble you're about to make, you can gain everything but can't lose it all. You must make sure, not only that you don't stand to lose too much, but that your ability to gain is not tempered. Never underestimate your own potential for success. Never underestimate the probability of losing everything if you gamble too much.

# #100

# WATCH YOUR COSTS AT ALL COSTS

*"Costs are like fingernails, they always have to be cut."*
—CARLOS SICUPIRA, BRAZILIAN BILLIONAIRE

Revenue goes up and down with seasons, economies, world events, buyer fatigue, competitors running sales, you name it. But no matter what your customers or competitors are up to, there's one thing you can always control: your costs. Watch them like a hawk.

When faced with having to repaint his television studio's building, media mogul Tom Murphy famously said, "Paint the two sides that face the road and leave the other sides untouched." He got it done for half price.

When naming his now ubiquitous store, Sam Walton decided on Walmart—instead of using his full name—because it was only seven letters. That meant fewer big letters to make, fewer letters to light, to clean, and fewer lightbulbs to change. Over hundreds of stores, this was massive savings, especially compounded over time.

In the 70s and 80s, Southwest Airlines saved money by using its regular receipt machine to print their plane tickets on receipt paper. When customers began to complain they lost their tickets amongst their other receipts, Southwest considered spending several million dollars to follow the rest of the industry with a multi-layered ticket machine. Instead, they decided to print **"THIS IS A TICKET"** in big red letters on the receipt. It worked.

If you run a Shopify store, you're constantly being pitched new apps. They all promise better data, more sales, higher order value, or better conversion rates. Some are $50 a month, some are $3,000. Some are worth their weight in gold, and some are nearly impossible to know if they're working or not. Treat them the same and audit them every month. Clip them if you're not getting consistent, measurable value, or you'll wake up one day with twenty grand missing from your account and no added revenue.

Consider what's a *need to have* and what's a *nice to have*. Just recently, I was paying $8,000 a month for an agency to run our email campaigns. We were unable to pay them on time. They suspended services. The same day they cut our services, we began to run our emails and SMS internally. We cut our costs in half immediately, and after inspiring my team to take courses on email marketing and design, the result is better. We thought we needed an agency for the last four years because that's what we've been told. Training your team to take something from external to internal can save you big bucks. What "need to haves" in your business are actually "nice to haves"?

When things go south, you'll naturally cut costs to survive. Necessity will make you more resourceful. The trick is to continue this practice when you are prospering. When you have millions of dollars in funding, human nature dictates that you spend it. Go against your nature. It's okay to be profitable.

A dollar saved is better than a dollar earned. It's a dollar all the same, but you don't have to take return on ad spend, shipping costs, taxes, or cost of goods out of it. The entire 100 percent of the dollar goes back to your bottom line.

# #101

# PEDAL TO THE METAL

*"Borrowing money is not a bad thing as long as you don't treat it as a life buoy to only be used in times of crisis, but instead use it as a powerful tool that you can use to create opportunities."*

—JOHN D. ROCKEFELLER

Being scrappy is great. Frugality through resourcefulness is where it's at. As a printer, Ben Franklin made his own paper and ink, Rockefeller turned oil waste products like Vaseline and tar into gold, SpaceX found out a $30 bathroom stall lock worked better to keep hatches closed on the Space Station than NASA's $1,500 one, and Jeff Bezos won't shut up about how he saved money in Amazon's early days by making employees make their own desks out of cheap Home Depot doors.

Sometimes though, you need to quit being a cheap fuck. There comes a time to break open your piggy bank and make a big bet. Founder of Seagram's Whiskey, Sam Bronfman's philosophy was to spend as little as possible on things that don't matter, like luxury office furniture, and as much as you have on things that do matter, like the quality of his whiskey and the talent of his team.

Take it from me. Do not take on debt to keep the lights on, pay payroll, or fund operations because you don't know when your situation will improve. If there are other steps you can take, no matter how drastic, do those instead. There is a time when it's worth taking on debt though: Investing in new technology, talent, an expansion of your market, or anything else that will improve efficiency and drive sales.

## NEW TECHNOLOGY

Technology, such as trying to automate too many tasks all at once at your factory, can be a costly mistake. Tesla tried to reduce their workforce by replacing many tasks with automation. It failed miserably. They went back to workers working in unison with robots instead of being replaced by them. However, when it's a proven technology that lowers your costs or expands your market, it's a no-brainer. Andrew Carnegie learned of a new furnace for making steel more efficiently, which his competitors viewed as an "extravagant expenditure." Carnegie made the expensive investment and found that "almost half of the waste could sometimes be saved by using the new furnaces. The expenditure would've been justified even if it had been double." Some years, Carnegie's profit margin was so slim that it was only by the saving grace of the new furnaces that they made money. By the time his competitors tried to copy him, it was too late for them.

## EXPANDING YOUR MARKET

In the early 1920s, in trying to solve a problem for the telephone system, Western Electric created efficient amplifying devices. They tried to interest film producers in the new tech, but none of the large studios were interested. "Why should they tamper with their satisfactory medium of silent films? The addition of mechanical audio would only be an expense." Studios thought of an improvement to their product as an expense. This was at a time when broadcast radio had just become the next big thing in American homes. Movie theater attendance was down because people were staying home and listening to the radio. "Theater men saw no advantage in going into the expense of installing costly equipment while attendance was falling off." They thought of radio as merely a competitor for their customers' time. Not perhaps that...maybe people wanted to actually hear audio??? Hmmm, what if you could combine that audio they love to hear on their radios with soundless movies? Wouldn't that be something that could maybe, I don't know, *fix your attendance problem*?

Well, one of the smallest studios at the time thought it would. A little company called Warner Brothers. They made a few short musicals, and here's what happened: "He faced the audience and for the first time spoke in audible words instead of printed subtitles. The effect was galvanizing. Suddenly the character was brought alive and made capable of giving vocal expression to the already tearful sentiments of the plot. The illusion was so effective that the audience cried and cheered." By others in the industry, this system of synced sound was regarded as a novelty, an unnecessary expense. Even with the audience having this crazy reaction. But Warner Bros knew that once audiences heard sound, they would never want silent films again. It's worth it, whatever the cost, if you know your customer will love it. An expense becomes an investment when it makes your entire market larger.

## TALENT

To riff on a Steve Jobs idea, the difference in quality of most things is rarely better than say two-to-one. The best burger you've ever had compared to McDonald's, a Mercedes SL compared to a '93 Honda Accord. Sure these things are better, but even twice as good is pushing it. However, when it comes to talent, there are people who are more effective in their role than others by a factor of one hundred. Some people on your team can make tens of millions of dollars of difference in your bottom line per year. A-level talent is everything, and therefore, it's better to overpay for true talent than to risk them leaving or joining a competitor. This does not apply to B or C players. How do you know what level someone is on? Imagine they walked into your office and quit. How you would feel about that is what level of talent they are.

Payroll is always going to be one of your biggest expenses. Watch your headcount like a hawk. When you hire someone, don't just factor in their annual salary; factor it over a lifetime. Add to the equation payroll tax, benefits increasing over time, raises, bonuses, and things like extra power consumption, increased HR costs, even down to how much extra coffee and toilet paper you'll have to buy for each employee. It's not just $100,000 a year, it's several million dollars over the lifetime of that new position. Think long term. An empty chair costs less than the wrong fit.

# #102

# ALWAYS HAVE A BUFFER

*"Fortify yourself fully to cover possible setbacks because you can absolutely count on meeting setbacks."*

—JOHN D. ROCKEFELLER

The world is complex. You can't predict or control what will happen. The reason most businesses fail is overoptimism concerning cash flow. You need to build a buffer, and for that, it's time to embrace your inner pessimist. Really channel your inner Scrooge here. Plan for unexpected expenses in your thirteen-week cash flow plan. Whittle your expenses down even when you're making tons of money and stack as much cash as you can. Not every dime needs to be reinvested. Your team doesn't need to grow. Your company coffers do. When the shit hits the fan, you'll be happy you're wearing a poncho.

Limiting spending when you're raking it in goes against human nature. You think you need to invest every dollar into scaling your business. You don't. You need as big a buffer as you can get. The time will come when you'll need it. It's not an if, it's a when. Every entrepreneur will make this mistake, so I am once again drilling it into your skull.

When it rains, build a reservoir, so you'll have something to drink in the drought. The drought is coming.

Goldman Sachs not only built a reservoir of cash, they built generators in their building. When Hurricane Sandy hit Manhattan's financial district, they were the only building still in business.

Now that you're on your path to building a massive buffer, you'll not only survive black swan events, you'll be able to take advantage of them. Do not let your buffer burn a hole in your pocket. Wait for the right opportunity. Be patient. It will come. Warren Buffett sometimes goes up to six years without investing a dime, then deploys billions all at once. The next recession is coming. It could be your moment to strike. While your competitors slash their marketing budgets, you can increase yours. While they're hosting fire sales to stay afloat, you can expand into new markets.

During the panic of 1873, Andrew Carnegie decided to do the unthinkable. He spent a ton of money on a new steel mill. Since it was near the bottom of a financial panic, he got huge savings on materials and labor, prompting him to say, "The best time to expand is when no one else dares take the risk." Do not, however, expand if you're losing money, only when your competitors are.

When I typed the first page of this book, I owed Ampla $300,000. At this exact moment, I have sent them the last six thousand bucks and paid them off for good. They asked if the transfer was done. I typed not a word and simply emailed back the "It's Done" Frodo GIF from the end of *The Lord of the Rings*. I am currently listening to "Good Day" by Ice Cube in a cold plunge with Palo Santo wafting through the air. I'm cleansing myself of their negative energy and my constantly negative bank account. Those days are over. From now on, I will follow my own advice and always have a buffer (bet you never thought *LOTR*, Gangsta Rap, and energy cleansing would be in the same paragraph).

# #103

# WHAT TO DO IN A DROUGHT

*"To be successful, all you must do is survive."*

—WARREN BUFFETT

If you're desperately reading this chapter, it's because you listened to your dumb human nature instead of me. You had money burning a hole in your pocket and wanted to strike while you were hot. You hired too many people, bought too much inventory, opened too many stores, or you really didn't fuckin' listen and launched swimwear. That's okay, I'm not your mom, I'm not going to hit you with a sandal or a belt. You're too far away. Instead, I will help you.

When you don't have enough money to accomplish it all, or even to make it to next week, you either need more money or you need to figure out which mouths to feed and which babies are going hungry. Here's how to drum up emergency cash.

## LAUNCH A SALE

This one's easy. Depending on the drought, you can do a flash sale, a month-long sale, or a sitewide sale. Get creative, make it fun, put a time constraint on everything you do, or no one will take action. Keep in mind, when you do too many sales, you become a discount brand, and people will only buy during sales. If you chase this short-term sugar rush too often, it can get tougher to sell during the evergreen period. Which is the most important time because it's most of the time.

## CLEAR DEAD INVENTORY

The following we copied shamelessly from Lululemon. Make a new section on your website for inventory you either have too much of or that isn't selling. You can call it clearance internally, but don't say that word out loud. People don't want what other people don't want. Lululemon calls their section "We Made Too Much." For us, it was on brand to call it STEALS. We start things at 30 percent off for a month, then if they don't boost sales, we move them to 40 percent, then 50 percent off.

You need to get rid of dead inventory. We've found that a print sometimes won't move at all until we price it down. Then it flies off the shelves. If you have something at 50 percent and it's still not moving, you can launch a "mystery" item and mark it down more. We sell mystery pairs of underwear when our prints get too size broken. When there's only XS or 4XL left, that becomes our mystery product, so it doesn't take up valuable real estate on the site. Just put a system in place so if someone orders three mystery products, they don't get three of the same. There are also companies that specialize in taking the stuff you can't sell at a big discount. It's better than it sitting.

## GIVE EVERYONE A HAIRCUT

*"All shared the burden of the recession. Good people were not released into a very tough job market and we had our highly qualified workforce in place when business improved."*

—DAVID PACKARD, CO-FOUNDER OF HEWLETT-PACKARD

Giving everyone a haircut sounds more fun than it is. My CFO told me we had to fire people. I said, "What if we just temporarily cut their pay, so we didn't have to do that?" He said, "Okay, but you have to bring everyone down by 20 percent today. I decided 12 percent would be the max without affecting people's lives too much. I decided everyone would get additional equity equal to their pay cut. Every team member agreed, and it was heartwarming because it proved they were truly missionaries, not mercenaries. Except one guy, one guy didn't agree. He's gone now. It was a hard moment for everyone but brought us all together in the trenches more. I didn't take a pay cut because I was already not getting paid and had invested every dime I had into the business.

It was only by my team's selflessness that we were able to survive; otherwise, I would've had to do the unthinkable. After six months, I was able to right the ship, get everyone back to normal pay, and we're all a more cohesive unit having gone through that shitstorm together. I owe all of them immensely for trusting me through that and agreeing to risk their own livelihoods for the company's well-being. It saved our asses, and thanks to their willingness to sacrifice, no one got laid off.

In 1970, there was a downturn in the economy, causing Hewlett-Packard's sales to dip. Faced with the prospect of laying off 10 percent of their workers, they went to nine days out of every two weeks; a 10 percent cut in workdays with a resulting 10 percent cut in pay. After only six months, their orders recovered, and they were able to bring everything back to normal. Some workers said that although they had to tighten their belts, they actually enjoyed the long weekends. Had I known of this story before I had to do my own round of haircuts, I would've drawn this as my parallel (Lesson #93) and chosen this version.

Hopefully, by following the advice in this book, you never have to go through that. But if you do have to make an equally hard yet ultimately rewarding decision that saves the day for everyone, promise me one thing: don't expect any praise. You won't get it. Every single time pay is late or uncertainty spreads amongst your ranks, the blame is not put on the economy or Tim Cook's iOS 14 update; it is put squarely on your shoulders. And when you relieve that uncertainty and restore equilibrium—no matter how hard the battle may have been, how much internal suffering you may have gone through to save the day—all you did was get things back to normal. Saving your startup from imminent demise is a thankless job. And guess what? It should be. Your team is right not to thank you. You haven't done them any favors. You just saved them from the hell you put them in. If they had chosen to work at a big corporation, they would have better job security, but they chose to believe in your vision. And for that, you owe them all the security in the world. So, swallow your pride, stop fishing for compliments, and get back to saving the day.

## LAYOFFS

Your last resort. But if you hired too many too fast because "We need to keep up with our growth curve," this may be your only option. As Felix Dennis says, "Overhead walks on two legs and it will eat you out of house and home." If you have to do this, be extremely matter of fact and don't leave anything up for debate. Don't place any blame or give any false hope of them returning. Simply say, "The decision's been made; we need to let you go." If you feel morally obligated to give a reason, you can add "because" and then say, "I'm an idiot who grew too quickly and forgot the principle that slow is smooth and smooth is fast."

My CFO said we needed a three-person accounting team: him, a bookkeeper, and an accountant. I was shelling out ten grand a month, and they weren't generating any revenue for us. After ad spend, shipping and cost of goods, our margin was 33 percent. That means to pay my accounting team $10,000, I have to sell $30,000 worth of underwear. You have to think like that with every expense. Not how much does it cost, but how much do you have to sell to pay for it? When our sales went from $800,000 per month to $400,000, I realized I needed to get rid of anything that wasn't generating revenue. My CFO would constantly tell me we needed to get our shipping and fulfillment down from 13 percent of revenue to 10 percent, and all these other ideal scenarios.

Well, that wasn't possible at $400,000 in sales, so I cut where I needed to. I cut him, our accountant, and our bookkeeper. I let go of three people who, to any other business, would be vital. People on my team thought I was psychotic to do this, but I didn't need monthly accounting, spending reports, or organized records of vendor payments. I needed to survive.

For more than a year, we had no accounting of any kind, no QuickBooks, and I made every vendor payment myself with a shoddily scraped together cash flow plan. We had debt payments that, if they went unpaid, would result in a hold on our revenue. At any given point, we had less than five grand in our bank account for an entire year with a business that was doing $8 million in sales, because so much was being automatically drawn out! It was insane in every way, but it was vital to keep our company in business.

## WHEN ALL ELSE FAILS, RAISE THE PRICE

If you've watched your costs, and bullied your vendors down with expert negotiation, gotten your CRO, ROAS, AOV, LTV, CAC/CPA and every other acronym in the best possible place, and your margin still isn't high enough to drive your company to astounding profitability, you have one more option...raise your prices. If your company is small, you can try this yourself. If it's bigger, I recommend using an A/B testing app that redirects a percentage of site traffic to different prices depending on your business. Try lower prices too during your test. You may find your ad spend goes down enough to justify this.

## TAKE ON DEBT

Debt should only be used for surefire, smooth expansion. It should not be used to keep your head above water, because you'll just be adding holes to your boat. The only exception is when you can consolidate existing debt you have and make lower payments over a longer period of time. If you're having trouble paying your existing debt, there are companies that can help with this, or you can talk to your creditors. You can get a longer-term SBA loan to pay off your shorter-term loans and make one smaller monthly payment.

One of our advisors says, "Debt is cheaper than equity." When Henry Ford needed to come up with five grand to pay the Dodge bros, he gave them stock. They got insanely wealthy. He should've taken on debt instead of creating future adversaries. However, you'll want to watch out for the flipside. When I met Daniel Hoverman from Texas Capital, he put it this way, "Debt is infinitely dilutive if you can't pay it back." Meaning, it will dilute you down to zero percent if you take on too much debt and go into bankruptcy.

## TAKE ON INVESTMENT

This is a safer route than taking on debt because the risk lies with the investor, but obviously, you're giving up part of your company and possible control. So, again, only do this if the money you raise is not just for survival but is spent to make your company more valuable. You want people who can help you grow. Does your investor know about manufacturing, retail, or international expansion? Cool, it might make sense. Just remember, debt is cheaper than equity in the long run, and an investment is a marriage. It's not like a marriage, it is a marriage. There are legal consequences if you want to break from it. It's more important to negotiate better terms in your term sheet than to get a better percentage or valuation.

## CONCLUSION

This temporary drought may feel like the end of the world. You might feel as if you're in a pit of despair and you can't see yourself saving the day this time. If you ever feel this way, just remember what Russian immigrant-turned-fruit-kingpin, Sam Zemurray, said, "You're never out of options, there's always something to be done." One time, Culprit was out of new stock to launch, we had ads paused due to nonpayment, and everything was bleak. In a flash of necessity, I came up with lifetime memberships. We launched them the next day for $2,000 a pop and made $30,000 that weekend off inventory we didn't even have. Tough times don't last, but tough people do.

# #104

# THE VALUE EQUATION

*"Make offers so good, people feel stupid saying no."*

—ALEX HORMOZI, AUTHOR OF *$100M OFFERS*

To charge more for your product, you need to provide more value to your customer. In Hormozi's book, *$100M Offers*, he explains how people will pay $25,000 for liposuction but won't spend $99 a month on a gym membership. They both have the same dream outcome: a shredded body. However, liposuction wins in the perceived likelihood of achievement. Results are guaranteed. Many who join a gym either don't go enough or eat their way through the results. The time delay for getting that dream bod from a gym is months, whereas liposuction is overnight. The effort and sacrifice to transform your body with weights is excruciating. Liposuction involves taking a medically induced nap and waking up looking sexier. Liposuction's value is astronomically higher than a gym membership. It's not about what's healthier. It's about being able to command a price tag that's an order of magnitude higher.

If you're making an incredible product that is differentiated, has an unfair advantage, and all the other lessons I've drilled into your skull, the last thing you want to do is compete on price. Instead, compete on value. Charge a little more and give much more. Here's what Hormozi's value equation looks like:

$$\frac{\text{Dream Outcome} \times \text{Perceived Likelihood of Achievement}}{\text{Time Delay} \times \text{Effort and Sacrifice}} = \text{VALUE}$$

Other ways to increase value besides simplicity, speed, and a guarantee include scarcity, a time constraint, and bonuses. I had lunch with one of the founders of Kith, and he taught me a valuable lesson: only make 50 percent of what you know you can sell. This guarantees scarcity, and by lowering the supply, you automatically increase the demand and therefore, the value.

Using a combination of time constraints and bonuses, here are some examples of how we've increased value at Culprit. For our seasonal drops, we have a countdown on the landing page. It lets our customers know they only have thirty days to preorder it to guarantee it in their size because we always sell out. Once we launch it, they have thirty days to purchase that drop, or it's gone forever. Often, it's already sold out in several sizes by launch day. Each drop comes with free expedited shipping to decrease the time delay. They also come with a surprise mystery gift. One recent launch featured a paisley print and came with a matching bandana. Our latest release had an adult-themed Valentine's candy print, which came with matching candies.

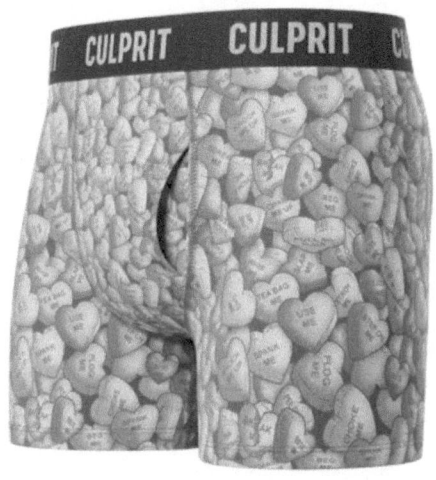

# #105

# INCENTIVIZE

*"Show me the incentives and I'll show you the result."*

—CHARLIE MUNGER

Give your people incentives to do well, and you'll be surprised at the results. Incentives can be anything from profit sharing to private praise, public accolades, to a robust company culture where everyone feels like part of an amazing team that only wants to do the best work. As much as Charlie Munger learned about incentives in his ninety-nine years, it wasn't enough. He said, "I think I've been in the top 5 percent of my age cohort all my life in understanding the power of incentives, and all my life I've underestimated it. And never a year passes but I get some surprise that pushes my limit a little farther." Here's how to incentivize your team.

## SHARE PROFITS

Les Schwab founded his multi-billion-dollar tire empire in 1952 from a single location in a small town in Oregon. His rapid expansion was due mostly to the incentives he gave his staff. While he owned each location, he shared 50 percent of the profits from a given branch with the employees who worked there. He also trained them extensively, resulting in knowledgeable team members committed to the company's success.

This profit-sharing system resulted in employees who worked hard and stayed with the company for the long term. He had low turnover, a more die-hard sales team, superior service, and as a result, a better customer experience. Instead of mercenaries for employees, Les Schwab had a team full of missionaries, speaking fabulously about the company at every chance. They became evangelists for the brand, not just tire salesmen and mechanics. How well did his incentives work? As of 2019, Les Schwab was doing nearly $1.8 billion in annual revenue. Not bad for a humble Oregon tire shop.

## OFFER PRAISE

*"Appreciate everything your associates do for the business. A paycheck and a stock option will buy one kind of loyalty. But all of us like to be told how much somebody appreciates what we do for them. We like to hear it often, and especially when we have done something we're really proud of. Nothing else can quite substitute for a few well-chosen, well-timed, sincere words of praise. They're absolutely free—and worth a fortune."*

—SAM WALTON

Not everyone is incentivized by cash, as illustrated by the founder of *Maxim* magazine, Felix Dennis: "Remember that not all employees respond well to incentive bonuses or a dangled carrot of any kind; they seek recognition, not bribery." Not everyone needs a seven-figure salary, a massive bonus, scrambled dodo eggs for breakfast, and an Uber-copter to work. Some people just need to be treated well, respected, and given their well-earned pat on the back. It's your job to figure out what each person on your team needs in order to achieve greatness. Making someone feel important and recognized for their unique contribution and talent with a few selectively chosen, honest words of praise can be enough.

Just don't praise too liberally or your team's egos will inflate, and they will think they're doing such a great job that they don't need to keep up the hustle. Only give praise when it's truly due. Jim Senegal waited fifty years to get praise from his mentor, Sol Price. That was overkill for sure. Meet somewhere in the middle.

When someone on your team steps up to the plate in an unexpected way, praise them and reward them. But do not give praise when someone does their job as expected. You are not training a dog not to shit on your couch; you are teaching your team to excel.

Don't celebrate every little thing they do; only when they truly excel should you commend your team. It will be more meaningful that way. But when they truly kill it, let them know how you feel. Don't hold back. Find a creative, well-thought-out way to honor your team's great work. And don't you dare throw a pizza party.

Steve Jobs understood this when he had the original Macintosh team sign their names on a piece of paper. He then had their signatures engraved and included inside the mold of each Macintosh case. The public would never know they were there, but the Macintosh team would, taking pride in their work and understanding they had not just made a great product, but a work of art, and as all great works of art, its artists needed to sign it.

## GET TO KNOW YOUR EMPLOYEES

No matter how big your company gets, this will always be true. All the way up from the newest intern to your executive team. People need to feel that what they are doing matters. It's up to you to tell them. It's also up to you to get to know them. This applies especially to your earliest team members. The people who really killed it for you and continue to. Get to know their hobbies, the names of their family members, remember their birthdays, and learn as much about them as you can. Don't try too hard or force it. Actually care. Ask open-ended questions, like, "What was it like growing up in..." to naturally become interested. Unless you moonlight as a method actor, you can't fake being genuinely interested. Ask the right questions.

With that said, inside your company, be vanilla. You are the boss, not the cool boss. Be professional, be gentle, but be firm. You're here to accomplish a goal, and your teammates are not your friends. Being too friendly with your team will make it harder when you have to give them a talking to, break bad news, or even worse, fire them. Remember in lesson #28 when I said to let your professional guard down to foster real relationships with other founders and your peers at other companies? Yeah, do the exact opposite with your team. Never make sexual jokes or innuendos with people who work for you. Don't date anyone who works for you. Plain and simple. It's the fastest route toward destroying your reputation and everything you've worked for. I'm sure there are exceptions on the dating thing, I just don't advocate for them. It's not worth it. What if they're "the one?" Settle for #2, pal. Don't Coldplay yourself.

Having a shared culture puts everyone on the same wavelength. Recommend books to each other, not just books that will help with productivity, business, and achievement, but share fantasy and sci-fi, share TV shows, movies, music. Get everyone thinking like the brand that you're creating. I've set up a Slack channel where everyone in my organization shares the best books, podcasts, shows, movies, quotes, and things they've learned that inspired them. We also share gifs, memes, and music. It makes us a more cohesive unit. I have a separate Slack where I share great copy I come across that I feel fits our brand voice. This allows me to teach the brand voice to anyone who comes on board in the future.

Once people know you care about them beyond the task you've hired them to do, they will be by your side during the inevitable crisis. When you care, they care. They'll help you out when your business goes through a tough spot. When they personally go through a tough spot, help them any way you can. David Senra distilled it down into this gem: "The strong rule the weak, the wise rule the strong, and incentives rule all."

# #106

# MAKE GROUP DECISIONS

*"My idea of a group decision is to look in the mirror."*

—WARREN BUFFETT

By group decisions of course, I mean just the two wolves inside you and no one else 🐺 🐺 ☺.

After concerned employees suggested he have a focus group test the salability of the Cyber Truck before committing to the design and announcing it publicly, Elon simply replied with these five words, "I don't do focus groups." Had he done a focus group, there would've been a convincing argument for a more moderate design, as that's likely what the group would have decided on. When you form a committee, focus group, or, in my opinion, any group larger than three, what you end up with is something everyone sort of agrees on and not a single person is burning with passion about. The Cyber Truck was designed to be radically different. To serve a niche that wants their truck to stand out. It's not a replacement for the Chevy Silverado.

Tesla stock went down 6 percent after the live presentation, revealing what many considered an unseemly trapezoid that belongs on the moon instead of suburbia. But it did get you talking. It did make you feel *something*. When's the last time you felt something as strong, whether love or hate, for a new pickup truck? Nobody was on the fence about it. It was binary, and because of that, it was beautiful. While the stock went down for a couple of days, the preorders climbed to 250,000 in the first week and reached nearly 2 million. I don't know if there's ever been that many preorders for a car, but what I do know is that if you want to stand out and be different, you'll never get there as a big group.

A small team can add to the flavor when designing a product, but ultimately, one benevolent dictator must make the decision. As the old idiom goes, "Too many cooks spoil the broth." And to keep too many cooks out of your kitchen, I shall cement this into your brain right now with a video. Google "Too Many Cooks | Adult Swim," kiss the next eleven minutes of your life goodbye, and thank me later.

This is not to say that all group creations are bad, however. Small groups are fantastic for brainstorming, designing, creating a prototype, planning a marketing campaign, and problem solving. It's great to have a few trusted voices bouncing ideas off each other. The optimal group size for efficiency is from four to seven people. Jeff Bezos calls this "the two-pizza rule." You should never have a creative, decisive meeting if you can't feed the room with two pizzas.

# #107

# THE MOST DANGEROUS FOE

*"Of all their enemies, the cold, the ice, the sea, he feared none more than demoralization."*

—AUTHOR ALFRED LANSING ABOUT ARCTIC EXPLORER, ERNEST SHACKLETON

Poor morale is the worst enemy your company can face, yet panic always comes from the top. If you stay calm and resolute in the face of even the grimmest circumstances, your team will stay cool under pressure. If you maintain supernatural positivity no matter how dire it gets, it will spread from the top throughout your company. You'll be able to face any obstacle and bounce back from any crisis.

In 1940, during the London Blitz, morale was at an all-time low. Though the German bombers were relentless, London's anti-aircraft guns were silent. Soldiers manning the guns couldn't see the planes attacking at night. Churchill made sure the anti-aircraft guns were firing regardless, whenever the Luftwaffe flew overhead, because even if they were just blindly wasting ammo, the appearance of fighting back boosted morale.

He boosted spirits further with a mission to bomb Germany soon after the first attack on London to bring the fight back to the enemy, no matter how ineffectual and costly that first mission was. Churchill knew it was worth it to renew the people's faith in the possibility of victory. He was "undeterred in the face of calamity." When the only news was bad news, Churchill would give a sober appraisal of facts tempered with reasons for optimism, something along the lines of "yeah, they bombed the shit out of us last night, but we'll read books in the bombed-out library and learn how to cream 'em right back across the Rhine river."

Churchill probably didn't say that word for word, but we don't know for sure. We do know he said, "It would be foolish to disguise the gravity of the hour. It would still be more foolish to lose heart and courage."

Londoners checking out books at the Holland House Library after an air raid (probably staged for propaganda, but that's the whole point).

# #108

# HIT THE GROUND RUNNING EVERY DAY

*"A company is never more vulnerable to complacency than when it's at the height of its success. The #1 threat is us. We must not let success breed complacency, cockiness, greediness, laziness, indifference, preoccupation with nonessentials, bureaucracy, or hierarchy."*

—HERB KELLEHER, FOUNDER OF SOUTHWEST AIRLINES

Hit the ground running every day. Especially if you're already successful. If you think you've already made it and let your guard down, bad things happen quickly. UFC fighter Conor McGregor says, "Never go to sleep on a win." If you think for a second, *Damn, we're killing it*, you're about to experience pain. Never take your eye off the ball. If your revenue, valuation, or publicly traded stock is on fire, it can just as easily crash. You might get sued for something you least expect. If your investors just sent you millions of dollars, they might think they now own you. You don't know what fresh hell tomorrow brings.

Not going to sleep on a win does not mean don't enjoy your success. By all means, go out and have a good time. But when you do, don't stop doing the work that made you successful in the first place. And if you do go out and party, make sure you take Rough Night Recovery, so you can wake up fresh the next day and keep your work ethic strong. Yes, that's my new company. I only founded it because I needed it and nothing else was as good. How's that for a shameless plug?

When you do celebrate, pretend all you've won is the semi-final and you still have to practice harder than ever tomorrow for the championship game that is perpetually in the near future. After a game-losing shot, Kobe would practice early the next morning. After a championship game-winning shot, Kobe would be at practice before everyone the next morning. His reaction was the same whether he won or lost. He hit the ground running every day. Win or lose, Kobe always kept his cool like a penguin's penis. If I had a pet penguin, I would name him Kobe. Mark my words, when you meet my pet penguin one day, you won't have to ask his name.

# #109

# LEADERSHIP

*"The role of a leader is to change the status quo, step up the pace, and increase the intensity. Leaders are the energy bunnies and pacemakers of the organization. Some people drain energy from organizations; not leaders, they engulf organizations with energy."*

—FRANK SLOOTMAN, PROMINENT TECH CEO

General Sir Alan Brooke said Patton was, "A dashing, courageous, wild, and unbalanced leader, good for operations requiring thrust and push, but at a loss involving any operation requiring skill and judgement." Patton was luckily the right man for the job in most cases, and his mistakes could be swept under the rug. He struck fear in the hearts of the Germans at the mere mention of his name, but he made several catastrophic mistakes because of...drum roll please...you guessed it...his ego.

As a leader, you must confidently push your team in the fast, hard, energetic thrusts needed to take advantage of opportunities. On the flipside, you need to use your judgment on when to slow down, regroup, and make things smooth. To accomplish these contradictions, you'll need the 3 C's of Leadership.

## COMMUNICATION

Have smooth lines of communication with your team on every level. In the next chapter, you'll learn to break the chain of command. To go around your managers and speak directly to your team on the front lines to get a feel for your situation. Sometimes you just need information directly from the source. Make sure everyone is on the same page so when your plan adapts, your team is up to speed.

This weekend, we were supposed to run a big sale, and everyone on my team knew about it, but nothing happened because no one knew whose job it was to get it done. We didn't have the sale on the calendar. We just talked about it in one meeting and didn't make it actionable. We missed out on tens of thousands of dollars in revenue. I'd love to blame others because it would be better for my ego. But in reality, I'm the one in charge, so I take complete ownership. It's my fault for not giving clear-cut roles and making our conversation actionable. I failed as a leader to have clear communication with my team.

## CONTROL

A leader needs to be in control. No shit, Sherlock, but how do you retain control without being controlling? How do you have a firm grasp on every situation, no matter how bad it is? By not overloading yourself or anyone else. Understand the span of control; one person can't manage everyone. One book on leadership stated that a manager can only effectively manage five or six people at a time. Otherwise, you'll have too many moving pieces. You won't be able to effectively communicate all that's going on, and it will spin out of control. However, Warren Buffett doesn't share this belief. He says, "When you have able managers of high character running businesses about which they are passionate, you can have a dozen or more reporting to you and still have time for an afternoon nap. Conversely, if you have even one person reporting to you who is deceitful, inept, or uninterested, you will find yourself with more than you can handle."

In the time before Slack, both Alexander the Great and Julius Caesar ran massive empires from horseback while fighting multiple hostile tribes because they had effective communication, firm control, and of course the last C.

## CREATIVITY

Probably the most profitable and important tool in your box. However, to use it effectively, you'll need to get outside that box. The biggest cliché in business, folks, here it is: think outside the box. Bet you thought this book was going to be different and wouldn't have that whopper of bullshit in there. Well, it does. Now, here's how you actually do that: When presented with a problem, first spend five minutes thinking *inside* the box. Really get in there. Box your thinking up with only what you currently know, have done, and can solve. Now that you've done your in-the-box thinking, the only way to think of anything else is outside the box. Spend another five minutes thinking as outrageously outside of the box as you can.

Answer these dumb questions: What shouldn't we do? What's the worst way to solve this? What's the most tragically bad solution? What's a really dumb idea? Now that you've broken up the difficulty with some lighthearted idiocy, getting to that brilliant idea will be much easier. In fact, one of those dumb ideas might be the match that sparks the fire of brilliance. Then you can ask smart questions: How can I solve this? Who can help solve this? What's the end result I desire, and how can we work backward to get there? What happens if we invert the problem and look at it from another side? Feel free to get a fresh perspective by bouncing ideas off someone outside your team or an advisor. Just remember, the instructions to thinking outside the box are written on the outside of the box.

One of the best examples I've ever heard of a leader thinking outside the box is when the CEO of a Texas oil company was faced with an existential problem: his oil supply had been cut off. It was 1973, the OPEC oil crisis was in full bloom, and Libya had just cut off its supply to America. Gas stations had lines around the block, and oil companies had free-falling stock. This Texas oilman didn't panic though. Instead, he thought outside the box.

He asked his boardroom, "Alright, Libya won't sell oil to us Christians. Who's the most famous Muslim in America?"

His board replied, "Muhammad Ali."

"Great," he said, "get me a meeting with him tomorrow." His board made excuses as to why that was impossible and crazy. He simply repeated his request in his charming Texas drawl, and the next day, he was on the company jet to meet Ali at a gym in LA.

After sparring, Ali approached the CEO and said, "I heard you want to meet me. Everyone wants to meet me. What makes you special?"

To which he replied, "Muhammad, how much did you make last year boxing?" Ali replied with a number in the multimillions. "Cool, I'll triple it. All you have to do is come with me to Libya."

They flew to Libya, sealed the deal, kept the black gold flowing, and became best friends for life. I saw a photo of Muhammad Ali holding that man's son as a baby. It was the guy who told me the story. Fun fact, Muhammad Ali went to the Middle East again in 1990 to negotiate the release of fifteen American hostages from Saddam Hussein. And again, Muhammad Ali got the job done. If you're having trouble thinking outside of the box, just ask yourself, Who can be my Muhammad Ali?

Muhammad Ali and Saddam Hussein

# #110

# BREAK THE CHAIN OF COMMAND

*"Go as close to the source as possible for information."*

—ELON MUSK

When you're the boss of a large organization, most of your information comes from your managers. You lose perspective. You need to regularly break the chain of command and speak directly to the people actually executing your orders. General Patton was a master of this. He would routinely gauge the morale of his frontline troops. Sometimes he'd go overboard and slap shellshocked men in the hospital for being cowards. But at least he knew what was going on.

Since you're not on the real frontlines, you can do what the founder of UPS, James E. Casey, would. He'd go right up to the people driving his trucks and ask them specific questions. He'd ask:

- What am I doing that you like?
- What am I doing that you don't like?
- What am I not doing that you would like?

This technique let him better understand his team's challenges, gain insights for improvements, and ensure that his company's values were being upheld. Many times the drivers wouldn't even know it was their boss until afterward. This direct intel gave him unique insights that ivory tower CEOs just don't get. Serial entrepreneur Brad Jacobs similarly asks his frontline employees these two questions:

1. "What's your single best idea to improve our company?"
2. "What's the stupidest thing we're doing as a company?"

## SEE FOR YOURSELF

Sam "The Banana Man" Zemurray was a Russian immigrant who started a fruit import business that rivaled the biggest corporation of his day, United Fruit. He routinely broke the chain of command. Instead of being in a Boston skyscraper, riding the elevator down to the street only for lunch, he'd be riding a mule in Honduras, watching over his banana fields. Instead of using a pen and paper in a conference room, he'd be brandishing a machete, cutting through the jungle, and surveying the land himself. He would say about his rivals, "What do they know about what's going on here if they're all the way over there?" United Fruit experts would use their ledgers to make decisions, telling boat captains to sail slower so they'd save money on coal. Sam would be on the docks inspecting each ship instead. He realized that while slower boats saved fuel, it meant more time for bananas to rot. The money saved paled in comparison to the worthless, rotting inventory.

Sam knew how to find the richest soil, buy land from locals, clear fields and jungles, plant bananas, harvest them, transport them, and distribute them. Because he knew every single facet of his business, there wasn't a problem he couldn't solve. He made better decisions because he got his information from the source. United Fruit executives had their info filtered like a drunken game of telephone, hearing from yes men who cared more about not getting fired than giving the hard facts. Instead of using a ledger, Sam the Banana Man used his own eyes.

Later in his career, after a forced merger with United Fruit, Sam became frustrated with how the corporation was being run. Luckily, he had also learned a thing or two about company structure. During a board meeting, after executives ignored his suggestions and made fun of his accent, Sam let them finish their point. He knew every facet of the business better than they did. Then he enacted a hostile takeover and became CEO of United Fruit. Remember Lesson #43; be audacious and never let them make fun of your accent!

Elon Musk doesn't just get information from his managers; he speaks to the engineers and factory workers who are actually doing the designing and manufacturing. He walks the factory floor and sees the work being done. He makes sure he has a clear, unfiltered picture of what's going on so he can make better decisions. Does it sound like more work? It is. But it saves you from disaster and pays long-term dividends. Talk directly with those executing the decisions you made. The farther away you are from the source, the more your information gets filtered. The more powerful you are, the harder it becomes to get a straight answer about a problem. Every founder wants to be revered, but with greater success comes a greater chance of being feared.

If people are scared of being fired, they'll downplay a disaster. Hugo Sperrle, a Luftwaffe commander in World War II during the Battle of Britain, was fearful of Hitler's response to suboptimal results. He overreported British losses and downplayed German losses to such an extent that it skewed reality. The Germans kept up their balls-out daylight attacks, convinced they were winning. Had they gotten accurate information, they could've changed their tactics and switched to nighttime raids earlier. They found out too late that their supposed winning tactics were in fact giving their air force losses they'd never recover from. When they finally figured it out, the Battle of Britain was lost. They would never gain air superiority, and their entire plan to invade the United Kingdom had to be scrapped.

# #111

# BE A DICTATOR

*"Set exorbitant standards and give your people hell when they don't live up to them. There is nothing so demoralizing as a boss who tolerates second-rate work."*

—DAVID OGILVY

David Ogilvy says an organization will not produce a great body of work "Unless it is led by a formidable individual."

A *benevolent* dictatorship is the finest form of government there is. The only issue is that few people who come into power are actually benevolent. And those who are, die after one generation, and either their cokehead son takes over, or there's a coup, and a guy with real lion's heads for shoulder pads is the new dictator, and he sure as shit ain't benevolent. But assuming you are both a good person and an effective leader, for the brief flash in the pan that is your existence, you get to run your very own, successful, benevolent dictatorship.

Why is this form of running your company so great? Because you can move insanely fast. This allowed the Dodge brothers to design, build, and launch their own car in just eighteen months. When an Amazon manager needed approval to build a 300,000 square foot warehouse,

Bezos replied in four words, "You just got it." SpaceX used this system to get a rocket off the ground just four years after its founding. And if you stop asking everyone their opinion and just get on with it, your business will take off too.

Now that you know the best form of government for your company, would you like to know the worst? A committee. Just look at the inefficient shit-show that is America's Congress or Britain's Parliament. As put by hilariously named member of Parliament, Sir Barnett Cocks, "A committee is a cul-de-sac down which ideas are lured and quietly strangled." And as Felix Dennis puts it, "A group chosen by the unfit to do the unnecessary."

Ray Dalio had a different take on company structure. He ran the insanely successful hedge fund, Bridgewater, as an "idea meritocracy." Ideas and the merit of the people sharing those ideas win the day. Sounds like a dream. But if you think he wasn't secretly pulling the strings like a dictator on some level, then you know jack-shit about billionaires.

Being a dictator, however, doesn't mean being a dick. Focus on the benevolent part. Start by taking an active interest in your team, in their lives, know the names of their spouses, know what they're into, their hobbies, and their dream vacations. Know them so well that when their birthdays roll around, you know just what to get them.

> Book Recommendation: *Principles* by Ray Dalio

# #112

# TAKE CARE OF YOUR TEAM

*"Clients do not come first. Employees come first. If you take care of your employees, they will take care of the clients."*

—RICHARD BRANSON

It's hard to admit publicly, but I've failed at this. There have been times when I've had to sell every asset I own to keep my people paid. One of the problems was that I had too many people. Did we need a full-time graphic designer, full-time CGI artist, or full-time product developer? No. Slim down if you have to. Hire only when it hurts not to. Sometimes, unpredictable events happen, and you won't have enough cash to keep every mouth fed.

Do you think if you're late on paying your team or, God forbid, their healthcare plan goes unpaid and gets cancelled, they'll understand? You think they're going to give you a pass if the economy is in the tank, market conditions change, competitors outbid you on your keywords, lenders put a hold on your revenue, or levies get put on your bank account because you're behind on sales tax in thirty-eight states? You think they're going to understand, or care, or be compassionate to the stress you're under?

Not one bit. They're going to think you're an asshole. A deadbeat piece of shit that doesn't pay them on time. Especially when their tropical Zoom-call backgrounds are fake and yours are real. They don't care that you made money before your startup and are currently working for free, investing your entire net worth in the company so they still get paid. They are looking out for themselves and their families. And you have to look out for them.

Be transparent and understand they're going to get really scared if payroll is even a week late. They will also take it personally. To them, it is. You're responsible for *their livelihood*; forget about *your own* when you run a startup. Make sure they get paid even if you have to eat ramen, and I don't mean the fancy kind with a soft-boiled egg and pork belly. I mean the one with dried carrots and chicken flavoring but no actual meat. If you have to sleep in your car to make sure your employees get paid, I hope your seats go all the way down.

# #113

# RISKY BUSINESS AND THE BUSINESS OF RISK

*"The biggest risk of all is not taking one."*
—MELLODY HOBSON, AMERICAN BUSINESSWOMAN

The normal cycle in business: you have a disruptive idea, the idea takes off, the company continues to innovate and becomes a massive success. You bring on investors, a board, maybe sell all or a portion of it, or go public. Now the company is more focused on protecting what it has instead of continuing to make killer products and innovate. It no longer wants to disrupt, it just wants to maintain the status quo.

Herein lies the problem. By protecting what you have, you're more likely to lose market share to someone out there with a nimble arsenal full of energy, guts, and new ideas.

This happened to Apple. They risked everything they had getting set up, selling their most prized possessions. Steve Jobs sold his car, and

Steve Wozniak sold his beloved scientific calculator to build the first Apple I computer.

After taking this initial risk and succeeding, the brand took off and went public within four years. They continued to push the envelope with new products and iconic ad campaigns, but then, after Jobs hired John Sculley, a former Pepsi CEO, the board decided to move into "let's protect what we have" mode. They voted for Sculley to take over as CEO of Apple. In 1985, they kicked out their bold but immature founder, and instead of focusing on their mission of *insanely great products*, their mission became *insanely great profits*. They became risk averse and focused on hiring salespeople over product engineers.

Yvon Chouinard, founder of Patagonia, says, "When I die and go to hell, the devil's gonna make me the marketing director for a cola company. I'd be in charge of trying to sell a product that no one needs, is identical to its competition, and can't be sold on its merits. I'd be competing head-on in the cola wars, on price, distribution, advertising, and promotion, which would indeed be hell for me."

That's what happens when you get a Cola CEO. So, what happened to Apple? They started making everything from scanners to printers that no one needed, and a sprawling, confusing line of computers that looked like this (feel free to skim this): LC, LC II, LC III, LC 475, LC 630, Quadra 605, Quadra 610, Quadra 630, Quadra 650, Quadra 700, Quadra 800, Quadra 840AV, Quadra 900, Quadra 950, Power Macintosh Series, Power Macintosh 4400, Power Macintosh 5200 LC, Power Macintosh 5260, Power Macintosh 5400, Power Macintosh 5500, Power Macintosh 6100, Power Macintosh 7100, Power Macintosh 7200, Power Macintosh 7300, Power Macintosh 7500, Power Macintosh 7600, PowerBook 100, PowerBook 140, PowerBook 145, PowerBook 150, PowerBook 160, PowerBook 165, PowerBook 170 and many more totaling around 350 products.

When Steve Jobs came back to Apple in 1997, he said, "Okay, why would someone want a Quadra 630 instead of a 650, but not a 700? No one could give him a straight answer, so he decided to cut the entire product line down to four products. Not four products with different variations. Just four, that's it. He made a famous graph you may have seen that looks something like this:

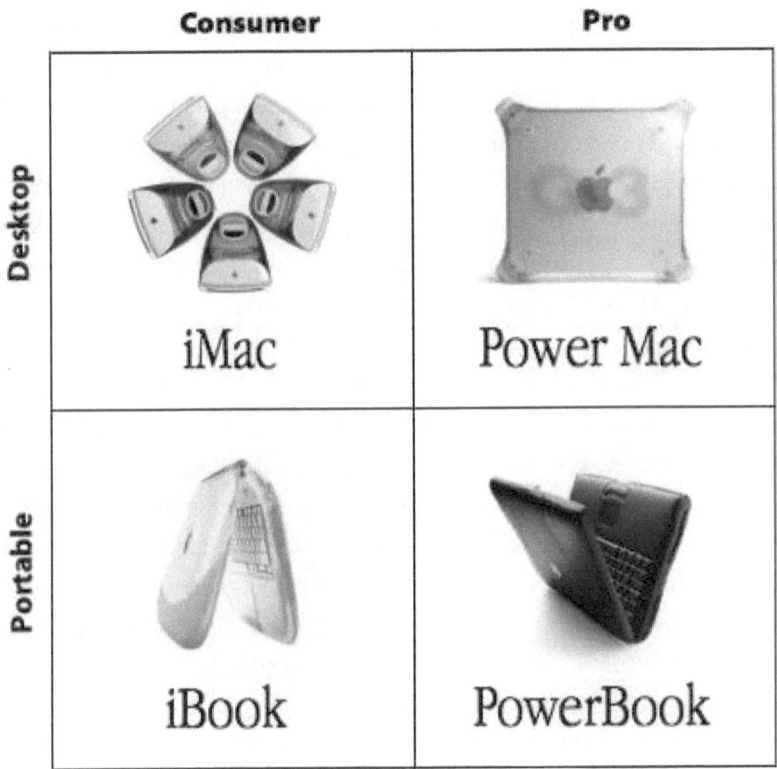

Was it a risky move? Hell yes, it was. Cutting your entire product line with nearly $10 billion in annual revenue is certainly risky. You're risking $10 billion! But in the long run, you're risking so much more by not making this monumental change.

Jobs realized it's better to be profitable at $6 billion in sales than hemorrhage money at $10 billion. Nowadays their product line has expanded a bit but still fits the Pro/Consumer model laid out by Jobs, and it's no longer confusing to be an Apple customer. Their revenue speaks for itself, topping out at $383 billion for 2023.

The mundane can be dangerous. When you're taking a risk, you're focused—you're doing your best work. Adventurers often die doing run-of-the-mill things. Lawrence of Arabia, a British archaeologist and military officer who led the Arab revolt in World War I, faced harrowing combat many times, yet died from a motorcycle accident near his home in England. Steve Irwin, who caught crocs, venomous snakes, and other most dangerous animals on the planet, was killed by a stingray during a routine nature documentary. Brad Gobright, a legendary free-solo climber, didn't die doing what made him famous: doing the most challenging rock climbs in the world alone without a rope or safety equipment. He died descending a well-known path with a safety rope and a partner.

Mistakes often happen in less dangerous situations when your guard is down. If you ever think, "Oh, I can do this with my eyes closed," trust me, keep your eyes fucking open. Sometimes the biggest risk is when you don't think there is one. Companies often die when not taking a risk. These slow, agonizing deaths arise because the executives in these companies don't want to get fired for taking a risk that ends up as a costly mistake. So, companies become set in their ways, afraid of a single bad quarter. Never thinking long term. Seldom investing in innovation while the world around them goes through the inevitable seasons of change. If things aren't working or if your market share is slowly evaporating, take a risk and make a change. Never do nothing.

While writing this today, June 15, 2025, over a year after "finishing" this book, I'm about to take one final roll of the dice with Culprit. We have a crowdfunding campaign on WeFunder nearing $100k, which will take at least thirty days to get us the funds we desperately need to restock our dwindling inventory. It's not soon enough. I can't take on more debt because I've learned to stop digging. I'm out of stocks and crypto, I'm already all in. I have one option. I'm selling my most prized possession: my 1962 Lincoln Continental Convertible.

This is the car in which I wrote the first words of this book. It's all coming full circle. The car that started the journey with me is now giving its last gift to me, a final chance at massive success. That car is like The Giving Tree in a way. I could easily take that money and live a year on it while I figure out the rest. Or invest it in my next venture, which is ready to go. But I've worked too fucking hard and put out too many fires for our candle to flame out into a wisp of smoke. By the time you're reading this, who knows what will have happened. All I know is I'm more focused than ever, and no matter how impossible things may seem, if there's a chance, I'm going to take it. And so should you.

T.S. Eliot said, "This is the way the world ends, not with a bang but a whimper." A business can have a similar fate, but I'd prefer to go out the same way I came into this world...with a bang.

# PART FOUR

# THE AFTERPARTY

# #114

# DON'T LET THE GRIND AFFECT YOUR MIND

*"The time you put in is the single most important, controllable variable determining your future."*

—MICHAEL BLOOMBERG

There are two schools of thought regarding work. Successful people always write about work-life balance and how important it is. Unsuccessful people are obsessed with how hard they grind, how they forgo sleep, how busy their schedules are.

The successful people are wrong. They were once unsuccessful. They forgot what got them there. Now they're in this great place in life where they can set boundaries, have time for family, and enjoy the fruits of their labor. But to get fruit, you need to plant a shit-ton of seeds and toil the soil through all the turmoil. You have to work harder before you get to work smarter. At first, you must work to the point of passing out.

At a certain point though, you do need to protect your brain power.

Warren Buffett is happy if he makes one good decision a year. He spends 80 percent of his time thinking, not working. But he's ninety-five and has been a billionaire longer than you've been alive. Once you build a competent team and master delegation, you can take yourself away from being *in* your business and be *on* your business instead. Make a couple of important decisions a day and be happy with that. Deciding not to do something is as important as moving forward.

You will be more prolific if you get yourself out of the weeds and day-to-day minutiae of your business. But that's impossible in the beginning. Work-life balance should not exist in the first years of your company. As soon as you can, though, hire an operator who can do the daily grind so you can use your mind. A well-trained assistant can also really help you take back your time.

Also remember to *not* work—at least a few times a year. Take a proper break. Be there for your family. Paul Orfalea, the founder of Kinkos, said, "Success in life is after your kids grow up, they still want to hang out with you." But they won't want to hang out with you if you aren't there for them growing up. Be there. If you absolutely, positively have a mission that is so important you must go all in with your time, bring your family in with you. Involve them. Bring them to work. You're the boss. Invite your spouse to work in your company or have them support you however you need. Teach your kids your business.

I'm not saying don't let them do their own thing in life. I'm saying give them experience by working with you, so you don't have to be the absentee parent. No matter how many zeroes you add to your bank account, if you have zeroes in family attendance, you, my friend, are the zero.

This goes not only for hanging out with your family, but also for getting to travel and accomplish your personal dreams. By the time most people retire, they're less mobile. They can't gallivant around the globe like they once could. If you can, take mini-retirements in between projects. Time off is powerful. It can reinvigorate you, inspire you with fresh ideas, and keep you from getting burnt out.

There's no excuse for unplanned laziness, but feel free to take breaks and as many vacations as you can afford. Time spent thinking can be more valuable than time spent working, but only in between savage bursts of work.

No matter how successful you become, however, never be hesitant to jump in and get your hands dirty. It's good to do the hands-on work sometimes so you don't get rusty or complacent, and it can inspire your team to see their leader working in the trenches alongside them. Never be the ivory-tower boss. It's good to do the occasional, serious, all-nighter grind.

# #115

# SAY YES TO NO

*"Learn to say 'no' without explaining yourself."*
—PAULO COELHO, AUTHOR OF *THE ALCHEMIST*

I'd like to introduce you to your new best friend: the word NO. Every other book out there tells you to say yes to everything, open your heart, your mind, your soul to new experiences, people, and ideas. Fuck that. Too much noise, not enough time. Finish reading this book, then stop ingesting so much content and go create something beautiful. Make your default answer no. To everything. You can do this politely, but you must make this a habit. Take back your time one "no" at a time.

Saying no is especially important the more successful you get. When Steve Jobs said, "Focus is saying no," he wasn't talking about saying no to mediocre opportunities or good ideas. He was speaking specifically about saying no to fantastic opportunities and great ideas. Do you know what kind of opportunities would routinely show up on Steve Jobs's desk? Better opportunities than you or I will ever be offered. He said the only right answer back, "Nope."

Default to no. The more your star rises, the more people will come out of the woodwork with "once-in-a-lifetime" opportunities, like, "Bro, you should get into this new NFT." If you magically knew the exact time to buy and sell a Bored Ape, you would've made a lot of money, but watching prices go up and down on things will distract you from what you're put on this Earth to do. I made this mistake. I got into crypto early and made easy money. This rush made me focus valuable time and energy on researching the hottest blockchain companies. Then I was up a lot. Then I lost it all. Then this cycle repeated during the next bull run. Imagine if I spent all that time, energy, and focus achieving actual, long-term success, chasing down my dreams, and living out my purpose. Don't lose billions chasing millions. Lucrative distractions are not lucrative. If you want to dabble in crypto or stocks, have someone else manage it. Your time is better spent. You're here for something bigger.

The same goes for any amazing opportunity you come across that is not your main focus. Don't let the B or C idea take time away from Plan A. James Dyson could make billions licensing his technology, selling his electric motors to other companies, and everything in between, but does he? No. He makes ten billion in revenue each year, sticking to his main business that invigorates him still to this day in his late seventies. He doesn't waste time on anything else, no matter how lucrative. He's an inventor, so he spends his time inventing. Ultimately, no matter how much money he'd make off licensing, for him it's a waste of time. He lets nothing get in the way of his passion.

You have to pick your battles carefully. Every product or business you create will be harder than it looks. It will take more of your time than you realize. There will be unforeseen problems in each new venture. You have sixteen waking hours a day. You can work about twelve of those, but only four will be peak performance. Your hourglass is emptying daily. Focus only on the main thing and say no to everything that is not the reason you were put on this Earth, no matter how quick it might appear to get you rich.

I routinely get offered ad campaigns for major brands in the neighborhood of several hundred thousand dollars a pop. My answer each time: no, thanks. Why? I calculated the time spent on marketing someone else's product with zero ownership. It nets a fraction of what we'd make using the same time to market our own product. Which we own 100 percent of. Instead of making a hundred grand for a month's work, the company I'm building could be worth a hundred million in a few years. Meaning, the time I spend on my own brand instead of someone else's is giving me a 1,000x return.

Frame your decisions like that, and you will be much more successful in the long run. Every hour you invest now compounds later. Every no now is a yes to a happier you later. This applies to your personal time just as much. You may have read *The Power of Now*, but now you know the power of no.

# #116

# DON'T WHITE LABEL

"Bulova Radio Company Rep: 'Our company name is a famous brand name that has taken over fifty years to establish. Nobody has ever heard of your brand name. Why not take advantage of ours?'

"I understood what he was saying, but I had my own view.

"Akio: 'Fifty years ago, your brand name must have been just as unknown as our name is today. I am here with a new product, and I am now taking the first step for the next fifty years of my company. Fifty years from now I promise you that our name will be just as famous as your company name is today.'"

—EXCERPT FROM *MADE IN JAPAN* BY AKIO MORITA

When Akio Morita began making high-quality transistor radios out of a bombed-out building in Tokyo, he had a huge opportunity early on. American company, Bulova, offered to buy his entire stock, only they wanted to put their brand name on it, not Akio's. Akio turned down this massive win in the early days of his company because his goal wasn't to make money; it was to build a globally recognized brand that would single-handedly fix the poor reputation of the phrase "Made in Japan." That brand was *Sony*.

It's easy to get caught up in short-term success, especially when you're struggling, but if anything deviates from your vision, no matter how tempting at the time, you will regret it later. Akio reflected, "I turned down what looked like a chance to make big profits. The buyers thought I was crazy, but even though our company was young and I was inexperienced, time has shown that I made the right decision."

Back when future fashion mogul Ralph Lauren was making strange-looking neckties, Bloomingdale's wanted the whole stock. However, they wanted it to be under their in-house brand. As broke as he was, Ralph didn't want to be the designer for the Bloomingdale's house brand. He wanted to be the designer for Ralph Lauren. As the author, Jeffrey Trachtenberg, puts it, "The way he saw it, if he took off his label, he wouldn't stand for anything."

Always think long term. It's fine to get experience working for someone else if you need to add to your knowledge base, but once you set out on your own path, stay focused. Turn down tempting offers to white label for others. Your day will come, but it will be delayed indefinitely if you say yes to every potential windfall, no matter how much money is at stake. You're not building their brand, you're building yours, and there's more at stake than money.

# #117

# THE OTHER SURE THING

*"There is nothing sure, but Death and Taxes."*
—DANIEL DEFOE, AUTHOR OF *ROBINSON CRUSOE*

Besides death, the only other sure thing...sure is a bitch. Taxes are unfortunately inevitable. Sure, there are some really smart things you can write off. But if you're moving around the globe to avoid taxes, you're just adding stress to your life and essentially taking on a second job. The effort you expend getting around taxes will take you away from doing what you do best, your purpose, what you're put on this Earth to do.

Unless you were put on this Earth to avoid taxes, just pay them and get back to work. Factor taxes into the equation of your big fat payday. If you visualize a certain number you want to have in the bank after you sell or go public, make that number *after taxes* not before.

Or, if you can make your company insanely profitable, why sell it at all? Warren Buffett avoids taxes the smart way: by holding assets long term. James Dyson is keeping his company in his family and not selling it or going public. Can you guess who doesn't have to pay massive taxes? People who hang on to assets. You can borrow against them, and as long as you don't sell them, you don't have a taxable event. You borrow money, the asset goes up in value, you pay the money back, and then you can borrow even more. Rich. People. Hack. Remember when I mentioned Bill Gates would be a trillionaire if he hadn't sold stock and diversified? He'd also have that trillion in net worth without a dime in taxes.

I know founders who sold their companies for millions and didn't want to give half back to Uncle Sam, so they set up a life-insurance trust. They have someone else manage the trust, and they don't pay a cent in taxes. This loophole is currently legal, but is it ethical? Avoiding taxes is more trouble than it's worth and can result in real trouble. Even if it's currently legal. What if you find out the person you put in charge of your trust is untrustworthy or bad with money? What if the law changes? What if, because the IRS knows you're doing this, they decide to audit you every year?

There was another *legal* tax loophole in England that an athlete took advantage of. When they changed the law and found him in violation, he was denied knighthood. There are so many what-ifs when you try to avoid paying your fair share. Just get a killer accountant who knows what smart things you can write off, let them do their job, and you do yours.

Tax havens are another big draw for people, but usually way more trouble than they're worth. Do you really love the vibe in Monaco or Dubai? You really want to spend six months in Puerto Rico when everyone you know, especially your family, isn't there? What are you really trading? Is the tax haven crew sipping spicy margs on the beach for 180 days your kind of people? If you're about to have your one and only exit for all cash, maybe it's worth it, but it's still three to five years of living like you don't want to for 30 or 40 percent more money. Is that worth your and your family's time? Tax is predictable. Time is not.

If this is your one and only shot at making real money in your whole life, maybe. If you're a one-trick pony and you want to go through the hassle, stress, and time consumption, be my guest. But you could just put that same effort into your next venture and make even more money.

# #118

# KEEP THE CHAMPAGNE ON ICE

*"Don't sell the skin before you've shot the bear."*

—DUTCH SAYING

Celebrating too early is hilariously common in running.

Not *prematurely popping the champagne* has become my only superstition. It's a fact that superstitious people have *worse luck* than the non-superstitious; however, when it comes to popping the champagne too early, take a page out of my book and listen.

Keep the champagne on ice until the check clears and you've moved the money to a different account. If you're launching a product and it goes well, keep the champagne on ice until the thirty-day return policy has passed.

Keep that champagne on ice until your rocket has returned to Earth. Or in the case of SpaceX, don't prematurely build an ice luge to take shots from at the post-launch-success party. Which they did. Right before their third rocket exploded. The final one, they had money for. It nearly brought the company crashing down with the rocket. What did blow up with the rocket was Scotty from Star Trek's ashes, which were supposed to go into space. As the ice luge sat there melting in the silence of a $10 million explosion, the reality for Elon was, as Eric Berger puts it in his book, *Liftoff*, "He'd tried to change the world, and the world resisted." So yeah, definitely don't pop any bottles. Just keep them chilling until you're chilling in orbit.

David and I always wanted to make a movie. We knew no one was going to give us millions of dollars to make one until we had proved ourselves. So, we became hellbent on making the most cinematic commercials possible. We weren't a household name, but we grew our fledgling production company to where every big agency had heard of us. Like many other young visionaries—and future criminals, such as Martin Shkreli, Sam Bankman-Fried, and Elizabeth Holmes—we were honored by Forbes on their annual 30 Under 30 list.

This accolade gave us validation. Now, instead of having to fight tooth and nail for big accounts, they came to us. We did a global campaign for Starbucks, launched Stories for Instagram, and made the video for the largest digital billboard in America in Times Square for Beats by Dre.

We were at the pinnacle of marketing, so we decided to leave the industry once and for all and make our dream a reality: we would make a movie.

This was 2015, when social media stars were supposed to be the next movie stars. Digital stars were on magazine covers, Vine was the #1 app, and people thought Logan Paul was going to be the next "Rock." Having done countless ads featuring these "superstars of social," we became friends. Their managers had reached out, wanting to get their small-screen talent on the big screen, suggesting two or three of them for some low-budget horror-comedy that takes place somewhere easy to shoot, like a house.

I had just rewatched the 80s comedy *Airplane!* and had an idea. What if instead of putting two or three of these future megastars in a movie, we put in ALL OF THEM? And instead of a lame faux-horror movie in a house, we had them playing themselves on the same doomed flight á la *Airplane*. Inspired by *Airplane!*, the pilots die, and one of them takes over the controls to save the day.

This was a perfect plan. Everyone wanted in. We got the twenty-five biggest social stars of the day, with a combined following of 600 million, to act in the film and guarantee three social posts each on their biggest platforms and promote the hell out of the movie. We went on a financing tour meeting with forty agencies, studios, production companies, and distributors. We didn't get a single no. Literally all forty said yes. It was an unheard-of success.

However, they were adamant, we had to come in at a $1 million budget, and it had to be PG-13. We knew cult-classic comedies were all R-rated, and making a movie on an airplane, we needed more than a measly million. We stuck to our guns. We said, "Give us $2 million, and it's gotta be R-rated." *All forty said no.*

One unfruitful year later, and I find myself on a date. A few drinks in, I tell her what I'm up to and she says, "Oh, cool! My dad used to make straight-to-video National Lampoon movies back in the '90s. But he lost all his money on the last one he made, so he'll never do movies again."

I said, "Set a meeting with your dad tomorrow."

I met him, and he was extremely skeptical, but we put together a compilation of Logan Paul's best videos, our best work, and a few scenes we had written. He showed it to his *much younger* girlfriend and said to us, "She hates your idea…but she's an opposite indicator. Everything she likes sucks, so I'm in."

He gets us an extremely short thirty-second meeting with a billionaire as he's getting off his private plane at the airport. In those thirty seconds, we closed the rest of the financing.

We got everything signed from the investors, but getting twenty-five contracts signed from influencers was like herding really vain cats. We had backups for each, so if one wanted more money than *scale*—the lowest rate you can legally pay an actor, and all we could afford—we told them we would just hire whoever happened to be their biggest rival. This third-grade strategy of mixing tactical jealousy with FOMO got 'em all off the fence. We were in business.

We had written a really stupid, but funny script. After everything was signed, our producer told us we simply didn't have the budget for it. Most directors' first films are realistic to the budget and take place in one location. Speaking roles are limited because actors with lines get paid extra. This is why in many movies, the waiter won't speak when taking an order. You're also supposed to avoid budget and time killers like stunts, choreographed fight scenes, working with animals, and babies. Our script had ninety-eight speaking roles, massive stunts, choreographed fight scenes with wire work, a llama on a plane, and a baby as a major character. He bluntly told us, "There's no way you can do this film for $2 million."

So, we reached out to every company we'd ever worked for and said, "Hey, we have all these social stars, we're making this massive movie, and you can pay us to feature your products." We pitched our asses off and got another $500,000. It still wasn't nearly enough for all the stunts. So we bet on ourselves and put in the only money we had, $50,000 from making commercials.

Betting Our Life Savings: April 2016

Having never made a movie, we were so sure of ourselves, we knew we had a solution. Instead of shooting this over two months, like sane people, we would get it all done in fifteen days. That was all we could afford. It was psychotic, but it was either water down your vision, delay your dream indefinitely, or do something impossible. We chose the latter.

For those three weeks, I worked harder than ever. When we were running out of light and needed to get every missing shot for the day, I'd take matters into my own hands. I ignored people telling me the director wasn't allowed to touch lighting equipment. They were moving too slow. I went against union regulations and tossed sandbags and equipment out of the room like a man possessed.

In filmmaking, I always say, only one thing matters: what you get in the frame. Rules or people's feelings come second to the result. If you follow the rules and your movie sucks, no one remembers your good manners; in fact, everyone blames you. If you disregard everything and the movie is a success, all is forgiven. If everything is on the line, you need to grab the reins and see your vision through. As they say, "the mark of a successful person is how many times they've said, fuck it, I'll do it myself."

We had shot a killer movie. We made one crucial mistake though, we hadn't read *this book*. We didn't know the "A-players rule" and hired an editor based on a recommendation without properly vetting them. This editor's dad had done Oscar-winning movies. We hired his son. The apple fell so far from the tree that it fermented. And after weeks of editing, we thought, *Oh fuck, maybe the movie we spent two years making was terrible.* Self-doubt crept in. Then we edited some scenes ourselves and realized, wait, the movie is hilarious, the editor is useless. He would edit the worst scene imaginable and then laugh out loud the whole time like he was editing *Blazing Saddles*. It was disorienting.

We found a new editor but ran out of money and could no longer afford the studio. Not only had we put in every dime of our own money, which had not been paid back, but we also never got our director's fees. We wrote the movie, raised the financing, put our only money in, shot the hell out of it, and didn't make a dime. But that was okay, because we owned half of it and were about to make millions.

We moved the edit bay to the editor's house. We came over and edited every day for six months. There was a moment when our editor got impatient and tried to rush finishing it. I had to have a come-to-Jesus moment with him. Logan and David were with me for moral support. We were in his kitchen with his wife. This was a fifty-five-year-old man. I was twenty-nine. I had to berate him in front of his wife in his own kitchen. David and Logan felt so awkward that they had to leave the room. It was as uncomfortable as it gets, but the point was made. We would press on and take no shortcuts.

The movie was hilarious. A cult classic, ready to be blown up on the internet by its twenty-five stars. We sold it to YouTube originals for $4 million for a six-month exclusive. Then we'd put it on iTunes and sell it to Netflix. The movie was set to make $10 million. The ink was dry on the contract. So, we did the obvious. *We popped the champagne.* David and I bought a house in the hills and a 1997 Ferrari F355. Then, for New Year's, we went to celebrate in Thailand. Our movie was coming out in two weeks! We were on top of the world. Nothing could stop us.

Then the text message came through. "What did Logan Paul do?" It turns out that while we were celebrating, Logan was exploring the suicide forest in Japan with a Vlog camera. Well, he found what he was looking for—a dead body—and after posting that now infamous video, the entire world turned on him. We called YouTube to find out about our movie. "We're still good, right?" "No, we're not good. Your lead actor uploaded a dead body to our platform."

We never got paid, and our movie we'd now spent three full (never get that time back) years of our life on, wasn't coming out. We had quit marketing. I even told David one day, "So happy we never have to do marketing ever again." We found ourselves with no money from the movie, no job, no prospects, no $30,000 director fee, and missing the only money we had in the world, which we would never see again. Except it was way worse now because we had a house and a Ferrari we couldn't pay for. It was like we won the lottery, spent the money, then *lost the ticket.* We swallowed our pride and called up everyone we'd ever worked for to avoid losing our house and having the repo man come pick up our car.

We said, "Hey, we're booked solid the next few months on a shoot, but if you want to do an ad for your brand, we're free the next couple of weeks only and can give you a 20 percent discount." We were relentless. As soon as we closed one client, we'd call another. No celebrations in between. We had our best month ever, saved our house, and booked a Mercedes Super Bowl Commercial. Sometimes it's good to whore yourself out.

We had popped the champagne prematurely and had to work our fingers to the bone to put that cork back in. Our movie was eventually re-edited, made more "appropriate", and way less funny. It was watered down, and no social stars wanted to push the project. Still to this day, I've never watched it. But our hilarious director's cut still exists, somewhere in our investor's possession. We also had a film crew with us every day, and it might be the funniest behind-the-scenes footage ever, which we'll probably never see.

The same Hollywood execs who told us we were geniuses when we first put the project together now said, "How could you?" when we had future meetings. It was a disaster.

**The other side of the coin:** Jack Nicholson said, "Don't make the mistake of not celebrating success because it comes around so rarely." Just don't do it too fucking early. Okay? Make sure the success is real, tangible, and there to stay before you tear the foil on that Dom Perignon.

# #119

# EXIT STRATEGY

*"I detest the term 'exit strategy' when I hear young entrepreneurs bragging about theirs. As if a business is something one builds and casts off."*

—JOE COULOMBE, FOUNDER OF TRADER JOE'S

If you're purely doing this for the love of what you're doing, then you never need to sell! If this is your life's work, keep your company. Many founders have regretted selling. If your business is profitable and you own a majority, you can take money out whenever you please. If your business isn't profitable, make it profitable!

Always remember, 90 percent of your business's revenue lies in the future. However, if you want to do something else in life, and you want that big, generational wealth liquidity event, you have four options.

## SELL THE WHOLE THING ALL AT ONCE

*"Tomorrow when I wake up, I'm an employee."*

—PAUL ENGLISH, AFTER SELLING KAYAK, NETTING $120 MILLION, AND CONTINUING TO WORK THERE

When should you sell? As Felix Denis says, "When there's still blue in the sky... Try to sell before you have to. You're an entrepreneur. Your companies are not your 'babies,' they are tools for acquiring wealth. Try to sell them before they peak. Buyers require what is called 'blue sky' (further growth) to get excited and offer a great price."

## SELL BETWEEN 20–50 PERCENT TO PRIVATE EQUITY

Do this once you hit a number that has enough zeroes that you feel good but not necessarily great about. Take some chips off the table. Buy yourself something nice and get your mom that apartment in Paris she's always wanted. Fly private whenever you want, like you're Taylor Swift. But don't you dare buy a plane or boat...yet.

Then get back into founder mode, to the earliest days of your hunger, build the hell out of your business, add a zero over the next three to five years, and sell the rest. But remember to keep some blue in the sky.

## GO PUBLIC!

*"1987, the one year we were a public company, was our least creative year. We spent 50 percent of our time getting approvals when we should've just been getting on with it."*

—RICHARD BRANSON

Screw blue in the sky. You're here for the biggest payday imaginable. But don't underestimate the bullshit that comes with running a public company. You don't get to ride off into the sunset yet, cowgirl. You belong to the CORP now. And now you have to deal with rogue waves thrown at you from the freaky force of Mother Nature called The Economy. Welcome to Stress-town, population: YOU. You rich sonovabitch! I'm jealous.

Yeah, you're still the biggest shareholder, but you are now a public figure. You are the tall grass that will get mowed. When Home Depot went public, they lost anonymity. Suddenly everyone knew how much money they were making and started trying to clone their business.

In addition to giving up more control and adding more cooks to your kitchen, you now have a target on your back.

When Sam Walton took Walmart public, however, it was a Godsend. He was stressed, up to his eyeballs in debt, and then suddenly with his IPO, he had the cash to buy up competitors' entire retail chains and convert them into Walmarts to expedite growth.

## I'M NOT LEAVING!

I'm keeping this till I die, so my unmotivated kids can run it into the ground and besmirch my legacy! This is the most noble of the four options. Only do this if this is YOUR LIFE'S WORK.

If you have other fish to fry, go ahead, sell your catch, and cast another rod in the river. However, if this is your best idea, do not sell it, or you will regret it. *Never sell your best idea.*

Notable examples of this approach who own 100 percent of their multibillion-dollar empires include James Dyson, Gustav Glock, and Sara Blakely, founder of Spanx. Red Bull is also still a private company, and the founders and their families make hundreds of millions per year. Every year. Now to help you decide, here are some founders who sold their life's work:

Paul van Doren, the founder of Vans, has said, "The acquisition marked an end of my leadership of Vans. As chairman, I continued to preside over board meetings, but found more and more often that, no matter the topic, the board rarely decided to go my way. Was it tough for me to walk away from a leadership position at the company I founded? There's no denying it."

Joe Coulombe, founder of Trader Joe's, sold his life's work because of the threat of interspousal death taxes. Under President Carter, a new capital gains tax increase from 33 percent to 73 percent threatened his family's livelihood, and he worried that if he died, his leaderless company would have to be sold, and his family's well-being would be threatened. He was scared and decided to sell for his family's welfare even though it went against every fiber in his being, saying, "I wish I had the courage to just go with it. I knew I loved what I did, but I was scared."

He continued, "Do I regret having sold? Yes, I admit it. To my own self, I was not true when I sold. I regret not having the guts to ride out the loss of the tax exemptions, the employee ownership problem, the threat of death taxes, Carter's threat to eliminate capital gains preferences, and all of the other fears, real or phantom, in late 1978. I have to admit the truth that I regret having sold Trader Joe's. And I've had to pay something for this beyond the loss of my shadow."

There's no one-size-fits-all answer here. Listen to your gut and pick the exit strategy that's right for you. Even if that's death.

# #120

# TAKE THE STOCK

*"How many millionaires do you know who have become wealthy by investing in savings accounts? I rest my case."*

—ROBERT G. ALLEN, BUSINESS AUTHOR

Whenever Rockefeller bought up a competitor, he said, "You can have cash or take the stock." If you decide to sell your company to a competitor, I recommend that you take the stock. Most people were too proud to get forcefully bought out of their life's work and took the cash. They died poor. Don't be too proud. Everyone who took the stock from Rockefeller—and didn't sell it the first time it went up—became a millionaire many times over back when that meant something.

When Instagram sold for a billion dollars in 2012, it was a big deal. An internet app was suddenly worth more than *The New York Times*. It was an insane prospect. But when WhatsApp was sold for $19 billion just two years later, you may have thought to yourself, *Oh wow, it was dumb to sell so early*. But was it? They didn't just get cash, they got Facebook stock. Think about where that stock is now. If you decide to sell your company to a publicly traded company, think about where the stock might be in a decade before you decide to cash out. Also, remember that cashing out equals taxes.

# #121

# THE UNUSUAL HAPPENS, USUALLY

*"Nothing sedates rationality like large doses of effortless money. After a heady experience of that kind, normally sensible people drift into behavior akin to that of Cinderella at the ball. They know that overstaying the festivities, that is continuing to speculate in companies that have gigantic valuations relative to the cash they are likely to generate in the future will eventually bring on pumpkins and mice, but they nevertheless hate to miss a single minute of what is one hell of a party. Therefore, the giddy participants all plan to leave just seconds before midnight. There's a problem though, they're dancing in a room in which clocks have no hands."*

—WARREN BUFFETT

In Nassim Taleb's 2007 book, *The Black Swan*, he outlines what he terms a *black swan event*. It's when something extremely unpredictable and rare happens, especially in a global market. Pretty wild that his book came out a year before one of the most massive black swan events many of us have lived through, 2008's great recession.

Several years prior, the dot-com bubble burst. Who could've predicted that? Well, one of my mentors, sports management mogul Marc Roberts, saw it coming. How? Because his mailman was telling him which internet stocks to buy and bragging about how in a few more months he'd be so rich, he'd no longer be Marc's mailman. Well, the bubble burst. Lo and behold, he was still Marc's mailman. Marc knew not to get into it simply because too many people were making money off something they didn't understand. It made no sense. What did his mailman know about internet stocks? Here he was trying to advise *him*. I similarly knew it was time to sell my crypto when Uber drivers were telling me which alt coins to buy. It soon crashed. When everyone gets greedy and the market is only moving up, there's only one other place it can go: the floor. Remember COVID? No one saw that coming except for a few stock-trading senators.

Hetty Green, one of the richest women to ever live, was known as "The Witch of Wall Street" for a reason. She could seemingly predict booms and busts. But could she really predict them? No. She just sat on cash because she knew that, as she put it, "The unusual happens, usually." You cannot exactly predict the top of a bull market or the bottom of a bear market, but you can predict that it will happen. You can always know the crash is coming, even if you're off by a couple of years. She became so rich that in 1907, she single-handedly saved New York City from financial ruin.

This doesn't just happen in the stock market though; there will similarly be booms and busts in your business. Keeping your team small, your office minimalist, your margins high, and your expenses in check will let you ride out any black swan event. Warren Buffett lives by his mantra, "It's better to be fearful when everyone is greedy and greedy when everyone is fearful." If you followed my earlier advice to sit on cash, you'll be ready when the economy's trap door suddenly opens. You'll have cash to buy assets you know are going to go back up. Similarly, when things seem too good, you'll know they'll soon be too good to be true and that it's time to start converting assets back to cash.

It's highly unusual for these black swan events to happen, but it's more unusual for them to never happen. They will always happen. Markets will shift against everyone except you. Because you know it's coming…eventually. And you're prepared.

# #122

# GET LUCKY

*"I am a great believer in luck, and I find the harder I work, the more I have of it."*
—THOMAS JEFFERSON

We've all heard the more work you put in, the luckier you get. Well, some of it is just straight-up random chance. Let's use Steve Jobs as an example. If he doesn't get kicked out of Apple, he doesn't learn what he needs to mature as an entrepreneur. If George Lucas didn't happen to be getting a divorce at the time, Jobs couldn't have affordably bought Pixar. In 1997, Jony Ive was about to leave Apple when Steve Jobs came back. If Jobs had come back a couple of months later, he would've never met Ive. Without that meeting, Apple's renaissance isn't the same.

In my own story, if I hadn't met my future business partner on the first day of college, I wouldn't have accomplished 1/10th—correction, 1/100th—of what I have. And neither would he. If I hadn't found David Senra's podcast, this book would never exist.

So yes, there's a certain amount of real luck involved. But it's generated by exposing yourself to new ideas and meeting new, inspiring people who will change your life. It's you putting in the blood and sweat to be ready for each opportunity. It's you picking up books like this, so you know when to say yes and take a terrifying leap of faith, and when to say no and turn down a multimillion-dollar opportunity. It's you having the wisdom on how to spend your time. It's you knowing it's a long game and to never despair because there's always something to be done. The more doors you open, the faster the right opportunity will present itself. Increase your surface area for luck.

If you're stuck in a rut, a dead-end job, or an awful situation, whether financial or personal, remember that one thing leads to another. One phone call or cold email could change everything. Reach out to your peers, reach out to the people you want to meet in your industry. Make friends with them. Attend the events the people you want to meet will be at. Going to the right dinner or cocktail party can be the first step to a new life. But remember *good input leads to good output*. You'll have better chance encounters hanging out with successful friends and new acquaintances than you will at a nightclub.

> **HACK:** Those who keep in contact with more old friends and meet more new acquaintances have better luck. Follow up with new and old friends regularly. If you suck at following up, put it in your calendar. A trick I use is whenever someone pops into my mind, I give them a call and catch up. Even the most introverted can talk to their old friends.

Some people think they're unlucky and complain they never win anything. The people who are lucky and win contests are simply the people who enter more contests. The more chances you take and the more you visualize yourself achieving the win, the more likely you are to get lucky.

> Book Recommendation: *The Luck Factor* by Dr. Richard Wiseman

# #123

# THE ART OF THE PIVOT

*"And those who urge entrepreneurs to never give up? Charlatans. Sometimes you have to give up. Sometimes knowing when to give up, when to try something else, is genius. Giving up doesn't mean stopping. Don't ever stop."*

—PHIL KNIGHT, FOUNDER OF NIKE

Should you ever consider quitting? Yes. Not on your mission as a whole, but on whatever isn't working. I gave up on swimwear. Microsoft gave up on their Zune because it couldn't compete with the iPod. SpaceX gave up on parachutes for booster retrieval. Google gave up on their Facebook competitor, Google+, their smart glasses, Google Glass, and they got rid of Google domains, and thousands of other things that weren't working. They have an entire experimental department devoted to trying new things, which most likely will not work. Figure out if what you're doing will have a big enough market and make sure you have product-market fit as fast as possible. If not, it's time to pivot.

When Honda launched the Super Cub motorcycle, they had a problem. People who rode bikes didn't want that dinky thing. They wanted a Harley. Driving through the hilly streets of San Francisco, a Honda engineer was stopped by locals who were amazed at how the Super Cub could navigate the steep inclines. This led to an idea. They pivoted their strategy and instead of going after motorcycle enthusiasts, they rebranded motorcycles entirely and went after a much broader market. Their campaign "You Meet The Nicest People on a Honda," was a smash success, and they made motorcycles mass market.

One of the best pivots in tech began when makers of a video game called *Glitch* realized their game wasn't commercially viable. They had, however, built an insanely effective internal communication tool so the team could collaborate while working remotely from different cities. They decided to launch that instead. I use it every day. It's called Slack.

# #124

# YOU DON'T DESERVE IT

*"I feel like I've stolen a really nice car and I keep looking in the rear-view mirror for flashing lights."*

—ANTHONY BOURDAIN

Bourdain's infamous words on success strike a chord. Imposter syndrome is real. You might feel like you don't deserve the success you either already have or will soon achieve. We all feel that way. It's weird to become suddenly more successful than your friends, colleagues, or peers, but remember, you've fought for every square inch of territory. You deserve it, no matter how opposing your feelings may be. You've fucking earned it. Here's how to get rid of imposter syndrome: outwork everyone else, and it will go away.

This is why I don't currently have imposter syndrome. The sheer number of hours, psychotic levels of stress, and personal sacrifice I've endured make me feel like I've earned it. In fact, I feel like I've earned the next ten levels up already, and I'm just waiting for those success bonds to mature. But if there's anything to know, it's that success isn't a waiting game, it's an accomplishing game. So, I'm going to stop my writing session for today and get back to work. Keeping that imposter syndrome at bay. And when your next venture is successful, you can pat yourself on the back—you earned it. Just don't go to sleep on that win.

## THE OPPOSITE OF IMPOSTER SYNDROME?

When asked by *GQ* if he felt like a freak growing up, Tom Ford replied, "I thought I was fabulous and everyone else was stupid." Instead of Imposter Syndrome, it's healthier to have Tom-Ford syndrome. To take it one step further, on a Reddit thread that asked what's the best non-sexual sensation one can feel, user r/invasionbarbare said, "The feeling of sheer ecstasy and invincibility after successfully achieving something you've put your heart, soul, and uncountable hours into. Suddenly the dots connect—you now know you took the right forks in the road—those random moments were not by chance at all—but carefully orchestrated by a universe that conspired to put a crown on your head."

# #125

# REMEMBER THE HARD TIMES

*"What helps me is to keep the hard times in the front of my mind because it allows me to go into these big moments that I worked my ass off for...with a different perspective."*

—DWAYNE "THE ROCK" JOHNSON

Whenever any big milestone happens, such as a major movie premiere, Dwayne "The Rock" Johnson always reminds himself where he came from and the hard times he had to endure to get to this celebratory moment. It allows him to be present and remember this is the stuff he dreamed of in the past. He reminds himself that he was evicted at fourteen, had no place to live, and was arrested several times by the age of sixteen. He had his dreams of professional football crushed. He was playing for a Canadian team, making $250 per week. Then he got cut from that shitty team and had seven dollars in his pocket. He named his production company Seven Bucks to remind himself where he came from. He keeps the hard times in the front of his mind in order to go into these milestone moments with perspective instead of sniffing his own farts. It also keeps him driven to keep on accomplishing as if his back is up against the wall, even though he's already "made it."

Sony founder, Akio Morita, started his future empire out of a bombed-out Tokyo department store where they had to use umbrellas over their desks when it rained. In 1947, while creating their first tape recorder, Akio needed a way to make his magnetic recording tape because this was cutting-edge technology in war-torn Japan. Everything was scarce. Beer was strictly black market. No one had enough rice. How are you going to make professional recording tape? Well, you get magnetic material, grind it into powder, cook it yourself in a borrowed frying pan, and apply it to the tape with a paintbrush made from "the soft hairs of a raccoon's belly," duh. You read that right. The founder of Sony was cooking his own chemicals in a borrowed frying pan, and applying it to the tape himself, by hand, with a raccoon-belly paintbrush.

For me? I don't need to remember the hard times. I'm still in 'em. I'm no longer living with three dudes in a crummy two-bedroom apartment on Hollywood Blvd., running a production company from my couch, which doubles as my partner's bed, but I am on the struggle bus every day to keep my team paid and my business alive.

If you're already successful, pause reading for a moment, and reflect on one of the hardest moments you thought you'd never recover from. Now use that as fuel and get back to work. You lazy bastard.

# #126

# SEND THE ELEVATOR BACK DOWN

*"A candle loses nothing by lighting another candle."*
—JAYSON GAIGNARD, AUTHOR OF *MASTERMIND DINNERS*

Go out of your way to bring up those less successful than you, inspiring the uninspired, and enriching the lives of everyone you meet. Many entrepreneurs are stingy with their knowledge until they're living on borrowed time. Whether they're old or terminally ill, some of the most successful people wait until their light is fading to share their knowledge and wisdom.

I know for a fact that no matter what I share here, you won't make better undies than me, so I have nothing to fear. Neither should you. Once you break the code of success, it's your duty to share your knowledge. That's how we as a species get to be smarter—and cooler—than all others. We might not have as much carefree fun as elephants playing at a waterhole or dolphins passing around a puffer fish to get high, but neither of those mofos invented jet packs, the 63-corvette split window, SR-71 Blackbird, or skydived to Earth from space like Joe Kittinger. So help a homie of your species out and teach 'em a thing or two.

Without Chuck Silvers, we don't have Spielberg. Without Larry Ellison, how far does Elon get? Without Edwin Land, where does that leave Steve Jobs? Without Sol Price, Home Depot and Costco do not exist. Without Edison, does Henry Ford have the will to create the modern age as we know it? Where is the human race without mentorship or, before that, apprenticeship? Do we get to have Ben Franklin? Probably not. If you don't send the elevator back down, the next generation has to take the stairs.

Want to help bridge the widening gap between the rich and poor? The best way is to take yourself from poor to rich. Then, send the elevator back down for the next poor bastard, and show 'em how it's done. We will not fix the rich/poor gap through higher taxes on the rich. The wealthy will just move to tax havens. The best way to lessen this gap is for more people to read this book so I can become rich, and my riches can trickle down Reagan-style. Just kidding. It's for more people to start their own businesses. The founding of new companies is at a forty-year low. It's up to you to fix that. Teach your team everything you know so they can become great in their own right. And if they want to start their own company one day, support them. The world needs it. Otherwise, the economy will devour your children.

# #127

# NOVICE VS. MASTER

*"Learning is not memorizing information, learning is changing your behavior."*
—DAVID SENRA

I didn't write this book for fun. I wrote it because I was pissed off and I didn't want anyone else to go through the suffering I endured. I wrote it so you could save ten years of your life and avoid my countless mistakes while soaking up the lessons of history's wisest entrepreneurs. I've done my best to write it in a fun, memorable way so that if you're hearing it for the first time, it sticks with you, and if you're hearing it for the hundredth time, it's still entertaining.

When a novice hears something they already know, they say, "I already know that." When a master hears it, they say, "Thank you for the reminder." You might already know more than half the wisdom in this book, congrats! Pat yourself on the back. However, it doesn't mean you've internalized each lesson. In fact, it doesn't mean anything. If it's familiar material, consider it a refresher course. I still haven't internalized each lesson, and I'm the fool writing it. It's not a waste of time to remind yourself of important things you already know. Repetition is key to learning. My grandmother said, "It takes varied iterations to force alien concepts on reluctant minds." Flex the muscles in your mind by reminding yourself. Learning once isn't learning if you aren't putting it into practice on a daily basis.

In Malcolm Gladwell's *The Tipping Point*, he mentions the "'Blue's Clues' Approach." If you're my age or older, you might remember this as your annoying sibling's favorite show. It was unique because it played the same episode on repeat every day for a week before moving on to a new episode. This had never been done before, as most children's shows aired new episodes daily or weekly. Here's why this show's approach was so novel.

Children learn through reinforcement and seemingly mindless repetition. By watching the same episode several times in a row, kids absorbed the lessons more effectively. They'd pick up on what they missed during the first viewing and reinforce what they already learned. Experts thought this approach was stupid and the show would fail, but the repetition was a valuable tool, and kids ate it up because most little kids are smarter than most experts. Studies showed the kids who watched Blues Clues had improved problem-solving skills, and the show's counterintuitive approach made it a massive hit. The network made more money too, because they got paid to run ads five times for the same episode.

As a fully developed adult, there's no way you'd watch the same inane bullshit five times in a row unless you're rewatching The Office as a coping mechanism. Reinforcement learning works no matter what age you are. It's one thing to learn, it's another to internalize it and put it into practice. You can build up each brick of knowledge in your brain, but without cement in between each brick, the knowledge won't stick. Repetition is the cement that holds whatever the hell you just read in place. Putting it into practice hardens it.

Come back to the lessons that resonate with you the most. Reread them and internalize them so you can take action without hesitation. The only better way to learn than by repetition is by doing.

Become a beginner again. After noticing the quality had dropped while visiting several of his restaurants, Wolfgang Puck decided to make sure his staff treats every guest, every order, and every meal like it's opening night.

# ALMOST THE END, MY FRIENDS

Alright, no more time to lose. It's go time. I'm publishing it. I've never been so proud of something as I am of this book. I finished this last year, but put it on hold because my company was and still is facing its biggest challenge yet. But this book was written to prevent you from going through what I have. So, regardless of the problems I'm facing, I'm putting this out now for you. And if you've been inspired by this book, please support your humble author by treating yourself to your new favorite underwear from Culprit, delicious, healthy snacks from my latest venture, Mortal Munchies, and hangover pills that actually work from Elxxr. How's that for a plug? I personally guarantee you'll love all three, and as a parting gift, here's a golden ticket discount code that will work for all three brands: Shortcut20. You'll love the undies, you'll be obsessed with the snacks, and you'll definitely be needing those pills if you're celebrating like me after finishing this book! 😤 For deleted chapters, videos, and even more tips on attaining your inevitable success, head to myshortcut.co.

## FINAL WORDS

The end of a book should satisfy the reader and offer the main character a chance to shine one last time. As this is the end, the main character will indeed shine one more time. However, I am not the main character. You are. The spotlight is on you. Now, go do some main character shit. **Slam this book shut and go take the next step, however small, toward turning your wildest dream into your living, breathing vision. Do it now. Why are you still reading? If you're doubting whether you'll be successful after finishing this book, remember one thing...belief comes before ability.**

# ACKNOWLEDGMENTS

I'd like to acknowledge David Senra. Your passion has sparked ideas and future successes I can't even see yet, and of course this book. It's been an honor getting to know you and to call you a friend. Thank you to my editor, Holly, without whom you'd still have another one hundred pages to go. Thank you, Eric Jorgenson, for believing in this project and in me. Thank you, Dave, my platonic life and business partner, who's supported my vast valleys of stupidity because he saw there might be some small rolling hills of genius. Dave, thank you also for your brutally honest feedback. I'd like to thank my dad, Vance, for delivering me into this world before a doctor could get there, and for teaching me math on a McDonald's napkin. I'd like to thank my mom for being my rock. Thank you to my sister for giving me a funny rival growing up that helped evolve my sense of humor, only to become a really cool friend later in life. Sorry for peeing on you when you changed my diaper. I didn't mean to ruin your ice-skating outfit before your meet. I'd like to thank Rob, my bro-in-law for being such an inspiring and actual bro. Thank you to everyone who always told me I had potential and talent. And thank you even more to the people who pissed me off. In trying to hold me back, you've only propelled me forward!

# ABOUT THE AUTHOR

Like many of the lessons in his book, **DYLAN TRUSSELL** is a walking contradiction. He is a lazy hard worker. Brilliantly braindead. Stubbornly open-minded. Yet seriously hilarious, though it depends on who you ask. If you asked his creditors in 2022, you might get a different response. That was hilariously serious. Why haven't you shut this book yet? The author already overshared.

For bonus resources, tools, and updates go to: Myshortcut.co/bonus.

www.ingramcontent.com/pod-product-compliance
Lightning Source LLC
LaVergne TN
LVHW041958060526
838200LV00019B/385/J